Prisoners
of Santo Tomas

by CELIA LUCAS

**Based on the Diaries of
Mrs Isla Corfield**

LEO COOPER LTD. LONDON

First published in Great Britain in 1975 by
Leo Cooper Ltd
196 Shaftesbury Avenue, London WC2H 8JL

Copyright © 1975 by Isla Corfield and Celia Lucas

ISBN 0 85052 166 1

Printed in Great Britain by
The Barleyman Press, Bristol

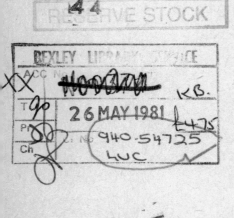

To my husband, Ian, the growl
behind the typewriter

CONTENTS

LIST OF ILLUSTRATIONS

Between pages 68 *and* 69

Between pages 164 *and* 165

MAPS

ACKNOWLEDGEMENTS

Firstly, I must express my heartfelt thanks to the wonderful American soldiers who saved us all when most of us were expendable.

I would like also to thank all the Australians from Townsville, North Queensland, to Sydney, who showed so much kindness and generosity to myself and my daughter during our four-month stay in their country.

My greatest thanks, too, are due to my friends Brigadier George Chatterton DSO and Mrs Chatterton without whose encouragement and help these diaries would never have come to light. Also thanks to Celia who somehow read my writing and made a story from the diaries.

Isla Corfield
London, 1973

CHAPTER ONE

And they sailed away

(December 1941–6 January, 1942)

GILLIAN CORFIELD ran excitedly to the telephone. The Manila afternoon was as hot and sticky as usual and she was looking forward to a pre-tiffin swimming party with her teenage friends at the Club.

Quickly she dialled a number.

"Wendy. Can I speak to Wendy? It's me, Gill Corfield."

Suddenly her eager expression changed to one of shocked bewilderment. For the voice at the other end of the phone was Japanese.

"Concentration camp. All gone to concentration camp. Not come home again." And the telephone clicked like the turn of a key in a prison cell. Gill was stunned. She dropped the telephone and ran through the flagged hall, across the sitting room and out through the french windows into the garden where her mother was writing her diary.

"Mummy, Mummy, they've taken Wendy. She's in a concentration camp. He said she wouldn't come back." And bit by bit, in breathless gulps, she told her mother what had happened.

The news came as no surprise to Isla. It had been that sort of year. Ever since the fateful Sunday morning in December when the Japs had destroyed Pearl Harbor things had gone from bad to worse. That was the reason why the ship taking them from Shanghai to India had been diverted to offload its human cargo in the Philippines, why they were now penniless lodgers in a house in the Manila suburbs and why they would soon, no doubt, join Wendy and the rest of the Gates family in a concentration camp.

It was 4 January, 1942, Isla Corfield's nineteenth wedding

anniversary. She put her arm round her daughter who, in her distress, seemed suddenly much younger than her fourteen years. How she wished now she had kept her at boarding school in England.

"I'm sure it's not nearly as bad as it sounds," she said reassuringly. "They're probably only checking in. Perhaps the Jap you spoke to didn't know much English."

In many ways Isla and her daughter were alike, both tall and slim and with a directness of approach which was sometimes quite disarming. Isla was just 41, a handsome woman with light brown hair streaked fair by the sun. Her eyes were fascinating for a reason not at first clear: one was green and the other hazel. She had high cheek bones and a clear skin, a good figure but legs which she always described as "racehorse top and carthorse bottom".

Gill, on the other hand, had the luck to have racehorse legs all the way up. She was a golden blonde and wore her thick, naturally curling hair at shoulder length. Her large eyes were a deep blue – a pretty girl by any standards.

Looking at her more than usually dishevelled daughter, who ten minutes before had been so full of fun and plans and who now seemed so downcast, Isla's mind raced back over the last six weeks.

It seemed no time at all since she was sitting in her comfortable flat in Shanghai, at that time one of the most sophisticated cities in the world, with her husband T.D. His name was really Gerald Frederick Conyngham Corfield but he was called T.D. because the year he was born the London Zoo acquired a Tasmanian Devil, a fierce jackal-wolflike animal, and the name stuck. He was an official in the Chinese Maritime Customs, an international service which at that time controlled all shipping on the River Yangtse and that part of the China coast collecting customs dues. He and Isla had lived in China, in some comfort, since their marriage nineteen years before.

If only they had not let themselves be persuaded into booking passages for herself and Gill on that evacuee ship, thought Isla, they might still all be together in China with a chance of repatriation now that hostilities had been formally declared.

And what of their son, Richard? At 17 he had just left his English public school to join the Gunners. As far as Isla knew he was now on his way to India. A sudden panic that she might not be able to get letters out to either T.D. or Richard seized her.

T.D. had never liked the idea of the evacuee ship. But the warning that the *Anhui*, sailing on 3 December, would be the last ship out of Shanghai overcame their better judgment. Isla and Gill had, after all, intended to leave Shanghai for India before Christmas due to the increasingly tense situation in the city.

Although no formal state of war had been declared between Japan and China, hostilities had existed between the two countries since July, 1937. Japanese ambitions for aggrandizement first settled on the provinces of northern China. By July, 1939, the whole Chinese coast was in Japanese hands and inland the Yangtse Valley up to and beyond Hangchow was under Nippon control. President Chiang Kai-shek and his government had fled to Chungking and the Japs were pressing for a settlement that would reduce China to the status of a colony. By December, 1941, not only was the situation in Peking and Shanghai critical but greater war clouds were looming.

In Europe the conflict with Nazi Germany had raged already for over two years. Britain and France had declared war on Germany on 3 September, 1939, after the invasion of Poland by Nazi troops. Since then the Allies had taken a terrible battering. Denmark, Norway, Luxembourg, Holland, Belgium and finally, in June, 1940, France itself fell to the Nazis. That same month Italy joined forces with Germany and between them, by the end of 1941, they had overrun Greece and Crete and, under the formidable leadership of Rommel, much of North Africa. In June, 1941, Hitler made the inexplicable decision to invade Russia. Within four months the Ukraine was overrun and Moscow and Leningrad were threatened. Only winter kept the invaders at bay.

In the East, too, some sort of confrontation was inevitable. In August, 1940, Japan occupied northern Indo-China. In September she signed a Tripartite Pact with Germany and Italy. In April, 1941, came the non-aggression pact with Russia and finally in July, 1941, the declaration of a joint protectorate with the French Vichy government of the whole of Indo-China. This brought an immediate reaction from the United States who, seeing her interests in South-East Asia, particularly in the Philippine Islands, threatened by Nippon imperialism, severed all trading relations with Japan. Britain and the Netherlands concurred in the stringent restrictions. The most serious consequence for the Japanese was that they could no longer import oil from the Dutch East Indies and no oil meant no empire. Sooner or later Nippon would have to bow to America and give up her ambitions in China or make a bid for the inviting oil fields of the East Indies.

Mrs Corfield and Gill found themselves caught in the thick of the landgrab.

They were a day's sailing from Hong Kong and the *Anhui* with its overload of passengers – 300 on a ship designed for 70 – was making heavy weather through rough seas when Skipper Evans called a special meeting.

It was Monday, 8 December.

"The Japs have attacked Pearl Harbor," he told his passengers, 90 per cent of them women and children. "America is at war. We may be bombed or torpedoed at any moment."

He said he had orders to take the ship to Manila, the capital of the Philippines, on Luzon island, but could give no guarantee that passengers would be taken on to India.

The evacuees rallied immediately to the crisis. A committee was formed and extra look-outs posted on the bridge and fo'c'sle. Isla took her turn on round-the-clock black-out duty patrolling the decks, while Gill was detailed to the baby department and given a baby to look after in the event of the passengers having to take to the life boats. When she finished her black-out shift Isla joined the decoding team unscrambling messages.

At last, on 10 December, they sighted Luzon. "At least we might be able to swim ashore now," Isla thought.

There were a great number of ships waiting to come into the harbour. The whole civilian fleet of the Pacific seemed to have been diverted to the Philippines. As the captain steered the *Anhui* safely through the minefield the passengers sent up a great cheer. They did not know what lay ahead.

At 12.30 all hell broke loose. A perfect formation of 27 Jap planes was circling Cavite, the U.S. naval base, dropping bombs. Suddenly the planes turned course and began making for the ships in the harbour. Three bombs fell. The *Anhui*'s sister ship, the *Anchung*, just eighty feet away, got two direct hits. Four people were killed and six injured in the raid. A

4

Filipino ship exploded in a mass of flames. She blazed for three days and three nights, a beacon light to the Japs.

The next day everyone was told to leave the ship, taking their hand baggage with them. Isla begged the captain to let her and Gill stay. She had an uncanny presentiment that once they left the *Anhui*, whatever its disadvantages and dangers, they would never get aboard again.

"I can't force you, ma'am," said the skipper, "but the ship's got to be cleaned and you'd be better off ashore, for a while at any rate. I promise I won't leave without you."

So Isla and Gill with their two little suitcases and some light hand luggage went ashore. Their passports were taken and in exchange they were given a bit of paper on which they made a finger print.

The next thing was to find somewhere to stay in Manila. They were both desperate for a bath and a good night's sleep. The filth and smell on the crowded *Anhui* had been indescribable and, with all the alerts and the bad weather, sleep had been something they only got when their eyes would not stay open any more.

Isla had an idea. Clark Lee, a journalist friend of theirs who worked for *Associated Press* and had been covering all the war fronts in the Chinese/Japanese conflicts, was in Manila. She got directed to the British Club and from there rang the Manila Hotel.

"What on earth are you doing here?" said Tick, as he was known to his friends. "Didn't you get my two cables telling you to leave Shanghai long before this?"

"No," said Isla. "I imagine the Japs wouldn't let them through," and briefly she told him of all that had happened in the last incredible week.

"Well I've got a room here," said Tick. "You'd better have that and I'll find a space with a friend. Stay where you are and I'll pick you up."

After a few stiff drinks Isla began to feel more cheerful but her optimism was short-lived. Just as she was beginning to relax came the news that the *Anhui* had gone. In spite of the Consul's assurance to T.D. in Shanghai that the *Anhui* had safe conduct to India, she had set sail within an hour of the last passenger embarking, with only the crew on board, leaving all the evacuees in Manila. And all their baggage had gone with

5

her in the hold. Gill and Isla were left with a couple of night-dresses, four suits and a few dresses between them. Luckily Isla had had the good sense to pack all her jewellery in her suitcase. Its value in bartering terms was to save their lives in the months ahead.

They stayed three days in Manila. All night long the alerts sounded. The smack of bombs never ceased. The air was black with smoke and the fumes and dust seeped into clothes and hair and eyes. The battle for the Philippines was all about them.

Staying in the hotel at 30 pesos or £5 a day was expensive – even a swim in the pool was charged on the bill – and Isla's supply of traveller's cheques was diminishing rapidly. So she applied to the Red Cross for lodgings.

Frank Hanson and Patrick Sullivan were two business men in their late 30's. They had offered the Red Cross a room in their house in the Pasay district of Manila when the evacuees arrived; their kindness to Isla and Gill did much towards softening the heartache and shock of the past weeks.

Frank was manager of a shipping firm. He was a great worker and had a tremendous sense of responsibility for his Filipino staff. He always looked about to burst into tears.

Sully was quite the ugliest man Isla or Gill had ever seen, tall with that slightly dislocated look that protruding bones produce, with glasses and sticking-out ears and stubble that never seemed to smooth over. He was Irish, a devout Catholic and he fussed.

The radio bulletins came every evening. Hong Kong was in desperate straits, Penang had been evacuated. The little group felt the inevitability of disaster.

Christmas Day was a sombre affair. Five times they listened as the sirens raised their plaintive wail across the stricken city, five times they heard the crash of bombs and falling masonry and saw the sky lit up with flames.

By 27 December the raids were up to six or seven a day. On New Year's Eve the U.S. troops blew the oil installations at Pandacan. For days a heavy pall of burning oil hung over the city.

Isla, Gill, Frank and Sully stood with their brandy glasses raised to welcome in the New Year – 1942. It came with a deafening roar of bombs. In the morning they learned that the cables had been cut and the radio towers destroyed. Now rumour would replace news. There would be no more wires, those lifelines of hope, from T.D. in Shanghai. Richard had still not answered his mother's cable.

On 3 January the Japs occupied Manila. Since the bombing of Pearl Harbor on the morning of 7 December, they had known no setback. Their brilliantly planned attack on a Sunday morning had caught the Americans literally napping. Only one battleship, the *Nevada*, managed to escape the holocaust of naval power in the harbour. Hardly a plane or a flying boat remained undamaged.

On Formosa, 400 miles to the north of Luzon, the main island of the Philippines, General Masaharu Homma had orders to launch his attack within hours of the strike on Hawaii. His first objective was the airfields and within three days the American air forces in the islands had virtually ceased to exist. At Clark Field on Luzon row upon row of B-17 flying fortress bombers were caught helpless on the ground. Nichols and Nielson Fields near Manila were immobilized.

Everything went according to plan for Homma, Commander of the 14th Imperial Army. With orders from General Sugiyama to take Manila within 50 days of the first shot being fired, he landed at Lingayen, just north of the capital, on Christmas Eve. A second force under General Morioka landed in Lamon Bay to the south and east of Manila. A third group landed at Legaspi in south-eastern Luzon. The capital was caught in the Japanese pincers. General Douglas MacArthur, Commander of the U.S. Forces in the Far East, declared Manila an open city and by 3 January, U.S. troops had retreated to the peninsula of Bataan and Manila was in enemy hands. The campaign had lasted just twenty-two days.

Meanwhile Guam and Wake island in the Pacific had fallen. The great British battleships, the *Prince of Wales* and the *Repulse*, were sunk off Malaya on 10 December. Kowloon on the Chinese mainland was captured and Hong Kong surrendered on Christmas Day. Penang and Kota Bahru in the Malay states had been overcome by General Tomoyuki Yamashita's army and Singapore was threatened. Brunei in Borneo was occupied on New Year's Eve. The fate of Sumatra, Java, the Celebes, Burma, the Solomons, hung in the balance and even Australia felt the oppressive rays of the Rising Sun across the Coral Sea.

*   *   *

7

The boy had just served tea when a knock came on the door. Sully answered.

"We want this house cleared in two hours," Isla heard a Japanese voice say. "We need it for airmen's barracks."

They planned to take over the whole row of modern houses but Frank and Sully had their argument prepared. They told the soldiers that many of the houses were owned by Spaniards, third party nationals, and one belonged to the British vice-consul. In any case, they argued, they were too far from the air-fields to be of any use to airmen. Finally the soldiers contented themselves with taking Frank's car.

Later that evening they had a phone call warning them to have a bag each packed ready for three days in case they were taken away to register. Register? Isla prayed that was not a euphemism for something more sinister. Now she understood some part of the icy fear the Jews under Hitler must experience listening for the bang of the S.S. mailed fist on the door. Every hour or so Sully would say: "If they haven't come by noon we'll be all right until 3 o'clock." And then: "If they don't come by 6 we're O.K."

On 6 January at 3.30 in the afternoon the order came: Be ready by 4.00. At precisely 4 o'clock a uniformed Jap arrived with an interpreter.

"Out, out, go out," said the interpreter indicating the door.

As the sad little group waited for the car to take them away, the Jap handed Isla a paper lampooning President Roosevelt. The words were revolting, the lowest form of propaganda. Disgusted, Isla handed it back and the Jap giggled foolishly. It was a giggle that was to grate on their nerves in the coming months till their reflexes were numbed by the effort of self-control.

A brand new red Cadillac screeched to a halt outside the gate. Two friends of theirs, Wyndham Stopford, an English business man, and his pretty, young Texan wife May, were al-ready inside. Isla, Gill and the two bachelors piled in.

The Stopfords had three children, Neville, aged nine, Anne who was five and Craig, three, but wisely, when she saw the way the wind was blowing, May had put the two youngest in the care of a convent. She had arranged to pick them up after the registration formalities were over. Neville was away at boarding school in Baguio in the mountainous north of the island.

The car took them to Rizal Stadium which the Japs had converted into a grand registration centre. On the way they saw a drunken Japanese general who had got hold of an American gun and with shrieks of maniacal laughter was firing round after round into the air. If officers behaved like that what could they hope for from the men?

From Rizal they were bundled into another car which took them north through the bomb-pitted city to Santo Tomas University. The tall iron gates swung back as they approached and they drove in. Santo Tomas – an institution, a concentration camp, a place of internment for enemy aliens. They were prisoners.

"Oh well," said Isla, "we're only here for three days."

CHAPTER TWO

What you can't have you're better not wanting

(*6 January–6 May, 1942*)

MAY STOPFORD stood at the entrance to the main building beckoning to Isla and Gill.

"I've found a space for you," she called. "It's in one of the lecture rooms on the ground floor."

They hurried over to join her. With all these people milling about sleeping accommodation was obviously going to be at a premium.

"We're in with some of the top Manila society," their guide whispered as she led mother and daughter along a wide, stone-floored passage. "Ours is considered the most desirable residence on campus!"

They came to a halt at a room marked "5". Inside was one of the most extraordinary sights Isla had ever seen. The floor seemed literally awash with women all busily unpacking the few belongings that would stake their claim to territory. At the far end of the room were two high windows and diagonally opposite the door, where Isla and Gill stood gaping in amazement, a large, dusty blackboard was embedded in the wall.

"Here's the space," said May, triumphantly indicating a gap of about four feet just in front of the blackboard.

Few people had had the presence of mind to arrange for a bed or mattress to be sent in and that night Gill and Isla, like many others, found themselves sleeping on the cement floor. Luckily a woman was able to lend them a small grass mat which took off the worst of the chill but, after a couple of hours of acute discomfort, Isla decided she could stand it no longer. She spent the rest of the night on a bench in the hall chatting to other women internees from her room.

She took an immediate liking to Ida Lennox, a fair, good-looking woman of about her own age from California. Ida's horrifying account of her three-day ordeal at the registering stadium of Hai Alai made Isla feel *they* had been lucky. Hai Alai was where the Japs had taken anyone they picked up away from home or people they had decided they wanted to question. For the entire three days the captives were given nothing to eat and for 24 hours they were forbidden to speak. Ida was suspect because the Japs had found a sheet of music written by her daughter in the waste-paper basket. They insisted it must be a secret code and were only satisfied when Ida sang it for them, her finger following the notes to try and prove the truth of her statement.

Thelma Koons was another suspect because she kept an album of foreign stamps. She was cross-examined for two hours before the Japs were satisfied the stamps did not conceal microdot messages or represent counterfeit currency.

Partly because of the Jap grilling and partly because they were unknown to the society set in Room Five, Ida and Thelma were regarded as fifth columnists. Isla and Gill, although they did not know anyone either, were given *carte blanche* by May who knew everyone in Manila and went character bail for them.

This did not prevent the "Rich Bitches", as the top people in Room Five came to be called, from looking down their noses at the two provincials from Shanghai who had nothing but a couple of small suitcases and a few travellers' cheques with which to bless themselves.

But with close on 3,500 internees herded into the camp this was no time to think of class prejudice. Even the jails had been emptied of enemy aliens, including one murderer, and there were at least 300 V.D. cases in camp. In the classroom next to the Corfields a gang of prostitutes squabbled over their charges to clients.

Life was spartan. Twenty-two women shared Gill and Isla's room; morning call was at six, evening roll call at nine, and lights out at ten. They had to queue for the one shower and three basins that were supposed to cater for the washing needs of all the women in the half-dozen lecture halls on the ground floor. Privacy was non-existent. It was a case of strip off in front of all or stay dirty. The situation did not bother Isla much but poor Gill, who suffered acutely from teenage modesty, went through agonies of bashfulness. The water, of course, was always cold.

Santo Tomas, a university run by the Dominican fathers, covered an area of 250,000 square metres. It had been approved by United States officials as an internment camp during late December and the directing fathers had no hesitation in giving their consent. Their monastery and its garden was within the campus and for the time being, at any rate, the Japs made no objection to their staying, effectively cut off as they were from the internees by a high barbed wire fence.

Before the war the University had had nearly 6,000 students and over 300 professors. Now it housed 3,430 internees and their 200 or so guards. Though the buildings were twentieth century the foundation of the University was much earlier and, since the American occupation of the Philippines in 1898, Santo Tomas had been known affectionately as "the oldest university in the United States".

It consisted of three separate blocks – in the centre the Main Building, where Isla and the other women were housed, to one side the Education Building, which was the men's quarters, and, to the other, the Monastery.

Behind was an Annex, assigned to the mothers with children under 10, and various store rooms and additional lecture halls, one of which was destined to become first the general hospital and later the children's hospital. Outside, between the Main Building and the Annex, were rows of small washing troughs and clothes lines. Soon a canteen and dining sheds would complete the scene.

The gymnasium, where most of the older men made their home, was just in front of the fathers' territory at the edge of the campus. Dotted about the grounds were various sports fields – for football, baseball, basket ball and even a three-hole golf course.

The Commandant's office was strategically placed between the Main and Education buildings.

The day after internment, 7 January, Sully managed to get a pass out and he brought back a single mattress and a mosquito net for Isla and Gill. The mattress, Isla found, had to be propped upright until they were ready for bed since once it was down there was no space to undress. It was a terrible squash for the two of them and, lying top to toes, Gill managed to kick her mother in the face twice on the first night. But it was a vast improvement on the concrete.

Sully also collected a few tins of bully beef. Isla and Gill had eaten nothing since their last tiffin at the Pasay house and they tucked into the humble fare with relish.

Three days passed, then a week. It was clear that the "three days to register" story was rubbish. One pessimist had brought with him an enormous supply of pills, saying he had collected enough for three years, his estimate of the length of the war.

It was obvious the camp would have to be organized. The Japs, apart from making sure everyone was dumped there, seemed to have no interest in how it was run or what became of their captives. It was time for the Anglo-Saxon spirit of order-liness to take over. An Executive Committee of prominent pro-fessional and business men was created as a governing body and an American, Earl Carroll, elected first chairman. Next came committees or departments for Police, Sanitation, Public Health, Discipline, Construction, Feeding, Fire, Welfare, Education, Library, Entertainment and Religion, each with their own elected chairman. An additional refinement was an Ombuds-man's department in the shape of a Committee for Internee Relations whose function was to help internees understand the workings of the Executive Committee!

All dealings with the Commandant and his staff were to be done through the Executive Committee. It was considered unethical for an individual internee to go direct to the Comman-dant, though, on occasions, some, including Isla, did.

Justice was to be carried out by a Court of Order and in due course a panel of judges, both men and women, was appointed.

The Americans took the lead in running STIC – the internees' name for the Santo Tomas Internment Camp – as they were greatly in the majority, accounting for 70 per cent of the camp population. They numbered 2,225 in all – 1,453 men and boys and 772 women and girls. The British, with 436 men and 460 women, accounted for 28 per cent and the remaining 2 per cent were Dutch, Polish, Russian, Mexican, Belgian, Nicara-guan and Cuban.

One of the first concerns of the organization men was garbage. More than 2,000 lbs had to be disposed of daily. The task fell to the Sanitation department and soon a labour force of trench diggers and garbage tippers had been rounded up to empty dustbins and clear the mountains of old tin cans that defaced the grounds. Later a chemical substance was introduced to rot the "soft" garbage and convert it to a brown earthy powder. The internees' constant dread was that they would still be confined when the monsoon season started in June. It was imperative, if disease was to be kept at bay, to have an efficient garbage disposal system in force by then.

The second major campaign was against bugs and vermin. In six weeks gangs of men working in half-hour shifts cleared the camp of rats and reduced the thick undergrowth behind the Education building, a breeding ground for mosquitoes, to an orderly vegetable patch. One man patented a fly trap which sent millions of flies to an early grave.

Isla was not surprised to learn that the Philippine Islands were regarded as an entomologist's paradise with the most varied and plentiful insect life in the world. Snakes, including giant boa-constrictors and pythons, abound in the islands, and parts of the mountainous areas are populated by huge vampire-like bats, some measuring six feet across their wing span. Santo Tomas, being in an urban area, was fortunately spared the worst excesses of wild life. But with all that warmth and garbage and human flesh to feed on the bugs loved it. There were cockroaches, mosquitoes, beetles, head lice, bed bugs, crab lice. In Isla's room when they took the blackboard down they found millions of bugs nesting behind it. In the room next to the barber's shop nearly all the women caught head lice and had to go round with their heads bandaged. When the sanitation squad disinfected they found crab lice on the walls and many of the women decided to shave all over to avoid infestation.

The bug problem highlighted the need for strict cleanliness which had to be enforced at room level as well as committee level. The floor monitors, the room monitors and the bathroom monitors assumed, in this respect, the role of local government officers with responsibility for keeping order and seeing that cleanliness was maintained in their own areas.

In Isla's room Caroline Wolff, a small, dark American woman of about 50, got the room monitor's job and Ida Lennox was lumbered with the thankless task of bathroom monitor.

Room cleaning was to be done by every woman in turn. Caroline made out a duty roster and gave instructions that cases and boxes were to be lifted out of the way so the day's cleaner could wash and sweep under the beds of those lucky enough to have such things and round the mattresses of the less fortunate. All too often some lazy or careless female would forget to move her boxes and Isla found it exhausting picking up the heavy things and shifting beds about in the stifling tropical heat which never seemed to let up even in the so-called cool season of the winter months.

Though charring was completely new to her, having lived in houses with servants all her life, Isla was meticulous in her cleaning. It made her wild to see some of her room mates trying to get away with a cursory cat's lick. She was appalled by the thought of bugs and decided, in addition to her rota "char", to heave her mattress outside at least once a week and give it an airing and the floor beneath it a really good wash with chlorax or any other super-powerful disinfectant she could find.

Bathroom duty was one of the camp details. Every able-bodied internee was supposed to have a detail or job doing cleaning, working in the hospital, the kitchen, the school or whatever else they were suited to. Isla found herself on bath-room detail with the 7 to 8 am shift. It opened her eyes to how dirty and inconsiderate some people could be. Worst of all was the woman who gave herself an enema each morning right in the middle of the getting-up rush hour.

As she wiped seats and handed out toilet paper, Isla thought how curiously life changed. A month ago she had never so much as cooked a dinner or washed clothes or even made a bed. Now here she was on her hands and knees disinfecting a smelly lavatory!

Life seemed one perpetual battle to keep clean. The humidity was so oppressive that Isla found she needed a shower at least four times a day. It was a great relief when the Red Cross in-stalled five extra showers in the women's quarters.

In camp food, not godliness, came next to cleanliness. For the first couple of days internees had to fend for themselves, making do with tins of bully beef and whatever else they had managed to bring in with them. Then the Red Cross got a canteen going. Finally the internees' Food Committee took over the running of the canteen, leaving the Red Cross to cope with the children's and teenagers' meals.

By 2 February, 2,500 internees – over two-thirds of the camp population – were eating on the canteen line. The staple diet was mush, a sort of corn meal porridge which tasted a great deal better than it sounded. Meat was scarce and, all too often, unrecognizable, and for vegetables there were mungo beans, baby marrows which the Americans call squash and the English courgettes, camotes or sweet potatoes, pechay – a Chinese-type cabbage – and talinum, a sort of spinach which the camp started to grow for itself in the cleared vegetable patch. The optimistic "fruit in season" proclaimed on the menu was another way of saying "banana".

In addition to – or, if you had the money, instead of – canteen food, supplies could be got from outside. At first Filipinos would bring things to the gate for their former employers – pots and pans, cutlery and charcoal stoves as well as fresh and tinned foods. If the guards found nothing suspicious the parcels were given clearance and their owners allowed to collect them.

After a few weeks, however, the system was considerably extended when Aguinaldo's, the Harrods of Manila, was allowed to open a branch in the hall of the Main Building, not far from Isla's "bedroom". Other traders followed suit, building little *tiendas* both in the grounds and round the periphery of the camp. Many internees, themselves former tradesmen, also started stalls in the grounds or in the passageways. Isla's corridor, with fifteen different sales counters, looked like Petticoat Lane on a busy morning.

There were boutiques for clothes, an ice-cream stall, bakeries, peanut and candy vendors, hot-dog stands, cake shops, dairy counters and a butcher's. There was a laundry service, a tailor's, a dyer's, a hardware shop, a manicurist, a masseuse, barbers' shops and hairdressing salons, tobacconists and drug stores, and numerous restaurants and coffee bars. One of Isla's first purchases were two plates and two mugs for herself and Gill. They were sick of drinking out of tin cans which made everything taste metallic.

One internee, Mr Blossoms, specialized in saucepans, fixing handles to old tins to make elegant cooking utensils. Robert Wygle made knitting needles and crochet hooks out of bamboo; another man sold wire clothes pegs, another did shoe repairs and, with the empty cotton spools discarded by the Sewing Department, a craftsman carved chessmen.

The Sewing Department itself was a hive of ingenuity. In

the time left after taking in the men's trousers – some waistlines had diminished by as much as eight inches – the sewing women made shirts out of sheets and transformed khaki remnants into tobacco pouches, or gloves for the lumber carriers. To save the children from mosquito bites they made nets eighty feet in diameter to cover whole rooms of cots in the Annex and Holy Ghost Convent nurseries.

Isla never ceased to wonder at the organization and ingenuity of the internees who, in a few weeks, made of a wilderness a well-ordered community, offering, within its limitations, all the facilities of an established small town. Sometimes the place reminded her of Blackpool at the height of the season with the loudspeaker blaring popular music from a tree opposite the Commandant's office, groups of people picnicking on the grass, the gaily coloured stalls, the queues at the canteen, the young people hand in hand, the strange holiday-atmosphere clothes, the bright posters for evening shows and dances.

All that was missing were bars and pubs. Alcohol was banned from STIC and internees were warned that anyone caught buying, selling or distributing liquor within the camp would be transferred to the military authorities for punishment. But the demon drink was not so easily exorcized. Gangs of bootleggers got to work almost as quickly as the prostitutes and even the Japanese ice-cream seller was known to conceal knock-out stout among his cornets.

Everything could be bought – at a price. Money was the great problem. Many, with their wages gone, had none. Others were able to draw on their savings or get money through their businesses. All Isla had was £300 in travellers' cheques and, at the rate inflation was moving, she could see herself and Gill being penniless before very long. The Filipino peso worked out at about six to the pound sterling or two to the American gold dollar and already simple provisions like a few cans of margarine, some fruit and a couple of kilos of sugar were costing over a pound. Her attempts to get a loan from the British banks in Manila had drawn a blank. They were incredibly unhelpful. Even if T.D. received her cable in Shanghai *he* could not wire her money with communications as they were. All she could do was rely on the goodwill of her business friends in camp – Fred Satterfield, her bridge partner, Frank Hanson and Sully, and Ida's husband, Stan Lennox, who were able to draw on funds in Manila and were prepared, for the time at any rate, to operate a system of I.O.U.'s.

There was food in the canteen and food on the stalls but it lacked the quality and vitamin content most internees were used to and, even for the rich, fresh fruit and vegetables, milk and fats were hard to come by.

It was not long before STIC fare took its toll on stomachs. Gill went down with dysentery and a mouth infection caused by lack of Vitamin B and had to go to hospital; even Isla felt her ostrich-like constitution rebelling. She was indignant that indigestion should have smitten her now after all the strange oriental foods she had consumed in the past to no ill effect.

Too much starch, sleeping on the floor and long queues for the lavatory was the doctors' explanation for all the stomach upsets. But the remedy, apart from a few helpful doses, was not in their power to give.

The women and girls had the additional problem of irregular periods. Many at first thought they must be pregnant but the doctors told them it was just the effects of the restricted diet and that they would adjust.

The possibility of a severe food shortage had to be faced. Research showed that with rationing there was enough rice in the National Corporation stores to feed the population of greater Manila, including the internees, for six months and enough sugar for fifteen months. But with an internment of as long as eighteen months predicted it was vital to conserve as many tinned foods as possible against emergenccy.

The newly formed Executive Committee laid down the rules. Line food was to be available for everyone but those who had the money to buy themselves hot meals from outside suppliers should try and do so. Fresh food and vegetables were regarded as supplementary to canteen meals and the Committee recommended all internees to buy and eat as much of these as they could. Tinned foods, on the other hand, except special dietary foods, coffee, tea, margarine and milk were not to be opened and eaten but kept as stores.

After three weeks of internment Isla thought it time to apply for a pass. She badly wanted to collect some clothes and a prescription from the Pasay house. Passes for the town were granted after registration on a permanent basis on grounds of ill health or, as a day release, to visit the hospital or collect urgent supplies from home.

While she stood in the pass queue outside the Commandant's office Isla heard an elderly American grumbling that his request had been turned down. He had applied to be interned in the house of his Filipina fiancée on the grounds that if guards were posted at the door that would count as internment. In the Commandant's view it did not.

Luckily Isla had no trouble with her request. She reported to the bus leaving for town and piled in with all the other pass holders. With surprise she noticed that Commandant Yamaguchi himself was travelling with them accompanied by his interpreter, Mr Yamastuta. Yamaguchi was an elderly man. Obviously he had distinguished himself at some time on the battlefield since the front of his dingy green uniform was liberally decorated with service medals. The command of Santo Tomas Internment Camp, Isla supposed, was some sort of reward for an old soldier.

They reached Pasay at about 4 pm. Isla's was the last house on the list and her fellow travellers all begged her to take as long as she could collecting her things to give them more time. She rushed across the lawn up to the house calling for Pedro, the Filipino servant. His face creased into a delighted smile when he saw Isla but, on telling him the purpose of her visit, his joy turned to dismay. Wishing to save the possessions of his employers and their guests from the ravages of the Japs, Pedro had removed as much as he could into hiding and it was impossible for him to retrieve anything in the short time Isla had available.

She tore upstairs to see if there was anything left and found Gill's little red suitcase containing Epsom Salts, Calomel, a few photographs and some linen. She was turning to the dressing table when she heard Japanese voices in the hallway. Commandant Yamaguchi and Mr Yamastuta had followed her. Had she done something wrong? The best thing, she thought, is to act naturally.

"Would you like a cup of tea?" she asked faintly. They beamed their acceptance. Pedro made the tea and all three sat down and talked, Mr Yamastuta acting as go-between.

Isla was longing for news of Shanghai and thought she could lose nothing by asking a few questions.

"Shanghai, everyone interned," said Mr Yamastuta trans-

lating for the Commandant. "But soon you lose war and negotiations start."

Isla thought how cold it must be interned there – Shanghai
winters could be terrible. At least in the Philippines it was
warm all the year round. Would T.D. be interned, she wondered, or would he be repatriated? If the latter he would almost
certainly rejoin his regiment.

The Commandant and Mr Yamastuta gulped their tea
noisily. Isla did the same thinking it would show good manners.

"You find prescription?" asked Mr Yamastuta.

"No, it's not here," answered Isla, wondering if these kindly
inquiries were the start of a ruthless interrogation. "The boy
has probably sent it on."

"He taken *all* your things to *his* house?"

"I don't think so. I'm sure he hasn't. Everything we had is
here," Isla answered hastily not wishing to incriminate poor
Pedro.

"Would you like come out again?" The friendly chat continued.

"Yes, of course I would but I don't think I've got a good
enough excuse."

"If your daughter needs prescription she must be ill. Maybe
she qualify for pass."

Isla explained the prescription was only for ointment for
some burns; Gill was not really sick. And suddenly she realized
that these two Japs were kindly men, genuinely concerned that
she should have good treatment. They were not part of the
Imperial inquisition squad that had tortured Thelma and Ida.
That was one of the hateful things about war. You made the
unfounded assumption that just because people were officially
enemies they were also inhuman and personally hostile.

They had followed Isla to the house simply because it was
the last port of call. Later the Filipino bus driver told her she
had been lucky to get those two as guards and that they had
enjoyed their tea and conversation.

As for Isla, although the arrival of Commandant Yamaguchi
and Mr Yamastuta had given her no chance to talk to Pedro
and do the thousand and one other things she had planned, her
few hours of freedom made her feel like a nun let out on a joy
ride. She longed for another excuse for a pass.

Every day the bombers came over. Santo Tomas was on the

direct flight path to the American strongholds on Bataan peninsula and Corregidor, the tiny but heavily fortified island that guarded Manila Bay and without which the Japs could not claim complete victory in the Philippines. The camp was shrouded in blackout.

The only light relief for Isla were games of bridge. In the early days they played nearly every evening until roll call and Isla found herself piling up a nice little sum of winnings to be paid A.D. – after detention. B.C. stood, of course, for before concentration!

Her partner in most of the games was Fred Satterfield, an American from Richmond, Virginia, who combined a deep south accent with a surprisingly British attitude to life. His wife, Lewis, had gone back to the States before Pearl Harbor and he tried to cable her the news of his internment. One evening Fred confided to Isla that he and Lewis had lived many years in Japan and loved the Japanese and got on well with them. "But I wouldn't admit it to anyone else in here," he said. It was Fred who found Isla the little folding chair complete with footstool that was her prize possession. The relief of sitting on a real chair after those first endless days of sitting or squatting on the ground, shifting agonizingly from side to bony side, was intense.

Another great friend, whom Isla had never expected to see in STIC, was Don. Fortunately the Japs did not expect him either and failed totally to recognize in the "William Donald. A. Scot" who signed the register the former adviser to the Chinese national government whom they had been hunting for years and whose capture carried a reward of thousands. William H. Donald was, in fact, an Australian Scot. From the time he joined Dr Sun Yat-sen, "the father of the Chinese Revolution", as adviser after the overthrow of the Imperial Manchu dynasty in 1911, the Japanese had been out for his blood. Rewards were offered for his capture dead or alive. Now when they had him, a captive in Santo Tomas, they had no idea how big a fish they had netted and accepted him without question as Mr W. D. A. Scot. Isla knew Don well from her days in China when he had been one of the most powerful men in the entourage of the young Marshal of Manchuria, Chang Hsueh-liang, and later the trusted friend and adviser of President Chiang Kai-shek.

He was on his way back to China from New Zealand on his ocean-going yacht when he was caught in the Philippines by the outbreak of hostilities. With him was Madame Chiang's secretary, Ansie Lee, an extremely able and charming Chinese girl in her late twenties. Madame had loaned her to Donald to help him in the writing of his memoirs. Now the manuscript was locked away in a flat in Manila. If ever the Japs found it it would mean certain death for Donald and probably for Ansie too.

Don, as he was always known, was 68 when he signed on in Santo Tomas, but in spite of his white hair he looked a good ten years younger. He was a powerful man in build as well as personality, although not tall, and he was sun-tanned and weather-beaten from his days at sea. He used to fascinate Isla and Gill with his stories of China – of the great Manchu Empire in its dying days, of the revolution, of the intrigue – and amaze them with his knowledge of world affairs. Gill would spend hours in the little shanty he built in the grounds behind the Main building listening to his tales and helping Ansie with the cooking.

He had humour and wit, kindness and discretion. It was said of him that he talked like the wind and never betrayed a confidence.

Don started life as a journalist on the *Sydney Daily Telegraph*. The extraordinary way he moved to China via Hong Kong was typical of the life of this incredible man, who with his own hands dragged into position the guns that blew the Manchus out of Nanking. The editor of the *China Mail* wrote to him in Sydney offering a job in Hong Kong, which he had never applied for, and sending travelling expenses. When Don reached the office he asked the inevitable: "Why me?" The editor replied that he had been searching for seven years for a reporter like Don – a newspaper man who didn't drink!

From the *China Mail* Don moved to Shanghai as correspondent for the *New York Herald*. There he was spotted by Dr Sun and offered the job of publicist for the new government. For a quarter of a century he remained as chief adviser to China's rulers, yet in all those years he never spoke one word of Chinese nor ate any Chinese food. Isla admitted he never spoke Chinese but thought to herself, "He understands it all right, the rascal!"

Several books in the Santo Tomas library had photographs

of Don and it seemed too much to hope that he would not one day be recognized by a visiting diplomat or a sharp guard. Isla begged him to grow a beard or moustache to disguise himself in some way but Don was adamant. He had been clean shaven all his life and that was the way he was going to stay. Having successfully dodged his Jap pursuers for thirty years he had no intention of loading the dice against them at this late stage.

A complete opposite to Don was Ernest Stanley. He was no friend of Isla's but he fascinated her. She could never make up her mind whether he was collaborating with the enemy or if he was a British spy. He had landed in the Philippines with the Jap vanguard and at Santo Tomas he lived, ate and worked with the Japs in the Commandant's quarters. He was a small dark man whose eyes always shifted from the direct look – a habit he may have caught from his Japanese friends. He claimed to be a missionary but seemed to belong to no recognizable order. He said he came from Evesham in Worcestershire. His Japanese was fluent and, though he was possibly the most hated man in camp, there was something about him that appealed to Isla. It upset her deeply that he was English.

His official job was camp liaison officer but all he did seemed to be for the benefit of the Japs and not the internees. Often it was Stanley and not the Jap authorities who clamped down on an outside pass. The Americans swore it would be too bad for him if he did not leave with the Japs. He was Number One on their shooting list.

The lack of privacy in STIC was one of the worst hardships – the dormitories where the mattresses all but touched, the communal showers, the grubbing for canteen food. Even when Isla disappeared, as she often did, with her little chair and a book to the remotest corner of the campus she could not escape the crowd.

In one of the women's rooms, in an effort to cut down numbers, they traded four mestizas – half Filipina, half American women – for one full-blooded American, only to find their brilliant exchange was a notorious prostitute with syphilis. In the men's quarters the saying was: "If you want privacy, close your eyes."

There was, too, the irritation that comes from living at close quarters with almost anyone let alone twenty-two in the same room and another 3,000 or more on the doorstep.

The women in Room Five were part of Isla's life whether she liked it or not. She found herself practically screaming every time she heard Jenny McLeod, a pampered, whining snob, complain that she could not possibly clean her space.

"But, darling, it's my hands and my nails. I've spent years, but years, cultivating them. Can you imagine what my manicurist would say if I ruined them now in this perfectly beastly place? No, really, I simply can't risk it." She even got her husband, Alec, a kindly, gentle little man, to wash her smalls and either he or one of their two teenage daughters, Jane and Lydia, would stand in the food line for her.

"Be a darling and rinse through these few things for me," she would say to Alec or "Run along Lydia and get me something to eat from the line. I'm absolutely *exhausted* after my work at the hospital." Work, thought Isla indignantly! She cleans a bit of talinum or rice, says it's staining her hands or straining her eyes or giving her backache and packs up for the day, bringing with her a selection of vegetables that she has neither earned nor needs. As far as Isla could see she got all the food she wanted and seemed to be eating all day.

Jenny, English, fair, fat, and rising forty, with bright red talons, was surrounded by relations in Room Five. There were, of course, her daughters Jane, aged 14, and Lydia, 12. Jane, fat and greedy, with her insufferable social pretensions and strident voice was, in Isla's opinion, a real chip of the old block. Monty Gordon, a tremendously amusing woman and a great mimic, was Jenny's sister. With her was her 18-year old daughter, May, always dreaming of romance. Doris Hair, though a good deal older, was another of Jenny's nieces and she had brought her Scottish maid, Miss Margaret McWatt, with her.

A second family group were the Fairchilds. There was Lydia, another 18-year-old, shy and rather nervous. Her mother, always known as Sister, had registered with Lydia but subsequently got permission to stay at home and look after her sick and aged father. She was a pleasant woman, tall, good-looking and part Hawaiian. She was married to a Scot, Gordon McKay, now in the STIC Police Department but, for some reason, she was always known by her maiden name, Fairchild. Sister had installed her daughter in a bed next to Molly, the sister-in-law for whom her disapproval was ill-concealed. Why her brother Bradley had ever wanted to marry this fat Australian she could not imagine.

Molly Fairchild was the room's champion snorer and, unfortunately for Isla, Gill and May, had the space next to them. Her favourite topic of conversation was food. She loved eating and her figure bore witness to her ruling passion. She was envied as the only woman in the room with a bedside lamp which Bradley, a genius for inventing gadgets, had fixed up for her with a tin can, a battery, a flashlight bulb and a bit of wire. She shared her mattress with Doris Cooke.

Molly's earth-shaking snores may have accounted in part for Doris's appalling temper. She was always flying into rages and even when a quarrel was nothing to do with her she could not resist interfering. In her more violent outbursts she would go quite Billingsgate fishwife, shrieking abuse at anyone who crossed her. Outside camp she might not have been so brittle but here her natural touchiness was constantly being assaulted and her highly strung personality cracked under the strain.

Thelma Koons, one of the American women whom Isla had chatted to on the first night, was flippant and vain, obsessed by her assumed sex appeal and, Isla thought, not over-bright. When the women internees first came in they were told not to make themselves too picturesque as the guards might ask them to clean out their quarters and Thelma piped up: "I'd rather clean the Jap quarters. See me not looking glamorous!" Her husband, Harry, was an ineffectual little man who seemed incapable of doing anything without Thelma's advice. He was perpetually putting his rather stupid and inquisitive face round the door of Room Five and calling, or rather bleating, "Th-ee-eeel-ma, whe-e-e-re ar-e-ee you?" For this they nicknamed him the Carabao, the bleating buffalo.

Caroline Wolff, whose husband, Tony, was regional head of the Red Cross, was room monitor, elected for her ability to get things organized without in any way shirking the job herself. Her great friend was Flora Selph, a dignified woman in her 50's. She was scared stiff of the bombings and the noise and the little yellow men who paraded past the room with their bayonets at the ready but, valiantly, she was determined not to show her fear. The soft white hair that framed her face gave her the look of a handsome grandmother and her personality fitted the face. She was the peacemaker in Room Five, the one to whom others took their troubles, the one who soothed and reassured. Her husband, Ewald, was a prominent U.S. Manila lawyer and in camp he was immediately elected to the Executive Committee and put in charge of Discipline, the Court of Order and the package line at the gate.

Further down the room was Margot Ewing, whom Isla liked immensely although, to start with, her giggle got on her nerves. Margot was about 30, extremely good-looking in a model-like way, tall, fair, with good legs. She was also an expert on astronomy and would point out all the constellations in the night sky as they sat outside on the long, hot evenings. Her husband, Bud, was a stockbroker, dark and handsome, but at 5 ft 7 ins, a good three inches shorter than Margot. They knew all there was to know about the Philippines and Isla would always ask Margot if she wanted to locate a place or a battle or find out about some Filipino personality.

Madeleine Peters, with her two teenage daughters, Dodie and another Lydia, kept herself very much to herself. She had little choice since her husband, a thoroughly miserable individual, got violently jealous if she formed a friendship with anyone, even another woman. Isla liked her.

Another woman they saw and heard little of was Mrs Jamieson, a lone Scot with a husband somewhere in the offing.

Isla's greatest friends were Ida Lennox and May Stopford. Ida was one of the most conscientious women Isla had ever met. She was thorough in everything she undertook and was the ideal person to take charge of the bathroom detail. Married to a hard-living, hard-drinking business man, Stan, she was sensitive and rather nervous and would burst into tears at the drop of a hat. But at the same time she had a tremendous sense of fun and a great vitality which would uncharacteristically manifest itself in a plethora of swear words. Isla never ceased to wonder at the amazing quantity of doubtful expletives that this otherwise rather staid woman gave voice to. She even swore in her sleep, which seemed to be peppered with nightmares even when the bombing was light. Stan was another who had been chosen for the Executive Committee.

May Stopford was a great ally. One night, about a month A.D., when she, Isla and Gill were all tossing miserably on their cramped mattresses hemmed down by inadequate mosquito nets, May suggested it might be slightly more comfortable if they were to move the two mattresses together. So the following day the mattresses were duly joined up crossways on the floor and the mosquito nets sewn together and spread over the entire bedding system. During the day the nets could be hitched up onto hooks out of the way. They then pushed their chairs against the wall and moved the mattresses further into the centre of the room. The result was undoubtedly cooler and certainly a great deal more comfortable for Gill and Isla, though the join got them in the rump and if any of the three moved about too much in the night they were liable to end up hind quarters on the floor, their toes gripping the retreating mattress.

They were glad now they had not been able to get a corner. It would, perhaps, have been more private, but not nearly so airy and bugs were well known to prefer corners. Their only fear was that some nosy woman would decide they were *too* comfortable and should be moved. Isla thought it pathetic that she should be scared to lose so little.

It was soon after the new sleeping arrangements that Isla awoke one night with a jolt to find a bayonet pointing at her head and a flashlight searching the "tent". May was standing by the bed looking like a bewildered witch doctor, with all the face cream she had piled on as an experiment in beauty before going to sleep, in clown-like patches on her nose and cheeks. Isla remembered that she had also tried the new treatment and wondered why the little Jap guard did not take to his heels and run from these two apparitions of horror.

"He stinks, he stinks," cried Isla still bemused by sleep. "What do you want?"

"Esco," he said brandishing the bayonet. "Esco," and turned and left the room.

It turned out that the Jap guard, seeing May coming back from the bathroom, had followed her into the room. The word they thought sounded like "Escape" was more probably Japanese for "Come to my arms, baby" a Japanese-speaking internee told them.

"Rather a nasty reflection on my bed companion," Isla teased May, "in view of our friends next door!"

Next door, of course, were the prostitutes. As it happened there were only two, but, from the row they made, there might have been a dozen. It was not that they used the room as "business premises". The Jap rules on no co-mingling and their own long-suffering room-mates saw to that! But somehow, somewhere, the ladies of the town were finding ways and means to carry on their time-honoured profession and they brought their work problems home with them. The disputes were endless.

It seemed that the Russian tart, Volga Olga, a classic movie exponent of the profession, with dyed black hair, thick make-up and throaty drawl, was the more successful of the pair. In a bid to boost trade, her American counterpart, Chicago Lil, who never wore more than a dirty house coat and seldom even that, had cut her price from the usual two pesos to 50 cts (about 10p). A terrible slanging match started over Chicago's loss leader tactics and ended with the two rolling on the floor locked in mortal combat, tearing at each other's faces and gouging into the skin with their dirty talons. Finally the room monitor resigned in desperation saying it was impossible to keep order.

No sex or co-mingling, as the Japs put it, was indeed the rule and sleeping quarters were subject to strict segregation. But in spite of saltpetre in the coffee, which was supposed to dull the urges, the tides of passion could not be contained and desperate lovebirds sought romantic refuge in the Main Building's two sizeable, but scarcely discreet, patios.

The patio sweethearts came to be known as the Patio Petters Association. Their activities were severely frowned on by unpermissive internee officials and the Commandant's office alike, and soon patio petting, which threatened a population explosion in the already crowded camp, became a punishable offence.

A Morality squad of worthy volunteers was set up by the Discipline Committee to deal with the Petters and each night they trudged about their thankless task. One man greeted their reprimand from under his blanket with: "I've got my papers. It's all legal." But other dismissals were less civil.

The corridors were another favourite spot for love-making. The enema woman and her husband refused to move from their love-nest there, saying that they would only go on Commandant's orders. Finally, the desperate Morality men, taking them at their word, called in the Commandant and got them deblanketed, at least temporarily.

The rumour went that a great pile of empty saltpetre cans had been found in the "basoura" or garbage dump. At least the Morality men tried.

Room Five was gradually getting organized. May was quite

right about the desirability of the residence. Their room had only twenty-two people whereas others had forty and in some cases fifty cramped into the same hall. The ground floor had the advantage of being more airy and, of course, there was none of that dreadful business of dragging up endless flights of stone stairs, more often than not commandeered by displaced Patio Petters.

On 15 March, more than two months A.D., Isla, Gill and May got their beds. They were nothing more than wooden stands and, since there were only two, they decided to share as before. It was worse than a jigsaw puzzle trying to fit them in and once they were in place it was almost impossible to move them or anything else. Oddly enough, when Isla sank gratefully onto her third of the sleeping arrangement the first night she found it hard and uncomfortable. Somehow, after all the initial agony, she seemed to have made a niche for herself in the concrete.

In spite of its shortcomings and deprivations Gill seemed to love STIC. She had done well for herself on her fifteenth birthday on 31 January getting a slacks suit and chewing gum from her mother plus a promise of something more exciting A.D., a box of candy from Flora Selph and a beautiful birthday cake with "Happy Birthday Gill" presented by the Red Cross. If this was prison it suited her – as long as it didn't last too long. Often she told her mother: "I'm really enjoying myself here!"

The listlessness and boredom that had afflicted her in Manila had disappeared and she was making a whole range of new friends among the young people. She felt more free than ever in her life before. It was splendid not to have to go to school and to meet and mix with people of every class and walk of life.

Isla thought Gill was being ridiculous when she went on about "getting away from English school discipline", maintaining that their family had never been bound by such things in the first place. Gill's friends at the Cathedral School in Shanghai had been from all backgrounds, all nationalities. But Gill insisted that STIC was a better and braver new world and revelled in the liberty of its environment.

Often Isla would not see her daughter from dawn to evening roll call. Her casual attitude and offhand manner hurt her terribly but whenever she tried asking her about her friends or what she had been doing all day Gill simply replied with a shrug,

"Oh, nothing in particular" or "You wouldn't be interested" or, worse than all, a blunt "I don't feel like talking about my life."

Isla was utterly wretched. Lying in bed at night, with Gill by her side, she would hold back her tears.

Her main cause of concern was the amorous activity in the patio. Isla did not want Gill joining the Petters Association and getting pregnant or catching V.D. She tried to ask Gill whether she had any special boyfriend.

"Oh, mummy, no. We go about in a gang."

"Well, where do you *go* with the gang and what do you *do*?" Isla inquired, fighting back unwelcome visions of mass teenage immorality.

"Oh everywhere, anywhere. We just roam about."

In fact Isla need not have worried about the Petters Association. Gill and her gang were an innocent, unsophisticated lot. Nevertheless she was relieved when the patio was made out of bounds to the under-16-year-olds after 8.30 at night.

Gill's growing friendship with an American girl, Betty-Lou Gewald, was another source of encouragement. At 20 Betty-Lou was far too old to be in "the gang". Their common interest was cooking. Betty-Lou had been doing a domestic science diploma in Manila when hostilities closed the college and forced her and her mother, Myrtle Gewald, into STIC. Pretty and vivacious, she was engaged to an American soldier fighting in Bataan. They had hoped to get married in the autumn.

Gill had never done any cooking in her life. In Shanghai she had hardly been near the kitchen which was ruled by a cook and a bodyguard of servants. She was fascinated by all the dishes Betty-Lou showed her and amazed at how much she could make with so little. She found she loved cooking, following recipes, inventing new ones.

If Gill had devoted the same energies to her studies as she did to cooking and "the gang" her mother might have been better pleased.

Gill had signed on at the camp school for shorthand, book-keeping, English and algebra. When Isla found she had been flunking classes she was furious.

"It's too bad. These people give their services free and the least you could do is turn up. After all you've only got four subjects. What's going to happen when we get out of here and you find you're way behind all the other girls in the class? We'll have to fix you up with some sort of school in England at least until you're 17."

"But mummy, the children in the class are all American and I've done all the things we're doing now *years* ago. And shorthand's boring. I'd much rather get a job looking after children in the hospital."

Isla did not much fancy the thought of Gill working in the hospital but since at least it showed an interest, she decided to offer mild encouragement.

"Well, perhaps when you're 16 we'll be able to get you a job there."

By that time, she thought to herself, they were bound to be far from the Philippines and Gill safely back at school.

Isla had some cause for her optimism. In Bataan troops under General Wainwright were holding out against impossible odds. Corregidor, the Gibraltar of the East, where MacArthur had established his headquarters, had been bombed again and again yet the rock held firm. The talk in camp was all about the promises President Roosevelt was said to have made of hundreds of ships, thousands of planes coming to their rescue.

STIC spirits were hopeful and high. A story from one of the men's dormitories mirrored the mood. At roll call the guard found his numbers did not tally.

"There should be fifty in this room. I count only forty-nine," he said accusingly.

And one of the men replied: "Uncle Sam is missing but he'll be here soon."

"O.K., good, soon, Uncle Sam. Good, good," said the Jap, a reasonable fellow, and retreated giggling and satisfied.

As long as Bataan and Corregidor held the internees could hope.

On 15 February two events shattered the camp. Three young men, two British and one Australian, who had escaped in an effort to join up with the troops in Bataan, were recaptured. Gill saw one of them being led back with a noose round his neck. The Japs had warned internees that anyone attempting escape would be shot but, with many still out in the town and others on regular passes, the threat did not strike them as serious.

But there was no mercy for these three. By the time they were led out to execution, Tom Fletcher, Henry Wynox and Brecky Leacock, the Australian, were so beaten and tortured they could hardly walk. They were sentenced under military law for disobeying orders, disrupting the peace of the camp and trying to communicate with the enemy. The internees' petition to the Commandant for clemency was turned down. The prisoners were forced to dig their own graves and were shot at dawn with just their room monitor and Padre Griffiths as witnesses. The padre said they died bravely.

Isla and Gill went to the Requiem Mass the next morning. They had heard the news that two Japs had been found killed with notes pinned to their shirts, "This is for the Englishmen – there's a third to come", and all through the service Isla kept thinking of the Old Testament precept "an eye for an eye, a tooth for a tooth". Christ had rejected the old law – telling his followers to love their enemies, to do good to them that hate you, to pray for those who persecute and insult you. But Isla wanted the old justice. She could not forgive the killing of these three young men.

For days the camp was silent, sad. The internees knew now for sure that if they did not obey orders their lives were worthless.

The second blow was the fall of Singapore on 15 February.

Radios were forbidden in camp yet somehow the news filtered through. Isla had heard that there was a radio concealed among the stuffed birds in the Education Building but thought it better not to ask too many questions.

The diary she had been keeping daily since her arrival in the Philippines was dynamite enough. She had started it as a letter to her husband and now, after two months, it had become her closest confidante. But the Japs had an obsession about the written word and Isla knew that if they found the diary she was likely to be tortured and shot. Some of her friends, terrified that she had mentioned their names in the diary, begged her to scratch them out but she reckoned that her illegible hand-writing was camouflage enough.

There seemed no doubt about the Singapore news which was gleefully confirmed the following day by the *Tribune*, a Japanese-controlled newspaper in English, the distribution of which was encouraged both inside and outside STIC as a propaganda organ.

For a time the disaster caused a rift between the British and

American factions in camp. The Americans blamed the British for letting Singapore go when they were fighting tooth and nail in Bataan. "Those goddam British," one Bronx boy growled on the food line. "They ought to be turned over to Hitler to run."

The Japs relished their allies' mutual animosity and fostered it in a compulsory questionnaire. Internees were ordered to give a "frank opinion" on which country they considered more responsible for the war, America or Britain. While the majority of internees answered "Neither", some Americans blamed the British and some of the British blamed the United States, answering, in fact, just as the Japs wanted.

The more serious camp view of the war situation was that after Pearl Harbor Churchill and Roosevelt had decided to kiss Singapore goodbye. Some pessimists suggested they might well have done the same to the Philippines, that the policy was to concentrate on winning the war in Europe and deal with Japan later.

The news of further Allied disasters in the battles of the Java Sea and Sunda Straight at the end of the month did nothing to restore confidence. Now Japan would have complete control of Java's oil wells and enough oil to turn the Pacific into a Japanese marina.

The Filipinos were beginning to feel the same sense of abandonment. The Japs wooed them to co-operate with the New Order – or Odour as the internees liked to call it – dangling carrots of Independence and a new economic prosperity as part of the Greater East Asia Co-Prosperity Sphere.

Certainly as February drew to a close the prospects for the native population could hardly have been worse. Filipinos had to stand for hours in the sun for a quarter of rice and if anyone moved out of line he was soundly kicked by a Jap guard. One Filipino who stole two cans of food was branded and thrown into the river. And when the farmers refused to co-operate with the New Odour and burned their crops rather than deliver them up to the Japs, six men were taken from each village and shot.

Yet, in spite of cajolements and threats, the majority of the native population remained loyal to America and the current Filipino joke went:

Jap sentry: "Come back, little boy, you're swimming too far out, the sharks will get you."

Little boy, showing his chest marked *The Co-Prosperity of Asia*: "Not even the sharks will swallow that!"

The one hope that kept up the morale of both Filipinos and internees alike was that Uncle Sam was sending reinforcements. MacArthur had broadcast from Corregidor on *The Voice of Freedom* that however many Japs attacked he would push them back. It seemed only logical that the Philippines would be defended to the last to divert the Japs from attacking Australia.

Even when MacArthur left on 12 March, ordered by Washington to take command of the war effort in Australia, the internees could only believe it was for the best. If anyone could bring them help Doug would.

The month dragged by. Isla was desperate to get a cable or letter out to T.D. When she heard that the members of the British Consulate were being sent home under diplomatic immunity she thought her chance had come. The Commandant ruled that each internee might send a letter of 100 words. Not much to cover all that had happened in three months, but better than nothing. She set about condensing her news. But 100 words was too much to hope for. The letter allowance was cut to two words and even those were selected by the Commandant – "safe" and "well" – a description that Isla for one considered quite false.

Those with families and friends still in Manila were in a happier position, being allowed to send and receive letters through the gate. As with parcels, letters were subject to inspection and just to show they were doing their censoring job conscientiously the Jap guards would cross out words like "please" and "hope you're feeling well". But outwitting the enemy was part of the game and the internees managed to get in a host of uncensored material including broadcast transcripts. Notes were concealed in banana skins, under cakes and, it was rumoured, written in invisible lemon juice. Messages even got through from the P.O.W. camps of Cabanatuan and Bilibid.

Easter fell at the beginning of April. This year finding an egg, let alone a chocolate one, was like hunting the proverbial needle in a haystack. But Isla finally tracked some down for Gill and her friends. Ida, who had earned the nickname of the Cow's Tail because she was always last, drew and cut out some Easter bunnies for the children. Another woman made a chocolate Easter cake. An egg hunt was organized for the children in the Annex and in the evening there was a barn dance for the teenagers.

A few nights later they were all woken by the noise of a tremendous explosion. The earth shook and rumbled – it was an earthquake. All night long the quakes convulsed the ground, uprooting trees and sending the little huts that some of the internees had built in the grounds crashing to dust. The building itself swayed like the Empire State top floor in a hurricane but, luckily, it was quakeproof.

Disasters always came in pairs at Santo Tomas. On 9 April, the same day as the earthquake, Bataan fell. The help that the exhausted troops had relied on had not come. For nearly three months they had lived at first on half rations and in the latter stages on as little as 700 calories a day. Over half the troops – 12,000 Americans and 70,000 Filipinos – were sick with dysentery or malaria.

From his headquarters in Australia MacArthur sent this message to General Wainwright:

"The Bataan Force went out as it would have wished, fighting to the end of its flickering forlorn hope. No army has ever done so much with so little, and nothing became it more than its last hour of trial and agony. To the weeping mothers of its dead, I can only say that the sacrifice and halo of Jesus of Nazareth has descended upon their sons, and that God will take them unto himself."

In STIC the jingle ran:

> Poor brave bastards of Bataan,
> No poppa, no momma, no Uncle Sam.

The full horror of the Bataan Death March when 15,550 Allied soldiers were clubbed, shot or bayoneted down as they came to surrender was not yet known. It was to be told by the wretched few who survived the 65-mile march, on the barest rations, under the baking sun, to become prisoners in Cabanatuan and Bilibid. One of them was Betty-Lou's fiancé.

After the fall of Bataan only a few weeks elapsed before the fate of Corregidor was sealed. The end came on 7 May after six days of heavy air bombardment. General Wainwright surrendered the whole archipelago into Jap hands.

MacArthur wrote: "Corregidor needs no comment from me. It has scrolled its own epitaph on enemy tablets. But through the bloody haze of its last reverberating shot, I shall always seem to see a vision of grim, gaunt, ghastly men, still unafraid."

In Santo Tomas the internees remembered his parting words: "I shall return."

CHAPTER THREE

Tally-ho!

(May–December, 1942)

THE Fall of Corregidor marked a turning point in the lives of the internees in Santo Tomas.

Now they were alone on totally enemy-controlled territory. No longer could they get news from MacArthur's *Voice of Freedom* station. Their captors had the upper hand completely and they soon showed it.

Rumour never had a better breeding ground and her STIC progeny were worthy successors in the line. Every night Isla would join May and Wyndham, Don, Fred, Mitch and others in a Council of War where they would discuss the rumours of the day. Somehow at night the good news seemed so believable, so near, yet every morning it would fly out of the window like an evil night shadow mocking the hopes and dreams of the isolated internees.

"Rumourtism" was said to be the most common and most infectious complaint in camp. The condition naturally concentrated itself on the internees' hopes of release. The distant humming of a plane was enough to start a rumour that American troops had landed at Aparri. Even the Chinese, whose naval strength amounted to little more than a fleet of junks, were credited with taking Formosa and invading northern Luzon. Further afield the rumours were more ambitious – Singapore had been recaptured, Burma was ours, Guam had fallen to the marines, the Allies had landed in France, Germany was suing for peace. And there were casualty figures to back each hoped-for victory or conquest.

A more outlandish strain of Rumourtism proclaimed that King George VI had abdicated and the Duke of Windsor had been reinstated to make Anglo-American relations more cordial. Mrs Wally Simpson, now the Duchess, was to divorce Edward and marry the Pope.

As she recorded this strange *mêlée* of reports in her diary Isla recalled the lines from Virgil's *Aeneid*, "What some invent, the rest enlarge, Swift rumour, of all evils the most swift, Speed lends her strength and she gains vigour as she goes. She has a hundred tongues, a hundred mouths, a voice of iron."

The internees had their own version of the classics, composed by one of their number, Mr E. S. Saunders.

"I heard it stated yesterday by a man who ought to know,
    That by tomorrow afternoon we can pack our bags and
        go.
This information came to him from a most authentic
    source
    Via his house-boy's cousin's aunt – and verified of
    course.
Ten thousand flying fortresses flew over town last night,
    It's too bad we couldn't see them, because of their great
    height,
But they dropped a million leaflets, one of which would
    have been found
    If some Japanese civilians hadn't just then come around.
MacArthur's men made ninety miles on a fake reverse
    and run
    They filtered through Manila, and dug in at Sorsogon,
While somewhere in the Pacific (near the Marshalls we
    presume)
    A naval battle is being fought; from which one can
    assume
That the Russians, Poles and Slovaks with twenty million
    more
    Have joined forces in the Ukraine and retaken Singapore.

This may all sound like a rumour,
    But to me it looks all right,
So why wait until tomorrow?
    Let's pack our bags tonight."

Finally the source of the most optimistic brand of rumour was traced to two men in the gym who, convinced any news was better than no news, had been distributing typewritten bulletins announcing as fact the news internees wanted to hear. They justified their efforts and their consciences by calling their media war work, a harmless way of keeping up camp morale. In the Education Building another pair with less altruistic motives started rumours for the sheer joy of seeing them metamorphose as they went round the camp.

If news was the main subject of speculation, the possibility of repatriation ran a very close second. Here hopes were not entirely unjustified since a small band, including some close friends of Isla's, had been allowed to return to Shanghai. Indeed Isla was asked if she wanted to go but, thinking that the Philippines were bound to be relieved before China and assuming – for she had heard nothing – that her husband would be repatriated to England, she chose to wait.

Stories came back that the Shanghailanders had had a terrible time reaching China, packed together like cattle in a small coaster with no superstructure. Apart from a few Jap troops, who took the pride of the accommodation, their travelling companions were horses and mules. Isla was glad she had not risked taking Gill, whose health was a constant worry.

Her choice seemed particularly fortunate when she heard that another repatriation ship would shortly be sailing to India, a much more desirable destination from Isla's point of view since it was British territory, still out of enemy hands and was almost certainly where she would find Richard. She and T.D. had many friends in India and indeed India had been her objective when she and Gill boarded the ill-fated *Anhui*. As Isla filled out form after endless form she felt sure release was near. She would pack her bags tonight like the others. Why wait until tomorrow?

Tomorrow was the elusive factor. As with all tomorrows it never came and the repatriation ship acquired the spectral name, *The Phantom Maru*.

Meanwhile the internees built up their community. Those with sufficient funds staked out spaces in the grounds and built themselves primitive palm shelters. The camp magazines were full of advertisements for "modern nipa shanties", "prefabricated shanties", and precious building tools passed from hand to busy hand on a rota basis. By the end of 1942 there were close on 2,000 shacks grouped in tiny communities – Shanty

Town, Jerkville and Upper Jerkville, Froggy Bottom, Glamorville, Intramuros, Jungletown, Gardenville – each with their own mayor and governing committee.

Don had a shanty, so did Fred Satterfield. May and Wyndham built one in Glamorville. Although at first the building materials were not expensive – 50 pesos would cover the basic cost – Isla and Gill could not afford such luxury.

Often as Isla strolled down Tobacco Road and Broadway looking at the open cabins with their gay little gardens she wished she had sold some jewellery to finance a home. She comforted herself with the thought that they would soon be out. She set no store by Ida's depressing dream. Ida was always dreaming, usually nightmares. In this particular nocturnal mirage the war ended and the internees were taken back to New York to be each presented, for their heroism, with one of the latest Ford models – 1947 vintage!

The Japs did not object to shanties so long as the buildings conformed to their rules. The shacks had to be completely open, with no nipa matting at the sides and no curtains so that the guards could see that nothing untoward – by which they meant sex or listening to the radio – was going on. No one was allowed to remain in the shanties at night.

The ban on sex was as stringent as the ban on booze – and about as successful. In spite of the efforts of the much-abused Morality Squad and the Commandant's constant purge on rising shanty walls, a steady stream of pregnancies was reported at the hospital.

A less steady, but by no means irregular, stream of drunks and bootleggers appeared before the camp's Court of Order. The drunks were particularly unpopular with those who still had relatives outside and with mothers, like May, whose two younger children were lodged at the convent in town, for if the drinkers were caught by the Japs all passes out were cancelled, sometimes for as long as a week.

To preserve what little freedom of movement the others still retained the Court imposed heavy sentences on those caught drinking, drunk, or smuggling in bottles. Thirty days' hard labour or a month's jail for male offenders was not unusual and for women the penalty was fifteen to thirty days confined to quarters. All offenders were forbidden to use their shanties during sentence.

Isla was amazed when she was asked if she would sit on the court bench for the women's cases. Her acceptance of the job gave her a clearer insight into the problems of discipline in the camp.

The alcohol situation was a particularly tricky one. All along the line there were vested interests – from the Jap sentries at the gate who got backhanders for letting vendors come in with their wares, to certain members of the Executive Committee who guaranteed protection to bootleggers in exchange for supplies of rum, Hong Kong whisky or any other alcoholic refreshment they could lay their hands on. It came in hidden in sacks of charcoal or disguised in medicine bottles.

Things came to a head when three bootleggers – Wally King, Robby Robb and Bill Reece – were caught by the new Police chief, Jim Tullock, a blunt, no nonsense American in his mid-thirties. The Court of Order sentenced the three to thirty days' hard labour apiece and ordered their shacks to be torn down. King, insolent in his security, informed the Court that the sentences would be reduced or revoked by arrangement with the Executive Committee and, in confirmation of their collusion, the Committee demanded a moratorium. The penalties were broadcast on the tannoy system – the agreed method of announcing that sentences were about to be implemented – yet still the culprits went free to the mystification and indignation of the rest of the camp. Finally Jim Tullock issued an ultimatum: either the Executive Committee give the Police the proper backing or the force would resign in a body.

Tullock won. But King and his companions were not beaten. Even while serving their sentences they openly boasted they could get anything they wanted through the gate.

Private brewing was another matter. Every ambitious internee had his own favourite recipe. Doris Cooke swore by fermented pineapple juice, Isla and May preferred the Gym recipe of raisins, prunes and mush. It tasted like a mixture of gritty madeira and sour porridge but it was indisputably the stronger of the two brews.

There was no doubt that the spirits of Room Five needed a boost. Every day some new quarrel broke out – Doris Cooke had left her clothes lying all over the floor when it was Isla's turn to clean; Jenny moved Caroline's mirror while Caroline was in hospital to make room for a set of shelves Alec was putting up for her; Molly never ceased to complain about people bumping into her bed at night.

Molly's bumping was indeed the major issue of the summer of '42 for Room Five, taking precedence over the battles of the Coral Sea and Midway Island. Molly accused Gill of kicking her twice in the night but, as Isla and May had proved, it was quite impossible to kick through two nets.

"Someone else must have shaken you to try and stop you snoring," Isla told Molly.

Molly's incredible grunts and snorts kept everyone awake. Not a woman or girl in the room was beneath giving her a good shake. One night, indeed, Isla had woken to see Molly's unfortunate niece-in-law, Lydia, banging her aunt on the head in an effort to quench the noise. The poor girl's bed was in the direct firing line and even the ear plugs she wore every night could not muffle Molly. On that occasion Molly had accused Isla, who indignantly retorted it was not her but Lydia, and, amazingly, Molly had dropped the matter like a hot brick. For the one person whose disapprobation Molly dreaded was Lydia's mother, Sister, and she dare not address a cross word to her niece for fear of reprisals. Isla was tempted to play the same card again.

But this time Molly was convinced she had the culprit.

"I *know* it was Gill," she persisted. "I suppose she thinks it's some kind of teenage joke to wake people up in the middle of the night and then pretend to be asleep herself."

"I *told* you," said Isla in desperation, "it's impossible to kick through two nets. May and I have tried it."

"I might have known it," rejoined Molly, triumphant. "And after all the food I've given you!"

Isla felt like pointing out that all Molly and her gang had ever given them were scraps that would otherwise have been thrown to the pigs, but she and Gill had been grateful even for that and so she restrained herself. She wished now she had never accepted anything and cursed herself for going to Molly's birthday party and taking her ice-cream and cake.

From the protection of her nail file Jenny mumbled: "There's plenty of room upstairs if you don't like our company."

Isla's temper was up and this intervention by Jenny was the last straw.

"Why the hell should *we* move?" she demanded. "It would

be much more to the point if Molly moved herself and her beastly snores and gave us some peace. Gill didn't bump her, but even if she did hers wouldn't be the only bed to get bumped in this god-awful hole."

She turned to Molly. If bed-bumping was the issue she had something to say on the length of Molly's which stuck out of line from all the others in the row creating a terrible hazard in the dark room.

"If you'd cut six inches off the end of your bed so the mattress fitted you might not be bumped at all. As it is it's impossible not to trip over it. Don't blame us for your own stupidity."

She swore to herself that if Molly mentioned her wretched bed once more she'd shake her *every* time she snored.

"We're *always* being bumped," said Margot from her corner.

And May joined in: "You're lucky to have only been bumped t wice."

This gave Molly her opportunity: "You complain about *my* bed! *Your* bed with that great net over it takes up so much room it's no wonder you're bumped."

"Aren't we even allowed to live?" said Gill, now almost in tears. All the ganging up and the squabbles and the bitterness made her feel utterly wretched. She felt herself trembling with nervousness.

"Our bed is in line with our shelf," said Isla as if to settle the matter once and for all.

"It's too bad the room wasn't measured by the Committee," said Margot.

"*You* keep out of other people's quarrels," screamed Doris Cooke, who needed about as much provocation as a taunted rattlesnake to stay aloof from a good fight.

The Battle of the Beds was once again in its zenith.

The other great issue on which all took sides was the mah-jong sessions. Molly, Jenny, Monty Gordon and Caroline Wolff formed a mah-jong school which played regularly in the passage outside Room Five during siesta hour. It is a physical impossibility to play mah-jong quietly and the high-pitched voices of the Rich Bitches as they called out their sequences seemed to vie with the slap of the mah-jong tiles for maximum decibel count.

Isla was not the only one to complain. All the rooms along the passage were indignant, not only because the noise disturbed the siesta but also because the gaming table, right in the middle of the narrow corridor, made it almost impossible to squeeze by. Needless to say the Rich Bitches made no attempt to move out of the way for what they considered the lower orders and all suggestions by Elsa Schoering, the floor monitor, that they should play out of siesta hours were ignored.

When Mrs Schoering warned Jenny that if they did not stop the Police would be called in, she retorted: "Just let one of the red-arm-band men talk to *me*."

Even instructions from the Court of Order appeared to have no effect on the self-styled élite of Manila.

Their smug contempt for everyone else's comforts made Isla wild. When, one hot and steamy evening, Molly turned on her and complained that she was keeping her awake brushing her hair, Isla could contain herself no longer.

"You keep me awake all night with your snoring and all day with your hateful mah-jong. By the time I get round to brushing my hair you're snoring so loud *nothing* would wake you. Why can't you play your mah-jong in the shanties or in the evenings? Everyone's complaining. You make more noise than any Chinese. I've never met such an inconsiderate lot as you Manila crowd."

"You're always on about Manila people," said Molly, flouncing over to her still untrimmed bed.

As Isla got into bed she heard Molly muttering about China coast people.

The final straw came when the gang turned on Gill. Isla had been at the hospital all morning where she had taken a job as messenger/receptionist. It was hard work but better than cleaning out the lavatories and it included the priceless perk of a free meal. As she walked back along the passage towards Room Five she heard a chorus of screams of indignation and accusation that indicated a major battle was under way. She braced herself for the inevitable fight. In a way this daily fracas had taken the place of the ordinary stimulations of life and a really good screaming match had a twisted sort of purgative effect on the taut spirits. But her militarism turned to horror, then anger, as she heard Gill's tearful voice raised against the accusing throng.

"Wendy's not a thief. I know, I know. I was with her all the time. It's not fair. You're just ganging up again. She'd never do a thing like that."

"Funny that everyone but you says she is. Perhaps you're her accomplice," said Jane deliberately provoking Gill from the protection of her adult supporters.

"I'm not, I'm not. It's not true."

"Of course you can't blame the child when Mrs Gates keeps absolutely no control over her, or indeed over any of her brood," remarked Jenny with scantily veiled reference to Wendy's elder sister, Barbara, who was about to become an unmarried mother. Her fiancé was a prisoner in Cabanatuan.

"You're all the same, you Shanghai lot," yelled Molly, her bumped bed still irking. "Why don't you move in with your light-fingered friends?"

"Good idea!" "We can do without thieves here!" "Go and join your precious Wendy."

Isla burst into the room and found Gill cornered like a stag at bay, the hounds hungry for blood.

"Leave the child alone, you great bullies. It's got nothing to do with her." When Gill first told her mother about the accusations against Wendy stealing from the kitchens, Isla had advised her to keep well out of it.

"Take no notice of them, darling," she had said to Gill.

"I don't understand," sobbed Gill. "Why do they hate us so? I was only trying to explain. I know Wendy didn't do it. She's already been cleared. I was only trying to tell them but they won't listen, they just accuse and shout abuse about people from the China coast. I can't bear it. I don't understand."

Isla understood all right. She had seen too much of the ganging up, the illbred smugness. And her opinion of the Rich Bitches was shared by most of the camp who suffered from their imperious behaviour not only over the mah-jong noise but also in the food line whenever they deigned to patronize it.

"Everyone knows Jane McLeod's a trouble maker. Forget it. Let's find May and go down to Leftie's for hot cakes and coffee," suggested Isla, piloting her dishevelled daughter out of the room where the charged atmosphere was gradually subsiding.

As they walked out of the door they heard Molly having the last word as ever. "Of course, all Shanghailanders have a terrible reputation both with the teachers and the boys. It's just typical!"

Leftie's was one of the many restaurants that had started up

45

in camp. In a makeshift shack behind the Education block it served coffee and hot cakes, made from corn mush, and hot meals at one peso a dish. With John Hunter's *Wayside Inn* at the end of the Boardwalk near the boundary, it was the Corfields' favourite haunt when they had a few pesos to spare.

Isla could never understand how these restaurants managed to keep going but obviously there was still a lot of money around for those who had the right contacts.

By the summer of 1942 there were few services the camp could not supply. The stores had become more sophisticated than in the early days. Now there was a bakery specializing in muffins and a dairy which delivered Coconut Cow – "Milk from Contented Coconuts" as the adverts put it – each morning at eight at 15 cents a pint. The coconut shells and oil made excellent lamps and, of course, there was an internee who did good business in the lighting line. Al's Discount Store operated from the second floor of the Education Building, the package line at the gate was manned by a pick-up and delivery service. There were building contractors for the shanties, several lending libraries and book clubs, beauty salons, stationers and a fortune-teller.

Advertisements for all the different services appeared, often fully illustrated, in the camp magazine, *Internitis*, along with cartoons, competitions, a gossip column, jokes, cookery hints, short stories, crossword puzzles and horoscopes by Madame Zomara.

Dave Harvey, a tall thin young man of tremendous energy and good humour, was the publication's leading light. His column *From the Slime to the Ridiculum* helped to keep spirits high. The cracks were strictly topical – "Fish and rumours smell bad after the first day!" – "Hey, Joe, there's a bed bug on your neck." "That's no bed bug, that's a freckle." "Well, it's the first time I ever saw a walking freckle!" – "Look George, Andy had a ham and sent you a slice." "He sliced it? Looks like he darn near missed it!"

Isla enjoyed *Internitis*. She was not so keen on its successor, the *Stic Gazette*. The *Gazette* excused its, in Isla's view, atrocious style by announcing at the top of each publication: "Papershort condition demands abrupt unceremonious edistyle. Therefore curt, concise our slogan." "Stic" was used as a prefix for practically everything – sticeditor, sticouncil, sticommandant, sticmedic, sticappenings, sticistory.

However, along with the notice board and the internal broadcasting system it did serve to keep internees in touch with what was happening in camp. It announced and reported on the baseball and football matches, the boxing and croquet, the bridge, chess and checkers tournaments which were so much part of camp life. It billed the evening's musical programmes broadcast on records over the tannoy under the direction of music lover Geoff Morrison. It gave notice of the teenagers' barn dances, the shows, the parties. It ran competitions.

The shows were another Dave Harvey project. He and his pretty young wife were professionals and had toured the world with their song and dance routines. Soon Dave's "theatre" in the patio, with its makeshift scenery decorated with banana leaves and palm fronds and lactogen cans for footlights, became the hub of camp entertainment dispensing a brand of optimistic Anglo-Saxon cheer that the oriental mind could not fathom. His song, *Cheer up, Everything's Gonna be Lousy*, rivalled the rumour song in popularity. It went:

"Our lot is getting better and the county's getting wetter,
So I'm no longer sad and pessimistic.
Conditions are chaotic, but I'm very patriotic,
And I want to show that I am optimistic.
I wouldn't say a word to make you blue (oh no)
I've come to bring a word of joy to you –
Cheer up, everything's gonna be lousy!

You may have built a shanty, but it won't be there for long,
'Cause the sides are going higher, so they say;
You may have been the president of Manila's leading
    store,
But you've still gotta haul the garbage from the third and
    highest floor;
You may grumble now at beans and peas,
But wait till you start on the bark off the trees –
Cheer up, everything's gonna be lousy!

The rules are getting longer every day . . .
You can't do this, you can't do that . . .
You can't even romance in your shack

I know because I tried it yesterday.
The rumours may be all you need,
But soon you'll believe in what you read –
Cheer up, everything's gonna be lousy!"

The country was certainly getting wetter. After an insufferably hot spell when the temperatures shot up to nearly 104° Fahrenheit, the hottest Manila had known for 57 years, the weather broke on 15 June and the monsoon was in full deluge.

The internees had been preparing for the rain, building up their shanties on stilts and clubbing together to buy mediaguas or rain shields to fix on the windows so the water did not pour in when they were open. It was bad enough having to sit inside during the rain but without the windows open it would have been unbearable. They had built shelters for the food benches and washing troughs and made floors to keep the mud at bay.

But the rain was no respecter of worthy effort. In twenty-four hours seventeen inches fell. The gardens and paths were awash, the mud came ankle deep sucking off the flimsy bakias, the native sandals that most of the internees wore. The little shacks with their neatly laid-out gardens that had had so much money and care lavished on them were deep in water.

The congestion in the buildings was horrific. Shanty owners, who as a rule stayed out during the day, crowded into the passages with whatever of their possessions they could salvage from the encroaching mud. Washing, damp and steamy, hung everywhere. Baseball and football matches were abandoned. Tempers, already frayed, splintered and snapped. Tuck, Isla's Shanghai friend, summed up the camp feeling: "We could get our own back on the Japs if we gave them the Philippine Islands!"

The Japs, for their part, considered they already had the Philippines. The marooned islands were almost at the centre of the Mikado's empire surrounded as they were by an expanding girth of Nippon conquests – Burma, Sumatra, Java, the Solomons, the Gilberts, the Marshall Islands, north to the Aleutians, east to Manchuria, Peking, Nanking, Shanghai and Hong Kong.

As Corregidor struggled in its death throes another American stronghold, the air base at Port Moresby in southern New Guinea, was under attack. The ultimate object was to win control of the Coral Sea for the Empire, isolating Australia and providing bases in New Guinea, New Caledonia and the New Hebrides for attacks on Australia's northern ports and airfields. The Battle of the Coral Sea on 8 May, though claimed as a great Jap victory, in fact resolved none of Nippon's hopes and Port Moresby remained, albeit unsteadily, in Allied hands.

Garbled reports of the encounter came through to STIC – the United States had lost two carriers and several battleships, it was a sweeping victory for the Empire; and, from the other side, twenty-five Jap ships had been sunk and the U.S. Navy were triumphant. In fact losses on both sides were considerably less, with the balance, if anything, slightly in favour of Japan. But, though the internees were not to know, Nippon had suffered a catastrophic blow in the Coral Sea – the loss of hundreds of trained pilots whom she had no hope of replacing in the short time it was necessary to win the war. The tide was imperceptibly on the turn.

One of the original objects of the war – the capture of the valuable oil-fields of the East Indies – had been achieved with comparative ease and Japan now had all the oil she wanted. The next question was whether she would strike westwards towards India in the hope of joining forces with her Axis ally somewhere in the Middle East or whether she would concentrate her strength on a drive eastwards across the Pacific to Hawaii and the United States western seaboard. Alternatively she could simply consolidate her gains.

Admiral Isoruku Yamamoto, Commander-in-Chief of the Japanese Fleet, decided that the primary objective was the swift annihilation of the U.S. naval forces in the Pacific. He was convinced that it would not be long before the United States Navy, under its dynamic new commander, Admiral Chester W. Nimitz, took revenge for Pearl Harbor.

Already in April Tokyo had been bombed by a small fleet of B-25s commanded by Lieutenant-Colonel James Doolittle. Although the Japanese press mockingly referred to it as the "Do-Nothing Raid", the fact that the U.S. could launch bombers from their Pacific carriers to bomb Tokyo was enough for Yamamoto. He determined to destroy the U.S. fleet in the Pacific while the strength still lay with Japan and before America had time to compensate for the disasters of Pearl Harbor. As his target in this do-or-die contest he chose Midway Island.

Nimitz would be forced to defend it for beyond Midway lay Hawaii and the American coastline. Yamamoto was convinced that if he could snatch a victory here the United States would sue for peace.

On 3 June the great Japanese armada – its strength was almost double that of the United States forces and Jap carriers outnumbered American by nearly three-to-one – went into action. By 15 June it was all over. The Japs were in retreat. They had lost four carriers, a heavy cruiser, 253 planes and 3,500 men. The United States losses were one carrier, one destroyer, 150 planes and 307 men.

STIC heard the news through the usual mysterious channels. Obviously, somewhere in the camp, was an illicit radio, for the Jap-controlled newspapers said nothing of the battle. For days they did not even mention the Pacific.

Some news reached the internees through Filipinos at the gate or through internees on permanent passes coming in to register. One radio commentator, they heard, had announced that Midway was the beginning of the end for the Japs. Events were to prove him right. Another report told of a marine at Midway who wired Hawaii, "The Japs have lost their pants saving face."

But the *Tribune* still dealt out trivia as if nothing of importance had happened anywhere near the Philippines. "Americans cut one inch off their shirt tails to further the war effort", the headlines proclaimed.

The Japanese Naval General Staff had in fact gone to great lengths to conceal the disaster from the public, imposing a strict censorship on all mail and press reports. After the war Admiral Kondo, one of the Midway commanders, was to admit, "Our forces suffered a defeat so decisive and so grave that the details of it were kept the guarded secret of a limited circle even within the Japanese navy."

For the next six months the battle for the Pacific centred round Guadalcanal in the Solomon Islands. In August the *Tribune* reported an astounding naval victory for Japan at Savo Island. Captain Syoili Kamada, the Japanese Navy spokesman, announced that the night attack was so complete a surprise that the enemy in many cases did not even train their guns on the Japanese vessels. As a result, he continued, "Japanese warships smashed through the lines of the enemy transports to inflict great losses." He added that the losses must be great since the Americans were keeping so quiet. "Their unbecoming modesty and reticence is tantamount to a confession of catastrophic disaster. They are helpless against the invincible might of Japan."

The Allies had indeed suffered a severe setback at Savo Island. The inferiority of their night fighting was to manifest itself again and again over the next few months. The hastily trained, inexperienced crews of the U.S. ships were no match for Japanese veterans.

Mockingly the *Tokio Shimbun* for 9 October, the first U.S. Navy Day since the start of the war, commented: "The day could more fittingly be described as a memorial day to lament over the crushing defeats the U.S. has suffered since the advent of hostilities."

And on the plight of the American soldiers desperately holding the air strip at Guadalcanal, the *Tribune* reported: "As a result of reckless operations nearly 10,000 American soldiers are left helplessly marooned in the Solomon Islands group. The United States Navy is seriously encumbered by these ill-fated men."

Encumbered or not the U.S. Navy managed to hold Guadalcanal. By November it was clear that the United States, in Admiral King's words, had moved forward from the "defensive-offensive" to the "offensive-defensive".

In the European war the defeat of Rommel's Army at El Alamein at the end of October, 1942, and the successful Anglo-American landings in French North Africa in early November prompted Winston Churchill to announce "the end of the beginning".

In Russia the counter-attack at Stalingrad had begun. The armies were fighting in thick snow, the internees heard, the Red Army taking their city back house by house, rubble by rubble. German besiegers were dying at the rate of 15,000 a day from cold and disease, and Stalin had promised to be in Germany before the summer of '43.

The Japs, however, celebrated "one year of war" in December with much mutual back-slapping. In the Filipino magazine *New Era*, of which Isla managed to get a copy, Lt-Col Nakazima, Chief of the Department of Information, wrote, "One year has elapsed since launching the Greater East Asia War for the creation of the New Order. The brilliant war results achieved in so short a period have astounded the whole world. The arrogant Anglo-American foothold in the Orient was dislodged; their imperialistic designs frustrated; and their kleptomaniac influence completely wiped out. The first step toward building Asia for the Asiatics has been made."

News reaching STIC was sparse. The internees' best gauge of how the war was progressing was the attitude of their captors towards them. The increased inspections by Visiting Vermin – as the Jap top brass were called – searching for radios and anti-Japanese propaganda, the cutting down on passes to the town, the restrictions on the package line, all indicated that the rumours of Allied victory at Midway in June and the subsequent laboured but definite turn to the offensive in the late autumn were well-founded.

Frequent inspections made an early warning system necessary. The internees struck on an original, and apparently innocuous, scheme. All Japs were known as "Tally-hos" and if any internee saw a guard or an inspection party approaching he would call "Tally-ho". The reason behind this curiously British appellation lay in an old story about an American who, visiting a friend in England, was taken hunting. The next day he asked his host: "Did I do all right?" The Englishman replied: "Yes, fine. Your clothes were right, you took your fences well but you must learn to say 'Tally-ho' and not 'There goes that son-of-a-bitch.'"

Isla would often say "Tally-ho" to Donald if she saw a Jap approaching and he would turn his face away. Isla was always afraid for this remarkable man. There were people less trustworthy than herself in camp who knew Don and knew that there was a price on his head. One such man was C—— P——, who had spent many years in China, some of them in jail for forgery. He was also thought to have been connected with a sinister black magic murder in Peking. He was constantly annoying Donald, hanging round his shack, trying to get accepted by him. When his overtures were met with a cold shoulder he threatened to expose Don to the Commandant and showed him a recent article from the *Saturday Evening Post* describing Don as "China's No. 1 White Man". But fortunately P—— also had connections with the Old Marshal which put him on the Japanese black list and prevented him from carrying out his treacherous intentions.

The tally-hos' main objective was to unearth the radio sets they knew must be operating within the camp. Their second target was any written anti-Axis propaganda or unauthorized news bulletins.

At the gate a squad of tally-hos was posted to inspect every parcel and book that entered the camp. The internees found that the best way to smuggle anything through was to divert the guards' attention with "feelthy pictures". The problem was for supply to keep pace with demand.

Notes were inevitably discovered – one day as many as thirty-five – and immediately the package line was suspended. When it reopened it was enclosed by a fence so that outsiders bringing parcels could no longer see the recipients. A sort of Customs shed was built for the tally-ho inspections and the flow of parcels was limited to two-and-a-half hours in the morning. Packages were restricted to foodstuffs, laundry, medicines, toilet articles and empty food containers. Special arrangements had to be made for articles for resale such as ice, charcoal, coconuts, lumber and building materials. It was the writing on the wall for the shopkeepers.

The Commandant's orders on propaganda were stern: internees must refrain from any expression of sympathy with the enemy or hostility towards the Japanese; rumours and criticism relating to the Imperial Japanese forces and their movements, to the government of the Philippine Islands, to the living conditions of the Filipinos or to the internment camp itself were forbidden and those guilty of disseminating such rumours or criticism would be punished, "the form and degree to be determined by the Military Authorities".

Isla's stomach turned over as she thought of her diary. She had completed almost three large exercise books since her arrival in the Philippines, all of them full of rumours, news and criticism.

Her main fear centred on Cassy, the Ratcatcher. He had often seen her writing the diary and had teased her about it. Having been born, as he claimed, in Naples and educated in Germany, he was possibly pro-Axis and, Isla felt, might give her away to the Commandant at any time in spite of their bantering friendship. His American citizenship, he maintained, was purely a business convenience. And Cassy, who had run a beauty salon in Manila before taking up rat-catching for STIC, was also the worst of gossips.

But, Cassy or no Cassy, she could not burn it all now. She would have to take the risk.

The tally-hos were everywhere. A second contingent was appointed to guard those coming in to register and make sure they did not communicate with anyone inside the camp. The penalty for talking to an internee was withdrawal of pass.

By the autumn a pass was a comparatively rare document. Passes had even been withdrawn from married men whose Filipina wives still lived in the city – a situation which provoked some extraordinary tensions.

One day Isla was sitting in the garden on Fred's fine chair with Gill crouched on the footstool at her side when an extra-ordinary vision appeared. A Filipina woman ran out of the Education Building wearing nothing but a pair of pink pants pursued by three tally-hos, one carrying a gun. Her bra, hooked helplessly round one arm, flew out like a pennant behind her as she ran with her hands on her head like some demented ship's prow before the storm. As she came towards Gill and Isla she turned and fell on her knees before her pursuers. They could hear her gasping for breath.

The tally-hos had run their prey to earth. They kicked it to its feet. The woman was marched to the gate.

Later Isla learned that the Filipina had come in to find her husband who was shacked up with a little blonde American girl. Her protest took the form of a striptease in one of the main men's dormitories and the resulting riot not surprisingly attracted the attention of the patrolling guards.

Not only were those formerly on passes interned. More and more were brought in from the outlying districts of Luzon and from the other islands. In May came a pathetic band of 350 from Bataan and Corregidor – army and navy nurses and a few civilians. June brought another 500 from central Luzon. In July the hospital and the old people's quarters were moved to Santa Catalina, a school just across the road from the camp, to make room in STIC for a further 1,100 from the provinces. They came from Davao, from Mindanao, from Cebu.

The new hospital was vital. With all the disease in camp the little one in the Annex had become impossibly crowded. There was no means of isolating tuberculosis cases or indeed any other infection and the dangers of young children sharing wards with adult patients were obvious. Tuberculin tests showed 18 per cent of children under ten with a positive reaction. From every point of view a new location for an adult hospital had to be found. Santa Catalina, though still not nearly big enough to cope, was some help. The Annex hospital was kept on for the children.

The extra accommodation for the old people in Santa Catalina, together with the few repatriations, enabled STIC to keep below the 3,500 population mark.

Some space was saved when non-enemy alien Jews were informed they need not register. At first, following Axis policy, all Jews were told to check in at Fort Santiago, the Kempeitai headquarters. When a contingent of German and Spanish Jews led by their rabbi turned up at the prison they were asked by the Commandant: "Why do the Germans hate the Jews?" The rabbi replied: "Well, you see, the Hebrews are Asiatics and so the Germans have no use for us." This wily piece of information won them their freedom.

At STIC the missionaries were offered passes and, with the exception of Dr Thomas Foley and his wife, Mary Alice, who elected to stay with their flock, they accepted. They certainly knew before they had left that their action signified co-operation with the New Order and that they would not be allowed to return.

Other internees who had been born in neutral countries such as Spain, Ireland or Sweden were also allowed to leave camp. Among these was Isla and Gill's great friend, Sully. At first he had been asked to surrender his British passport but he told the Commandant: "I would rather stay here. The King has seen fit to give me a passport and I will not part with it." Finally he was told he could go with his passport.

There was no doubt that conditions outside were infinitely worse than in STIC. Filipinos who openly expressed their loyalty to the United States or who were caught listening to broadcasts other than those of the Empire of Japan or the Imperial Japanese Forces were severely punished.

A fourteen-year-old girl who ran out to throw armfuls of cigarettes to American prisoners from Bataan as they marched to jail at Cabanatuan was dragged back by Jap soldiers. One shouted: "We'll show you what we do to Filipinos who help

Americans." And they dug a pit and buried her up to her breasts and left her to die in the sun.

Another woman suspected of listening to illicit broadcasts was taken to Fort Santiago, known and feared as the torture chamber, for questioning. When she said she knew nothing of a radio a door was opened and she was shown a Filipino strung up by his heels. "And if you don't answer quickly that'll be your fate", she was told. *She* was one of the lucky ones. As she left Fort Santiago she was warned: "If you don't keep out of trouble not even your mother will know your face."

Others were less fortunate. In August the internees heard the news that six Filipinos and eight Americans on passes were to be executed and twenty Filipinos given long prison sentences for "listening to false propaganda broadcasts from the United States and putting it down on typewritten sheets which they distributed among government officials, the personnel of companies and private neighbours thus creating bad propaganda". One American, released from STIC on medical grounds, was shot for criticizing the Jap Military Administration. Others were executed for "joining bandit groups" or "gathering reports of Jap movements".

As in all wars there were atrocities on both sides. The Filipino guerrillas, of whom there were many holding out in small bands in the mountains, often took justice into their own hands and gave what they called "a traitor's death" to those who collaborated with the Japs. The wretched traitors were impaled on a stake and left to die. The grisly process was said to take about twenty-four hours.

With all the violence outside May became more and more anxious about her children. At least she got occasional passes to see the two youngest at the Holy Ghost Convent but she had not seen or heard from Neville at his school up in Baguio for weeks.

Then one insufferably hot afternoon in June just before the rains started a bus came in with about thirty children on board. May was busy on cleaning duty when it arrived and poor Neville was one of the last children to be claimed – they all had to be signed for. Isla spotted him, nose pressed to the window, his dark curly hair, which seemed to have grown alarmingly in the last six months, falling over his spectacles. She ran to tell May and soon the boy was signed up and delivered just like one of the gate packages.

Neville Stopford was nearly ten and very conscious of approaching double figures and of being the eldest child. His school had been converted into a temporary internment camp when the Japs took possession of the Philippines and enemy alien adults in the area had been brought into Baguio as they had into STIC. But, according to Neville, the régime at Baguio was far stricter. Men and women were only allowed to meet for one hour each Sunday and, for simply walking with a girl, a teenage boy was beaten so severely about the head that he went deaf. Every morning at roll call the children had to stand to attention and sing in Japanese, "Good morning, dear soldier, good morning to you". If they refused to sing or failed to stand to attention and bow when a Jap passed they had their faces slapped. Obviously Neville's conscience had troubled him about the treacherous nature of singing a Jap song and he explained earnestly to Wyndham and May: "If you sing the Good Morning song under your breath it doesn't count."

At STIC they were supposed to bow to the Japs but so far Isla had not done so. They were also supposed to stand when a tally-ho came past and Isla avoided this mark of conquest too by standing up long before the tally-ho came near. "Bloody but unbowed" was her motto.

Listening to Neville prattling got Isla thinking about Richard. 4 August was his 18th birthday and she remembered how when he was born she had looked at him and said: "Cannon fodder." T.D. was horrified but now, she thought, here they all were in another war and Richard was a soldier. In her diary that night she wrote: "I wish him so much health, happiness and long life and if that doesn't cover everything in this lousy old world I've brought him into I wish him the best of luck and all good things. Please God he'll come safely through the war. We need boys like him to try and make a better world than we have done." And she remembered how twenty-eight years ago she had heard of the outbreak of the first war. They had been on holiday in Yorkshire. She was only a year or two younger than Gill was now. And the weather had been beautiful, warm and rich like the South of France, and it seemed that nothing could go wrong and shatter the droning peace of that deep blue summer.

Isla felt utterly miserable. She was not one to weep but now she was conscious of the prick of tears and a telltale lump at the back of her throat. Where was Richard? Would she ever see him again? How did he talk? How did he laugh? She could hardly remember.

She longed for the privacy that STIC denied. Taking her chair and her library book, Kathleen Wallace's *Without Signposts*, she sought out the quietest corner of the grounds. Sadly she read Mrs Wallace's dedication to her son: "Not thus did I dream that it should be for him – I dreamed that he should reap a fair harvest but the passing of the armies has laid low the corn. The army is past my son and the earth remains and there shall be a new seed for him to sow and a new harvest that he shall garner."

Further on she read: "The only way to live is to live in the circumstances which are about you whatever they are and to recognize that they are life. For you, for me, for the whole world of this day, this is the inheritance into which we were born. So this, I think, to learn to live in a world of war . . . but the present has a value now it never had, every day, every hour of being a sane, adaptable human atom is an achievement, the future will rise from those atoms as its foundation."

Like all teenage daughters Gill was a mixed blessing. Isla put most of her grouses down to the fact that she was not getting the right food and that her health had been bad ever since the first weeks in camp. She had trouble with her teeth through lack of calcium, trouble with her eyes from Vitamin B deficiency. Dysentery struck particularly hard on young stomachs and teenagers, susceptible to boils and spots at the best of times, were now sitting ducks to every pustular infection going. Gill soon joined the fashion for walking about with bits of sticking plaster on face and arms to cover unsightly, and often exceedingly painful, boils. Luckily she did not, as some unfortunates, get boils in her ears. They were excruciating agony with no aspirins or other pain killers left in medical supplies except for emergency cases.

Under the circumstances Isla was prepared to be lenient with her daughter's whims. It was becoming impossible to keep her at school, although the courses offered everything a student could desire outside modern history and politics which were, of course, forbidden by the Jap authorities as being too close to propaganda. Geography, which could have meant following troop movements, was also banned.

Academic restrictions were, however, the last thing to bother Gill. The only form of instruction she would willingly submit herself to were Padre Griffiths' lectures on the poets. The young Anglican padre had a way of making everything interesting from Shakespeare and Dryden to Swinburne and Chesterton. His lectures never failed to draw a crowd.

In Gill's opinion a knowledge of poetry and her 100-days STIC diploma "in solemn proof of any stories the graduate will tell in future years about his experiences" was academic distinction enough. She pinned the fully illustrated diploma certificate proudly on the cupboard door. It stated, with fitting solemnity, that 100 days of rumour and anti-rumour was ample proof of the ability to manufacture convincing stories. Graduates were also said to have qualified in entomology or the science of bed bugs; structural engineering or the art of sleeping on a cot; philosophy or waiting in line and physical education or the missing drink.

Finally Isla gave up the unequal struggle of trying to educate an obviously unscholarly daughter and let Gill take the job she had always wanted working in the Children's Annex. She was taken on as a canteen assistant, waiting on the tables at lunch and supper with the promise that when she was sixteen she would be considered for a job in the hospital.

Gill was delighted. From Isla's point of view too it proved a blessing since, with the job, went three substantial meals. Isla hopefully thought that perhaps a well-fed Gill might be less petulant about helping to keep their little patch of home in order. At present her excuse for getting out of every household chore – shaking out the mattress, cleaning the floor, doing the washing – was: "Oh, mummy, you're upsetting my schedule." Though any invitation to discuss what this mysterious schedule might be was met with the usual teenage indignation that any adult should presume to question, or even show an interest, in the sacred activities of the under-twenties.

Gill found the food at the Annex a slight improvement on that of the line but there was no doubt that communal food in general had deteriorated greatly since the Japs took over from the Red Cross. The internees' only hope was that when they got control of food purchases and organization, as the Commandant had promised in July, the situation would improve.

The rice that came into the kitchens was full of rat droppings and alive with worms and weevils. Isla was amazed when she heard the de-weevilling process had been the subject of one of the many propaganda photographs the Japs were always taking of the camp. She wondered what the caption would be!

The endless mush and rice dishes made stomachs unable to accept the occasional delicious windfalls of bacon and egg, ice-cream or carabou milk that came their way. The sudden rush of animal fats into the system was too alarming and every party – and at first there were quite a few – took its toll.

One night in October Isla was woken by groans from Doris Cooke's bed. Molly Fairchild was up looking after her and, since there had been a party earlier, Isla thought no more of the incident. But the next day Doris was taken out to the Philippine General Hospital and within the week she was dead. Even with expert medical attention it was doubtful whether Doris, who had some complicated internal trouble, would have survived, but her sudden death, at the age of thirty-eight, shocked Room Five. Her husband was a P.O.W. in Hong Kong and was not to hear the news until the end of the war.

Shortly after this Isla began to feel rotten. It was dengue, an Asiatic fever, which has all the unpleasant symptoms of flu and acute rheumatic pain combined. Soon she was in hospital with a temperature of 105°. When an epidemic was in full flood Santa Catalina was not much better than the old hospital quarters. Patients were crowded fifty or more to a room. The heat was appalling and even liberal sprayings of chlorax could not disguise the all-pervading stench of sickness. There were no bed-pan amenities and the fevered men and women had to struggle out of bed and queue for the few lavatories and bathrooms. To make matters worse there was no restriction on visitors smoking and the wards were always hazy with cigarette smoke. As soon as the temperature subsided Isla discharged herself.

Gill was, of course, the next dengue victim. She seemed to get everything that was going from laryngitis to jaundice and hives. Her bouts of dysentery were regular. Isla was greatly relieved when checks to rout out carriers of amoebic dysentery were started on the kitchen staff, the candy makers and food vendors, in fact on anyone handling food. In the kitchen alone ten carriers of amoebic dysentery were diagnosed and subsequently dismissed.

The other great health hazard was V.D. In the main kitchen four of the staff were found to have syphilis and fourteen others gonorrhoea.

With all the talk of V.D. Gill was horrified one day in December to find her bottom covered in large red spots. After worrying about them all night she eventually told her mother: "I've got some dreadful spots. I do hope it's not venerable disease."

Isla assured Gill that she need not worry. Soon the two were back at Dr Robinson's surgery collecting yet another jar of ointment.

Doc Robinson was one of the most popular men in camp and certainly the most hard-working. He was an American from Peking University Medical College, blunt but kindly, sympathetic and helpful. His was an unenviable task. By the end of the year nearly everyone in camp was suffering from some form of vitamin or mineral deficiency and he had to limit his meagre supplies of calcium and thiamin – for Vitamin B deficiency – to the most severe cases. He was constantly urging the internees to eat, however unpalatable the food might seem. "Be good trenchermen," he would say. "The line food is not lacking in essential vitamins so long as every scrap is eaten."

Inevitably the Doc's advice inspired yet another STIC poem.

"Methuselah ate what he found on his plate
And never, as mortals do now,
Did he note the amount of the calorie count
He ate it because it was chow.

He was not disturbed, as at dinner he sat,
Devouring a steak or a pie,
If it proved to be lacking in animal fat
Or a couple of vitamins shy.

He ate mungo beans and all kinds of greens,
Unworried by doubts or by fears:
He never lost hope and he never would mope
And he lived over nine hundred years!"

As Christmas approached even Job, let alone Methuselah, would have complained. By the end of October sugar had been cut to three teaspoons a day. No egg was ever seen near the line and if internees wanted eggs they had to buy them at a price at the gate or in the restaurants. Even the Thanksgiving meal was the same old stew though, in an attempt to make the thing more festive, the Kitchen Controller ordered the menu to be written out in Spanish!

Soap was getting short and toilet paper, or issue of tissue, was rationed to eight pieces a day for women, six for men. At 40 cts for ten, plus 10 cts for a box of matches, cigarettes had become the preserve of the rich and Isla, a 20-a-day addict, had to resort to little cigars presented to her by Fred.

Both Isla and Gill, most of whose wardrobe had, of course, sailed with the *Anhui*, found themselves desperately short of clothes. Of Isla's two suits, one had a hole in the seat and the other was covered in chlorax stains. When one day she went to empty her ash tray in the garbage bin and saw a faded flowered creation lurking in its murky depths she could scarcely believe her luck. On investigation she found that Flora Selph had just thrown it away. Isla was not the handiest with a needle but a slight alteration of the waistline and the hem – Isla was taller and slimmer than Flora – and a new button on the jacket sufficed to bring the suit well up to internee standard. At least there were no patches on the seat. Isla called it her basoura, or garbage, outfit.

Flora was impressed by the transformation. She had no idea Isla and Gill were so hard up for clothes and immediately searched through her bags to see what else she could find. She came up with a pale blue linen suit and a cream silky blouse with a necktie. Neither could have been more than a couple of years old but Flora insisted that the outfit no longer suited her, was too small, and that Gill must have it. Gill was thrilled. If only her father could see her now.

Where T.D. was and what he was doing was a matter of pure speculation for Gill and her mother. They had heard nothing from him since internment and could only hope that he had got their pathetic "safe and well" spring message and that theirs had not been among the pile of letters found unsent in the Commandant's office when he moved to his new quarters.

Then on 1 November Isla's name was called in the mail list. She ran to the office. It was a letter from T.D. on a special form. In the appropriate slots her husband had written: "Arrived

Lourenço Marques safely. Fit and well. Sailing for England shortly. Hope you will be repatriated soon and are keeping well. Love to you both."

With the letter and the sight of the familiar handwriting everything came flooding back. Not for the first time Isla cursed herself for leaving Shanghai. If they had stayed they would surely have been repatriated along with T.D.

Meanwhile Christmas was coming and the internees determined to make it a good celebration. The contributions box for materials for making toys and gadgets for the children was started at the beginning of November. Mid-month brought a hobby exhibition for the adults and older children with displays of internee-made gifts of backgammon sets and cribbage boards, spoons, brooms and bamboo mugs. Isla bought one of the latter as a present for Ida and Stan Lennox on their twenty-first wedding anniversary.

But the December toy fair astounded everyone – especially the Japs. There were wooden engines and coal trucks made by Wyndham Stopford, hobby-horses, every imaginable stuffed animal including a supercilious camel and a beautiful sealyham, dolls of all nationalities except, of course, the Axis countries and one with six changes of clothes. There were soft balls of brightly coloured materials for the little children and wonderful jigsaws made up of magazine advertisements stuck on to cigar boxes.

With a host of presents to buy Isla was more than relieved when Padre Griffiths told her he had arranged to get her fifty pesos a month from outside. Without these friends Isla and Gill would have been totally dependent on the line for food and the Indigent Relief Fund, a camp welfare organization, for charity.

Christmas cheer was greatly improved by the timely arrival of Red Cross comfort kits from South Africa, one for each internee. Inside were tinned pears, bags of sugar, two tins of English jam, two tins of Nestlé's milk, bacon, chocolate, fruit drops, jam pudding, beef and turkey paste, biscuits, a packet of tea, a cake of soap, canned margarine, four tins of bully beef and a tin of Gold Flake cigarettes.

The gloom that had pervaded last Christmas seemed to have turned this year to cheerful optimism. Last year there had been five hours of heavy bombing. This year the Allies were on the offensive everywhere. Nearly every family or shanty had a tree, most of them betel palms. Many were brightly painted or decorated with paper shavings from the gaily coloured wrappings of the comfort kits. The biggest and most decorative tree was in the children's playground, complete with comfort kit wrapping fairy, star of Bethlehem and reindeer.

Gill, who was back in hospital, was allowed out for the day. She looked pale and wasted compared to the strong, pretty girl who had sailed on the *Anhui* just a year ago. Isla determined to try and give her a really happy Christmas. For a present she found some earrings and a gold brooch she had tucked away in her jewel-box, a flowered cotton skirt from one of the boutiques and some scent. Gill was delighted. Flora gave her some pretty spotted material for a dress and Doris Hair a Christmas stocking with soap, scent, powder and sweets.

They had Christmas dinner with Don and Ansie Lee in Don's shanty together with the Lester family and their four young children. Isla provided the chicken and some cake, Don the turkey, and the Lesters the vegetables, fruit and sweets. Don's Christmas card to Isla, designed by Don and drawn by Ansie, caused great amusement. It showed a bearded female with a plate of steaming turkey hotly pursued by a grimly determined Santa Claus. The moral: no man in STIC chases a woman unless she has something to offer – food.

It seemed no time at all to New Year's Eve and the fancy-dress party. Ida Lennox made paper hats for all the Room Five contingent out of comfort kit wrappings and a special toilet-paper dunce's cap for Mitch who, having been lumbered with the job of Controller of Toilet Supplies, went as "Issuer of Tissue".

As 1942 faded out and the New Year marched in, Isla and Gill, Don and Ansie, Fred and John Hunter, the Selphs, the Lennoxes, May and Wyndham Stopford, Mitch, Tuck Peters, Jack Peoples, Margot and Bud Ewing, Myrtle Gewald and Betty-Lou gathered round and raised their mugs to "A happy Japless New Year. May victory be the Allies' soon and may they make the peace a lasting one."

On 1 January the *Stic Gazette* headed its front page: "So steady, so brave, so full of complaint, A spirit lofty, a body free, Is our wish for you in '43."

CHAPTER FOUR

A home of their own

(*January–September, 1943*)

NEW Year ebullience was regarded with disfavour by the Japs. Certain manifestations of the party spirit in the shanties were even more unpopular. A lightning inspection caught several luckless couples engaged in amorous pursuits and further searches revealed large caches of illicit booze.

Retribution was swift. Commandant Kodaki called a meeting of the Executive Committee and harangued them for nearly two hours on the subject of shanty discipline. Finally he ordered the complete evacuation of the shanty area. The use of shanties at any time was forbidden and shanty owners were to move themselves and all their possessions into the main buildings.

A plea for the ending of segregation which dropped through the Commandant's letterbox earlier that day could not have been more inopportune. The petitioner suggested ending sexual segregation as after a year of restraint the temptation to break the rules was too great. "If the temptation is that great," Kodaki had replied, "we had better remove it altogether and separate the sexes completely."

The Jap authorities had no time for sentiment or passion. All pregnant women were ordered to report to the Commandant's office by noon on 11 January. The understandable urge to gamble on being out of camp before the condition became noticeable was scotched by the threat of punishment for failure to confess. Five women turned up to the Pudding Parade. They were given two hours to pack their bags for transference to the Holy Ghost Convent in town.

A sterner fate awaited the fathers. Even as one proud father celebrated the birth of his firstborn, Samuel Tomas, the order went out for his arrest. He ended the day of the happy event behind bars with six still expectant papas. The internees of Santo Tomas never quite fathomed how five mothers matched six fathers but the Japs seemed satisfied they had netted the culprits.

Only forcible restraint prevented Tuck Peters from enlisting as a seventh papa. "I must give myself up," he said as his friends plied him with raisin brew, "or my reputation will suffer irreparable harm."

One genuinely expectant parent did *his* reputation no good at all when he asked to be transferred to hospital. His claims to be afflicted by amoebic dysentery were immediately translated as "morning sickness".

The only pregnancy to escape censure was that of Basoura the cat, now on her fourth litter of kittens. Both Japs and internees regarded her prolific and rat-reducing efforts as "war work".

None the less the pregnancy purge, plus the birth of little Samuel Tomas, the first baby to be born in camp, prompted one wit to name STIC "the confinement camp".

Commandant Kodaki was not amused. The revelations of jailbird Owens, a thief and deserter, who attempted to bargain with the Japs by squealing on his fellow internees, enthralled him even less. Owens had been in the habit of hiring out his bed on the third floor landing of the Education Building to interested couples at one peso a time. With the aid of a little discreet curtaining, business had been good and now Owens was ready to exchange his list of customers with Kodaki for Jap protection.

But Kodaki was not to be bought. Disgusted by Owens' two-faced scheming he even relented a little on the shanty ban. He informed Carroll Grinnell, Earl Carroll's successor as Executive Committee Chairman, that mothers with children under 12 could use their shacks during the day and men over 50 would be allowed in the shanties between 10 am and 2 pm.

The shanty concession was in fact meagre since the majority of shanty users were within the age ban. Soon the corridors were piled high with cupboards, cookers and all the bric-à-brac that had accumulated in nearly a year of cabin homes. The patio looked like a junk shop and, with almost a third of the camp out of bounds, the crowding was appalling. The food line doubled immediately – for the majority had cooked in their shanties – and washing seemed to hang everywhere.

Finally, after four weeks of misery, the Commandant relented. The shantyites were allowed back on payment of a monthly licence fee of one peso and on condition they pulled down any curtains or walls leaving the cabins completely open to view.

The Executive Committee issued a stern reminder of the rules: "Shanty occupants must refrain from any appearance or suspicion of intimacy. Any pronounced display of affection in the shanties falls under this category.

"Internees occupying shanties should recognize that violations of this or any other shanty regulations may be penalized by exclusion temporarily or permanently from Shanty Areas or by even more severe penalties.

"It is the duty of internees not only to guard their own actions but also to report to their supervisors infractions on the part of others. This is a disagreeable task but it is necessary if this situation is to be kept under complete control.

"At the same time it must be pointed out that the above restrictions apply not only to Shanty Areas but throughout the entire camp. No matter how orderly our Shanty Areas, the result is largely nullified if the same rules are violated on the grounds or in the buildings. Our record must be particularly clean in this respect and internees are requested to see that it is kept so."

In an attempt to whiten the slate beyond reproach the Committee went further and banned the wearing of house-coats outside the main doors. As Police Chief Jim Tullock explained to Isla, some house-coats were exceedingly flimsy and provocative. One, he confided, had even been used to encase two people. Surveying her own shapeless, and now threadbare, garment Isla wondered at the ingenuity.

The pregnancy purge coincided with polling day for the new Executive Committee. In sound democratic tradition everyone over 21 had the vote. Results were expected the following evening and that afternoon Isla went along to the Lennox shack for a chat and some coffee. Jean Mackay, Jim Tullock's fiancée, an intelligent and able woman in her late twenties, was there with Ida. They were discussing the election.

"Well," said Isla settling herself in one of Ida's makeshift chairs, "we'll have a new Committee tomorrow."

"Oh, no we won't," retorted Jean. "It'll be stopped. Don't think Grinnell and all his cronies are going to risk losing their seats."

"But surely, that's impossible," protested Isla. "The votes are all in."

"You don't know American politics. You'll see, they'll find some excuse."

The words were scarcely out of her mouth when the tannoy boomed into activity. "Important announcement, important announcement. The election has been cancelled owing to trouble over the pregnancies. Repeat, election cancelled."

Isla was astounded. She knew from the bootlegger stories about corruption in high places. Ida's hard-drinking husband, Stan, was not above reproach in this matter and Earl Carroll was another always with a good supply of booze. But she never for one minute thought they would nullify a perfectly constitutional election!

It amazed her how little Hitlers and Mussos were born in camp. All down the line power seemed to go to the heads of these jumped-up bureaucrats. She recalled the incident with Ida only a few weeks ago when some dreadful little man in the Cleansing Department had refused to give her brushes and soap for her bathroom job "because she was not in the department". Isla had come on the scene to find Ida in tears and immediately took up the cudgels on her behalf. Finally, one of "little Hitler's" juniors hearing the row had come in and given Ida all that was needed. It was just one incident in a tangle of exceedingly red tape.

The Executive Committee stuck to the story that the Japs had called off the election because of the pregnancies but there was absolutely no evidence to suppose this was so. Grinnell remained chairman, Stan and Earl Carroll kept their jobs and life at STIC continued.

Continued but deteriorated. The appointment of Lieutenant Konichi, a vicious individual, as Supplies Officer, spelt certain trouble. All the Japs in STIC despised the internees for allowing themselves to be captured but Konichi's contempt showed a streak of the sadist. He would turn up to meetings with the Executive Committee in a dirty kimono and while they discussed the business of the day he would sit with his filthy feet up on the desk picking alternately his toenails and his teeth. Most of his front teeth, which stuck out at all angles, were gold. His gyrations with the tooth/toe pick were quite nauseating.

68

1 The Corfield family in Shanghai, 1941. (*Left to right*) TD, Gill, Isla and Richard.

2 The primitive washing conditions in Santo Tomas.

SIC STARVIO INTERNITIS

STO. TOMAS
INTERNMENT CAMP
SCHOOL OF HUMAN RELATIONS
APRIL 1942.

INTERNED...............
WEIGHT ......lbs.
RELEASED...........
WEIGHT......lbs.
OCCUPATION IN CAMP
- - - - - - - - - - - - -

This certifies that .... rm.....
HAS STRUGGLED THRU THE FIRST 100 DAYS OF INTERNEESHIP
AND HAS COMPLETED COURSES IN THE FOLLOWING SUBJECTS

KNOW YE.........

The board of regents, Sto. Tomas School of Human Relations, authorizes the graduate whose name is hereby affixed to exhibit this diploma in solemn proof of any stories he may tell in future years about his experiences. The board feels that 100 days of rumors and anti-rumors have given the student ample ability to manufacture convincing stories.

It should be noted also that internees have studied many additional courses, besides those required for graduation, including: Entomology, the science of bed bugs; structural engineering, the art of sleeping on a cot; chemistry and how to wash clothes; philosophy, or waiting in line; industrial engineering, opening a can, and physical education, or the missing drink.

This diploma may be used for entrance into any post graduate school for stevedoring, ditch digging or weed pulling. The board knows that in those fields particularly its alumni will justly honor their alma mater.

Sic Starvio Internitis!

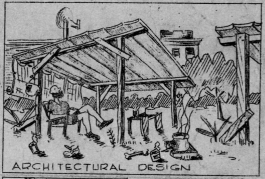

ARCHITECTURAL DESIGN

CHILD PSYCHOLOGY

THIS HAS HAPPENED

January
4 - First internees reach Sto. Tomas.
6 - First meal in old restaurant.
19 - Room monitors elected; library established.
24 - First issue of INTERNEWS.
26 - Executive committee, Earl Carroll, general chairman, formed from former central committee.
27 - Blackouts begin.
29 - First internee floor show.
31 - Central kitchen opens.
(Continued in Section 2)

WHAT! ONLY 4 SHEETS?

SANITARY ENGINEERING

PUBLIC HEALTH

3 The Santo Tomas Internment Camp Diploma that was issued to all the internees after their first 100 days of confinement.

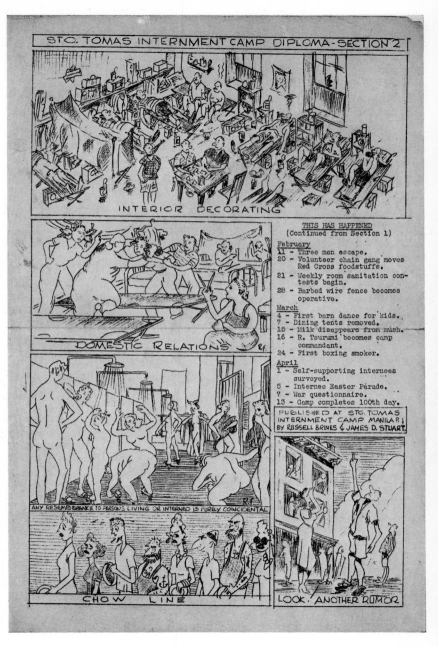

4 Section Two of the Diploma.

5 W. H. Donald and Madame Chiang Kai-shek in Nanking, the then Chinese capital. Donald was an economic adviser to the Chinese government and high on the Japanese wanted list.

When he stood up – and he was tall for a Jap – he looked like a skinny, scruffy ape, his long, gangling arms hanging well below his knees. His most sacred vow and ambition, of which he made no secret, was to "make the Americans eat dirt".

When Commandant Kodaki handed over to Karoda shortly after the pregnancy episode, he told the internees in his valedictory message: "So long as Japan is winning you will be treated magnanimously." With the tide hopefully beginning to turn in the Allies' favour the internees dreaded to think how Konichi would behave if encouraged to give full vent to his instincts.

Already Jap magnanimity was wearing thin.

Thanks to Owens' efforts as informant there was a round-up of any men connected with the military. Thirty-six, many of whom made no secret of their status when they registered, were marched off to the dreaded Fort Santiago. Camp rumour had it the tally-hos were looking for two men said to be directing the guerrillas.

At the gate internees and Jap guards were ordered not to speak to each other and friends bringing parcels were told they must register their names and declare where they got the money for the goods and whether they were employees of enemy aliens. The dossier against pro-American Filipinos was building up.

Outside in Manila enemy aliens were ordered to wear red arm bands and other nationals were forbidden to visit them. Soon the interrogation started. Groups of arm-banders, nearly all of whom were sick or elderly people out on health passes, were rounded up and taken to Fort Santiago. They were given no seats or beds and had to sleep on cement floors. The lavatory was a hole in the ground.

One woman was asked how she came to have a pass. "I've got bronchial pneumonia," she replied.

Her interrogator consulted the dictionary: "Oh, so your chest is bad. You smoke too much."

Then he turned on her: "Is the sun shining?"

"Yes, e-er, yes, it is," she replied.

"Don't answer in that tone of voice."

Others were asked how information got into Santo Tomas and when the Allies were going to win the war.

"It's the first time I've heard it admitted that the Allies *will* win," a wily old lawyer answered his captor.

And a negro came up with a good reply when baited about his nationality.

"You're not American," they teased him, "you're an African, why not admit it?"

"I'm not a white man," Big Joey replied, "but I'm not yellow either!"

The Jews who had previously been accepted by the Japs as fellow-Asiatics now came in for some of the odium heaped on them by Hitler's régime.

The *Tribune* reported: "There are indications that profiteering, espionage and other activities not in harmony with the policies of the Japanese Military Administration are being conducted by Jews who are parasites in the countries in which they reside and scathing penalties will be meted out to the offenders. . . . It appears there are a considerable number of Jews who harbour antagonism against the present German government. Moreover they even assume a similar attitude towards the Nippon Empire which is allied with Germany merely because they have been driven out of Germany and other Axis-controlled areas and forced to move to Asia."

The Axis whip was cracking hard. One by one the outsiders' passes were withdrawn on one pretext or another – chatting in the street, over-running the curfew, attempting to sell or transfer property forbidden to enemy aliens by military law. By the early summer of 1943 nearly everyone had been brought into STIC. The camp population touched 4,000.

More still were due in from the outlying islands. The situation was desperate.

It was imperative that no space should be wasted. The Executive Committee ordered that no bed should measure more than 32 inches by 72 inches and floor monitors were instructed to see the limits were observed.

Inevitably the newcomers clashed with the old-timers. Although conditions had been far from luxurious in Manila at least the pass-holders had been able to live in their own homes for eighteen months. They could not accept that in STIC there were no private apartments, no servants to carry baggage or bring tea, no hot baths.

In Isla's building the floor monitor was short with a woman who complained that she could not sleep at such close quarters to others. "There's an excellent place on the second floor," the monitor told her wryly, "two bathrooms and probably a southern aspect."

In the Gym an old lag gave his new neighbour no quarter when he asked if he could share his shelf.

"Oh, no," was the reply. "I've been in eighteen months while you've been out in comfort."

One bright spark asked for a job "with no mental or physical strain". The girl at the Labour Bureau told him: "Sorry, the Executive Committee is full up." Since the election farce the Committee was known as The Cave of Winds and its members as the Seven Dwarfs.

The hospital was busier than ever with queues of fifty or more people waiting to see the doctor, wanting blood tests, blood pressure readings, exemptions from camp duties. One shirker brought along a specimen in a bottle to which he had added stones from the path!

Room Five considered they got more than their fair share of newcomer trouble when Mrs Beryl Kidder, a loud-mouthed New Yorker, large, blousy and the wrong side of 60, moved in.

"There's no room to breathe in this place," said Mrs Kidder, flapping her sweaty arms like some outsize Jemima Puddleduck over her mass of bags and boxes that trespassed over at least three spaces. "It's like a pig pen."

"Everything is foul now," said Isla.

"It's not so bad for those who have a place of their own," retorted Kidder who resented the shanty community and consequently most of her neighbours in Room Five. "I'm a citizen of the U.S.A. and I'm wanting equal rights here and now," and the flab waved accusingly in Isla's direction as if *she* controlled the Shanty Board. "Next time England fight we're gonna have to make real sure they do it on their own."

Isla almost wished they *were* on their own if national friendships meant having Kidder as an ally. Not only did she spread her junk everywhere, she never put anything out to air and no one was surprised when she found her sheets covered in mildew. Thank God, thought Isla, for segregation. At least they were spared Mrs Kidder's shabby spouse who looked even dirtier and smellier. He always had a toothpick hanging from his mouth and spat every five minutes with unconcealed gusto.

There was no subject on which Mrs Kidder did not consider herself an expert. She would hold forth to anyone within earshot, arms crossed on bulging bosom, bun defiantly twitching, her lower lip in a perpetual pout even in full monologue.

"I wouldn't believe a thing that windbag Churchill says," Isla heard her confide to an uninterested Monty as she hurried away into the garden with her book.

As if Kidder was not punishment enough, Room Five found themselves lumbered with yet another Olympic-class snorer, Adele Baldwin. Mrs Baldwin was a nice woman and explained apologetically when she moved in about her stentorian slumbers but her concern was no consolation to Margot who found she had taken the space next to her and was desolate at the prospect.

"Never mind," said May who, now Craig and Ann were in to stay, was moving to another room, "perhaps *she'll* keep Molly awake."

But Molly could out-snore a rhinoceros. No one except Mrs Baldwin, not even Lydia with her ear plugs, could sleep through it.

Isla and Gill could hardly believe their ears when one day they heard Mrs Baldwin say: "I do like to hear you snore, Molly, it's so ladylike and comforting."

"And yours, Adele, is so gentle," returned Molly graciously. "And you sound so peaceful."

It seemed that everyone in the place was going quietly crazy. To Isla the snores sounded more like feeding time at the zoo.

The third newcomer was Sadie Moore, whom the Rich Bitches immediately cast as a spy. Sadie, a good-looking woman in her 30's, spoke fluent Japanese. She had worked both in Japan and with the Japs in the Philippines. Jenny was convinced she was employed by the Commandant's office to find out how news got into STIC and said she had heard that Sadie had taken a broadcast transcript to the Commandant. Certainly Sadie showed a great interest in news – but what intelligent person did not? Isla liked her. It was too horrible to think she was an informer. But at the same time she was careful to keep the diary hidden whenever she was around.

Mercifully Room Five was spared the addition of any missionaries, 500 of whom were scheduled to come in before the end of the year in spite of earlier assurances that they would be allowed to remain in their homes. It was bad enough having holy roller Mary Warner next door with her tuneless rendering of "All things Bright and Beautiful" and some dreadful hymn about

"When the Prison Gates shall ope!"

Isla knew the answer well enough to the Bible question "Why do the heathen rage?" "It's because the Christians are always nagging at them," she told Margot as the two stopped their ears against the crooning. "Why the hell can't they clean up the mess in their own lands before they go abroad pestering other people?"

Each month brought a new lot from the outer islands, all with their personal stories of horror and ill-treatment to tell. The Bacolod crowd of 119 came over from Negros Island on a filthy little tug covered in oil with only a plank stuck out over the side for a lavatory.

It took the internees from Davao ten days to get to Luzon instead of the usual three. Their water allowance for the journey, in temperatures of up to 104°, was one cup per person per day and nothing to wash with. The Japs on board used to hose themselves with fresh water. One day a woman caught the drops from the hose after it had been turned off and in half an hour of shaking the pipe she collected nearly half a bucket. She was just turning to take it to her two children, whose red hair was grimed black with the ship's dirt, when a Jap soldier who had been watching came over and tossed the bucket from her hand.

A Dutch priest from Iloilo told of a fellow-priest who had been ordered by the Japs to give up his house for a dance. He refused. He was given thirty-six hours to change his mind. When he still refused he was taken to the cemetery, made to dig his own grave and then hit on the head and thrown in. They left him covered in earth with just his feet sticking up out of the ground. Another man in Iloilo was strung up by his feet for having a disused aerial on his house.

To the Iloilo contingent of 109 STIC was heaven after their camp the size of a football field with little water and no showers. Those from Davao were amazed by all STIC's mod. cons., having had to carry their water half a kilometre over a hill.

STIC children were a major problem. After the mothers and young children had been brought in from the Holy Ghost Convent shortly after Christmas the place seemed to swarm with them. Their high-pitched squeals all but drowned Geoff Morrison's record concerts though these were played long after their bed-time. It seemed the parents were too exhausted and dispirited to do anything about disciplining them. Head lice, of course, spread like wildfire and there were few children without their heads bound up in bandages.

The numbers of children had increased so much that soon the Annex staff were complaining they could not cope with feeding them all. The Executive Committee solved the problem by decreeing that all children over 11 should eat with the adults. The mothers, already worried sick by the effect that lack of milk and vitamins was having on their offspring, went in a deputation to complain. "It's no good," the Food Controller told them, "we can do nothing now. When the kids get sick, *that's* the time to complain." The trouble, thought Isla, is that no one on the Executive Committee has young children. And they have more money than most to supplement the diet.

May's youngest, Craig, now four, was one of the most appealing toddlers in camp – and one of the most mischievous. His first exploit just after Christmas was to pull the toy cart his father had made him right across the path of an inspecting Jap officer. In trying to dodge the cart the officer tripped over his sword and fell.

And it was Craig who caused Isla to weaken on her own motto: "Bloody but unbowed." As she was walking over from the hospital one day she saw the little boy in a military car with one of the guards. Craig was holding the wheel and going "toot toot" while the guard, grinning broadly, was attempting to combat the airless heat by fluttering his fan on which was depicted, in Isla Corfield's terms, a large poached egg.

"Japanese flag, Japanese flag," said the guard indicating the blood-orange rising sun. Craig put out a chubby hand. The guard, flattered by his interest, handed him the paper fan. The next minute it was in shreds. With cries of delight Craig scattered pieces of Imperial sun out of the truck's window littering the ground.

A telltale shred fluttered to the feet of Commandant Karoda, Kodaki's successor, who was just passing. "Oh-ho, so you tear up our flag?" said the Commandant. "You should be taught better manners."

Isla hurried over. Karoda was a kindly man. He had shown justice and consideration to the internees on many occasions since his arrival in the new year. When a propaganda film showing the fall of Hong Kong, Manila and Singapore was shown in the camp cinema he apologized in person to Chairman Grinnell and promised to censor all films himself in future. He had turned a blind eye to the "cigarette factory" on the roof. And he seemed fond of children. But this was no time to take a chance.

"Say thank you to the guard for letting you play in the car and run along to your mother," Isla told Craig, blissfully unaware of the international incident he had just created.

Craig muttered his thanks. "Don't go away, don't go," he called to his guard friend as he ran off.

And Isla, praying Craig's sacrilege would be overlooked, bowed to Karoda. She had sworn she would never bow to a Jap. But Craig's misdemeanour must be purged. At least it had been Karoda, one of the decent Japs. He always wished someone would bow to him especially when there were visiting V.I.P.'s around. It upset him that the internees were not more conscious of their conquered status and he was pleased by Isla's obeisance.

Craig's third *tour de force* was a capital offence. Lesser mortals would not have survived to tell the tale.

One morning he was missing. May was frantic. She could not find him anywhere and none of his friends – and he had plenty – knew what had become of him. Then a woman said she thought she remembered seeing a little boy with brown curly hair sitting by himself in the bus waiting to leave for the Philippine General Hospital. Sure enough when the bus returned in the afternoon there was Craig flushed with popcorn and lemonade.

On the bus everyone had presumed that Craig, sitting as good as only a naughty adventurer can, belonged to one or another of the pass holders. Even the guard never thought to question him. It was only when everyone got out that it became apparent he was alone – with not the slightest sign of a pass. Others had been shot for less. But Craig spent the afternoon in the hospital canteen happily covering himself in all manner of sweet, sticky offerings. Back at STIC he was the camp's hero, the only one to go out passless and return unscathed.

Gill was scarcely a child any more. On her sixteenth birthday at the end of January her mother decided to give her a real treat. She organized a "beat-up" with ice-cream and cake and all the sixteen guests brought presents. They were recovering from the celebrations the following day when they heard about the cabana.

With all the extra people crowding into camp, Isla had been

anxious for some time to find herself and Gill a place of their own other than the few inches in the main corridor and the foot-space by their beds. She could not afford a shanty so the offer to rent a cabana in the Patio at one dollar a month seemed the answer to all their problems.

The cabanas were tiny open rooms about six feet square which the internees had marked out on the concrete path surrounding the grassed Patio. Overhead they had built a verandah to protect the rooms from rain and shine. The cabanas had started about the same time as the shanties and were speedily snapped up. It was a stroke of great fortune for Isla to find this one.

It belonged to an American woman, Soeurette Perkins, who was out on a sick pass nearly all the time. It was said, with some lack of charity, that Soeurette's yellow-grey complexion and the black rings under her eyes, which made her look like a walk-ing corpse, were achieved by liberal doses of iodine. Whatever the cause, Isla was happy to take advantage of the situation.

Gill, too, was thrilled at the prospect of having a place of their own to cook and try out recipes. She and Wendy Gates christened the first day in the cabana – 3 February, 1943 – with a fudge-making ceremony.

Ansie Lee presented the emergent cook with a lactogen can which served as boiler-in-chief. Isla ordered a grid, a broom and their own personal charcoal stove – up till now they had used Frank Hanson's or Don's. Barney, who, like Mr Blossoms, was in the tin business, said he would make an icebox if Isla could produce a kerosene tin.

As she surveyed her new residence in the corner of the crowded Patio, Isla wondered why possessions mattered so much in this world fraught with war and sudden death and she recalled a saying that had been worrying round her head: "Man's personal goods are vessels of the spirit."

When Isla got the cabana she gave up her space in the passage and moved her cupboard to the Patio. Though there was not much space, the cabana soon took on the appearance of home and in the culinary department fudge was quickly followed by papaya jam, which set like rock toffee, and gingerbread cake. The trick was to keep the charcoal at an even temperature. If the fire got too hot things burned quickly in the thin all-purpose lactogen can. Isla was grateful to the Filipina woman who came in twice a month to give cooking lessons, bringing recipes for dishes that could be made on charcoal stoves. Gill, who was the cook, was an apt pupil at this if nothing else. She quickly learned how to make the cassava flour lemon pies the Filipina brought with her as demonstration delicacies. Soon she had mastered the art of cooking with hot coals both underneath and on top of the tin – a method which proved ideal for cakes, soups and stews.

The Corfields' neighbours in the Patio were the Bisingers. In all STIC there was no more quarrelsome couple. Mrs Winifred Bisinger, alias Winnie the Bitch or Bitchinger, was past-mistress of the art of provocation.

She would sit all morning powdering her extremely plain face, giving orders to her husband George, and complaining about anything and everything. The more she taunted him the hotter and more irate poor George got until his nose, which had a tendency to wiggle under stress, was waffling up and down like a tormented rabbit's. Finally when he could bear it no longer he would burst out, "Winerfred, oh Winerfred," and storm out into the garden.

While the weather held George Bisinger's escape route was open. When the rains came he huffed and puffed about the Patio like a penned but cowardly lion. Mrs Bitchinger was in her element.

"Put that chair further forward, George. Prop it up against the cabinet," the Bitch cried between mouthfuls of peanuts. "Now the ice-box. We'll stop them pushing past, bringing their muddy feet through our clean cabana. Tell that man to stop. George, get them out. There's no public right of way through *here*."

Winnie the Bitch had no intention of conforming to the Patio rule that a clear passage should run through the cabanas during the rains to prevent people getting wet and muddy.

She would get George to barricade off the Bitchinger domain and infuriate the other Patio dwellers by barring them from shelter. Winnie, of course, showed no scruples about using her neighbours' cabanas as a passage. The delight in the Patio was unconcealed when one day the Bitch, carried away over an argument about the punishment of bootleggers which she considered unfair, protested with such vigour that she overbalanced, twisted her ankle and fell backwards into the mud. George's speed in coming to her assistance, the Patio noted, was not marked.

The shock of going in the "squash" she had been quite happy to see her neighbours wallow in, subdued Winnie the Bitch for perhaps thirty minutes. By evening she was back on full form. "There's a speck of mud on the floor," her raucous tones echoed over the Patio. "Clean it up, George. Go on, get on with it. Useless . . . stupid . . . what made me marry a man like you? Most husbands would mortgage all they had to keep their wives and families out of this dreadful place but not George Bisinger."

Privately Isla thought George would have mortaged any-thing to keep Mrs Bitchinger *away* from him. Though obviously the Bitch's appetites and pretensions were such that he had precious little left to barter. If sacrifices were to be made Winnie the Bitch was going to be the last to make them. While George was sent to eat on the line Winnie ordered food from the stalls and got George to cook it.

"Line eaters," she would snort contemptuously as Isla, Gill and other cabana dwellers brought the meal back on their tin plates. "You wouldn't *pay* me to eat that muck. Ugh, disgust-ing! You revolt me. Full of weevils. Only pigs could eat it!"

The Bitch's only friend was Soeurette Perkins. When Soeurette was in camp for the day to see the doctor and renew her pass she spent most of the time in Winnie's cabana lazing about being waited on by George. He was probably the only one in camp who, under orders from Winnie, would stand for her "I'm-so-delicate" act. For her part the Bitch thought that friendship with Soeurette would get her in with the smart polo set after detention, for Soeurette's husband, Peter, now a P.O.W in Cabanatuan, was an international polo player of some repute.

For three months Isla's cabana arrangement worked well. She and Gill had the place to themselves most days. Even with the Bitch's grumbling monologue, the cabana was heaven com-pared to perching on the edge of beds in Room Five or sitting huddled by the cupboard/dinette in the stuffy, dark passage.

The trouble started in mid-May when Soeurette, unable to renew her health pass, moved back into camp bringing with her her new boyfriend, Ken Huebsch. The two spread them-selves over the entire cabana, boxes, bags and bits of make-up everywhere.

Isla was miserable. Their home was a mess. She was even more miserable when the Patio Mayor, Mr Morrison, warned her to keep an eye on her space as he had heard Soeurette was trying to sell it. Isla was just wondering what on earth to do when she met Jean Mackay.

"You want to get down to the Shanty Board right away and stop the sale," Jean, always decisive, advised. "Come on, I'll go there with you."

At the office Isla's worst fears were confirmed. Soeurette had gone behind their backs to the Board and arranged to sell the cabana to Ken Huebsch.

"But he's only been in a week and there are people here who have had their names down for months," Isla protested, thinking miserably of how she had given up her meagre space in the hall for the chance of the Patio cabana. If Soeurette threw them out now they would have nowhere, they would be like orphans. She determined to fight tooth and nail for her rights.

She explained to the Shanty officer how when Tony Pratt moved from the site in February she took over as co-user with Mrs Perkins.

"It was only on the understanding that the arrangement was permanent that I gave up my hall space and bought equipment," she persisted. "On this basis alone, if there is to be a sale, I feel I have the right of first refusal. I've already, on several occasions in the past, offered to buy the cabana."

Her argument won the day. The officer agreed to suspend all transactions on the sale at least temporarily.

But Isla's troubles were by no means over. After a week's deliberation the Shanty Board informed her: "We do not see that Mrs Corfield has any claim."

Waves of anger and desperation overwhelmed her. She would *not* be moved. Any eviction order would have to be fought out in court. Whether she lost or won she wanted the whole wretched mess brought out in the open. Here she had been for nearly two years doing cleaning duty, bathroom duty, taking her share of camp responsibility in the Court of Order. In eighteen months she had taken no holiday from her job at the hospital. Soeurette, on the other hand, had been out nearly all the time. So had Ken.

And what of Tony Pratt? Why had he let her down? Why hadn't he told the Shanty Board of her offer to buy, of the assurance he had given her back in February that it would be safe to give up her hall space? Mr Pratt was going to have to answer in court too.

Winnie the Bitch was in her element. "Won't it be nice when they leave?" she was heard announcing in loud tones to George.

"I'd give them just five minutes to get out," she advised Soeurette. "It's disgraceful the way that woman is taking you to court. After all your kindness to them! You know I heard her saying the other day that you shirked your work. *You* shirk! Impossible! She doesn't realize how delicate you are."

"Of course, that's another thing we have in common," continued the Bitch confidingly. "The doctor had to give me a certificate to get me off rice detail. In my delicate state of health I simply couldn't cope. It made me quite ill to think of all these savages in here eating that stuff full of weevils. No, you and I, Soeurette, are a different breed."

What the Bitch did not tell her bosom pal was that she had been called off rice detail because she annoyed the other workers so. The doctor's certificate was an excuse.

"Take my advice," the Bitch waved an admonitory finger. "Throw them out!"

As the days went by it seemed the Bitch would get her way. The Court of Order, advised by the Shanty Board, ruled: "The claim of Mrs Perkins to the site is valid." Even Ewald Selph advised Isla that legally she did not stand much of a chance.

Finally a date was set for the hearing. Isla could not sleep worrying about the decision. After all, she was fighting for everything she had, the only thing that made life bearable, the home she had spent her last farthing trying to set up for herself and Gill.

She knew there were many on her side in the Patio including the Mayor.

As a last resort she decided she would appeal to the Commandant, invoking his ruling on "no selling". It was considered against internee etiquette to go to the Commandant but in this case Isla felt she would happily have gone cap in hand to the devil himself to avoid eviction.

As soon as Winnie the Bitch got wind of Isla's intention she was round the cabanas with the news: "Have you heard Mrs Corfield's going to complain to the Commandant about being evicted? Her excuse is something about an order against selling. Sneaking, I call it. If she starts a move against selling what's going to happen to all of us who have bought our spaces? I suppose she'll only be happy when we've all been evicted. Whining to the Commandant. It's the one thing an internee should never do!"

One woman pointed out that her friend, Soeurette Perkins, was constantly in the Commandant's office. Her passes out were knowingly said to be obtained in exchange for "certain favours".

"Oh, Soeurette just goes for a whisky soda," explained the Bitch as if social fraternization with the enemy was quite another matter. "You see she's so sick. She's an emergency. She can't take it here, you know. Too delicate. It's terrible those Corfields should have subjected her to such strain. I'll be glad when they're out."

Winnie the Bitch had her own reasons for wanting the Corfields dismissed. Soeurette had once again managed to get a health pass to move out of camp into her air-conditioned room in Manila. She felt certain she would be allowed to stay there as long as she wished. The new arrangement was that when Ken Huebsch took over the cabana and evicted the Corfields Mr and Mrs Bitchinger, who were not getting on at all well with their cabana-mates, the Richards, would move into Site 6 with him.

Already Mrs Bitchinger had pushed her table over the frontier of the Corfields' cabana. Isla resolved to ignore the insult. She would not be pressurized into moving.

Her friends rallied round her. Jean Mackay would not hear of defeat. The shanty owners, too, backed her resolve to go to the Commandant if necessary and the Patio Mayor told her: "You have every right."

At last, after a month of agonizing suspense and argument, the case came to court. Isla argued not for ownership but merely on the right to sell and evict. If someone had told her three years ago she would be taking on the role of defence barrister she would have laughed. Now her eloquence and the concise and pointed force of her argument would have been the envy of a King's Counsel. All her energies were concentrated on winning this battle. It meant so much. Apart from her own comfort, Gill had loved the cabana so. The tiny space had made up in a small way for having no home, no fun, no decent clothes. It had given Gill an identity, an address. It had given her a chance to develop an interest in something she loved and had a natural talent for – cooking. It was Isla's castle. She would defend her right to it to the death.

In the event the court decision was a compromise. For six weeks the Corfields were to share the cabana with Ken Huebsch. If during that time Soeurette returned Isla and Gill were to move out immediately. If she remained outside the cabana would be Isla's.

The decision, Isla thought, was typical of both the Court of Order and the Shanty Board. Neither had the guts to give a definite yea or nay.

The tension of the next six weeks was almost unbearable. Isla knew that at any time Soeurette might have her pass withdrawn and she and Gill would be homeless. Meanwhile the two of them had to put up with the boyfriend who, though a good deal pleasanter when out of Soeurette's company, was still a reminder of their precarious position. An added complication was that Ken had T.B. Mercifully it was not of the spitting and coughing variety but it worried Isla that Gill should be exposed to such a dangerous infection.

They lived on a knife's edge. Isla could not sleep. Gill was insecure and irritable. In the week before deadline Isla thought her nerves would crack under the strain. The hospital was crowded out with mental cases. Isla spoke severely to the nervy, super-sensitive being who had once been her robust, good-humoured self: "Get a grip on yourself, for God's sake, or you'll be joining those patients you keep signing in."

At last the six weeks were up. Soeurette had not returned. For 50 pesos the cabana was Isla's.

Ken asked if he might stay on but Isla's answer was a flat "No". He said he had nowhere to go. But Isla remembered how when she had told him and Soeurette that she had given up her space in the hall for the cabana they had replied: "That's *your* worry." Now the worry was Ken's. Isla had been given no quarter, she had asked none and was giving none. She was quite brutal in her refusal and felt no remorse. Hers was the "eye for an eye" justice. She had been through such torture.

Instead she gave a house-warming party with cake and coca-cola. It was 1 August, almost three months since the fuss had started. But all through the fight there had been another problem niggling in the background. Would they have to leave STIC altogether?

The camp was so crowded that obviously something had to be done to alleviate the situation. Enemy nationals still out on passes in Manila numbered 2,000. Soon either from choice or by coercion they would come into STIC. The solution proposed by the Japanese Military Authority was a new camp.

On 9 May Commandant Karoda announced that "a more spacious place" had been selected for the camp.

"The new site," the Commandant's adjutant explained, "is the College of Agriculture in Los Baños, Laguna, an ideal health resort noted for its hot springs where new buildings will be erected for your housing and where you will enjoy fresh air and find an easy access to fresh meat and vegetables, part of which you may be able to cultivate yourselves. . . . This change of location is entirely based upon the humanitarian consideration of your own welfare. . . . You are warned not to make any careless utterance which will distort the true intention of the Military Administration."

A pioneer group of 800 men was to be ready to leave within five days. The plan was that they should build barracks for the rest of the internees while themselves bedding down in the college buildings.

The Commandant called for volunteers. But the scheme was not popular, especially with the married men. At a conservative reckoning, it would be four months before the barracks were ready for the women and children. With the hope of an American invasion any day no one wanted to be separated from his family.

The bachelors signed on, 275 of them, but there the voluntary list stuck. Commandant Karoda ordered the remaining 525 to be press-ganged from the unattached men and the young married men. On the night of the 11th all the names of the eligibles were put in a barrel. One by one they were called . . . Bud Ewing . . . Jim Tullock . . . Harry Koons . . . Martin Hearn . . . Bill Stumpf. The scene reminded Isla of a mine disaster with all the women, white and strained, waiting to hear if their man was all right or not. The lots continued until one in the morning.

The next day as Isla walked over to the hospital to open up reception she was horrified to see a colossal queue outside the doctor's surgery. Literally hundreds had lined up to get exemptions from Los Baños either on grounds of their own ill health or that of their wives or children. One man who had been playing football the previous afternoon claimed he was not strong enough to work on a building site. Another was brought in on a stretcher after drinking quantities of soap and water administered by his desperate girlfriend. After a couple of hours in the lavatory he was told: "You're perfectly fit. No exemption."

Harry Koons, the carabou, burst into tears on hearing he had been selected. And Isla's building rang with the loud howls of women who were losing husbands or boyfriends – or in many cases both. Isla felt decidedly unfashionable having neither. In the next-door room a woman had hysterics because the husband she had not spoken to for seven months was among those selected. Perhaps, Isla thought unsympathetically, he did all her washing.

Isla found she had no patience with these over-emotional women. "Anyone would think the men were going to the front the way they carry on," she thought angrily. "Too bad some of them aren't."

On departure day the camp was awoken by the "Tiger Rag Bugle Call" at five o'clock. From then on the loudspeaker blared out "Red, White and Blue", "Onward, Christian Soldiers", "The Battle Hymn of the Republic" and, for light relief, "Shuffle off to Buffalo".

The men mustered in their squares. At the gate the lorries lined up ready to take them to the station. The loudspeaker called for attention and Karoda took the microphone.

Finding his English words with difficulty Karoda cleared his throat and addressed the waiting band: "I congratulate you boys on good behaviour here. I hope in new camp you will be good also and acquaint yourselves with new rules. I congratulate too on short time you are being ready. You will have hard work to get new camp ready for your fellow internees. I myself go back to Japan. This is probably the last time I speak to you. I wish you good luck and much health."

The music struck up again and, amid cheers from the internees and the Filipinos clustered outside, the 800 drove off. Somewhere in the distance a native band was playing "The Star-spangled Banner". A Jap guard at the gate was so overcome by the scene that he returned the "V" sign given by one of the departing men and then burst into tears.

The camp seemed quiet and subdued after the men's departure. There was nothing to do but wait until reports of Los Baños filtered back.

It seemed it was in the mountains, about 100 kilometres south of Manila on the shore of a great inland lake, the Laguna da Bay. There were 25 acres on which to build barracks and the possibility of extending even further if more accommodation became necessary. The climate was said to be much cooler and healthier than Manila.

The Commandant appointed to the new camp was Lieutenant Colonel Narusawa of the Religious Section of the Japanese Military Administration. Mr Calhoun, or Cal as he was always known, an American banker and one of the few popular members of the Executive Committee, was appointed Los Baños chairman. Doctor Leach and Doctor Doyle, the dentist, led the medical team.

Soon the internees at STIC were reading the *Tribune*'s account of the move and reactions to it. Cal's statement was reported: "At Los Baños the air is pure and camp grounds are spacious. There are hills, streams, playgrounds and gardens. The place is ideal from the point of view of health provided we internees lead a disciplined life. We are grateful for what the Jap authorities have done for us. I would like to express my gratitude, on behalf of the internees here, for the help and consideration given us by the officers and men of the motorcar corps who helped us in moving today."

Certainly the move at the STIC end had gone like clockwork. All the internees were impressed by the Jap efficiency.

At Los Baños the organization was not so streamlined.

The 800 arrived in the pouring rain and had to stand in the trucks that took them from the station, their possessions at their feet, in ever-increasing pools of water, while the college faculty, who had not realized the men were arriving so soon, cleared out of the bungalows which were to be their lodgings. Two truckloads of gear – pots, kettles, tins of food and the two refrigerators for the hospital – went astray on the journey and ended up in the next village some 15 kilometres away across the mountains. It took a couple of days to retrieve them. And to increase the complications Commandant Narusawa spoke no English and the interpreter either would not or could not interpret.

The main problem at Los Baños was the water. Supplies were barely enough for 600 men let alone 800 plus guards and there was no hope of getting the wells drilled for at least a month. It would be September, Cal reckoned, before the water had been tested and the pumps were working. Electricity and sewerage would also have to be fixed up for the new barracks. The whole operation, including Filipino labour, it was said, would cost the Japs two million pesos.

In spite of primitive conditions the chits coming back from the boys were optimistic. The food was good and the scenery beautiful but work was hard and discipline strict. Morning call was at 6 o'clock and lights out at 11 pm. Visitors of any kind were banned and talking to Filipinos was forbidden. The men were warned that anyone attempting to leave camp would be shot on sight.

The chits, now known as "diamonds", were mostly unofficial. They were smuggled in among coconut consignments by George, the incredibly scruffy American-Filipino bus driver. When petrol ran out George had the brilliant idea of running his bus on charcoal and, steaming along like a rear-engined puffing billy, the vehicle worked tolerably well. It could be heard chugging towards Santo Tomas miles away and by the time George arrived the "building widows" were so anxious for their mail they could scarcely contain their excitement. Poor George was badly let down by the internees when STIC tannoy broadcast that no more notes should be sent via him on the Los Baños bus.

Up till then Karoda, always lenient where he could be, had turned a blind eye to the chit traffic. Now he was forced to investigate. George's bus was searched and a six-page letter found in one of the parcels. Immediately a ban was imposed on all parcels and George, though allowed to carry on chuffing his bus between STIC and Los Baños, was under constant surveillance and suspicion.

Why *did* the internees have to be such fools? thought Isla irritably. They forced investigations on themselves through their own stupidity. A prime example of idiocy was the mestizo boy who went to the Commandant with a letter saying his sister had died. Could he go to her funeral? Naturally Karoda wanted to know how he got the letter and in his confusion at his mistake the mestizo blurted out: "God sent it to me."

One of the big attractions of Los Baños was that there were to be married quarters. Couples would be allowed to marry and even produce offspring if they wished without fear of jail sentence. Gill showed her mother an uncensored letter she had received from Bill Stumpf saying they were planning for married apartments, a maternity ward and a cemetery.

"Hatches, matches and dispatches," commented Isla.

At first the wives were told they would be leaving in four weeks' time. But the rains and high winds of June and July slowed down the building programme and finally, after many false rumours, the women were informed that no one would be moving until after the rainy season.

Jean Mackay was desperately disappointed. She and Jim had hoped to be one of the first couples to marry in Los Baños and Jean had had her thick dark hair permed specially for the occasion and resigned her job as floor monitor. Isla had become fond of Jean who, though somewhat bossy, was a woman of great intelligence and energy. Isla promised her that when she and Jim got married she would give them her gold signet ring to make into a wedding ring.

As for Thelma, she made no secret of her feelings about the postponement.

"We American women are so spoilt," Isla heard her confide in a loud whisper to an unsympathetic Madeleine Peters. "We are so used to *certain* things that we can't do without them. It's a *disgrace* the Executive Committee haven't asked for contraceptives. But *do* you know what I was told?"

"No," replied Madeleine shortly, hoping fervently that Thelma was not going to embark on one of those acutely embarrassing accounts of her sex life with which she delighted to regale anyone too polite to administer the brush off.

"Cocoa butter and vinegar," answered Thelma with a knowing nod. "Safe as houses. About a 95 per cent success rate. A Filipina woman . . ."

Madeleine, who did not care to talk to anyone for more than a few minutes, had had enough. Making an excuse that she had arranged to meet the girls at Lefty's she hurried off.

Thelma, now obsessed by the need to find contraceptives in time for the autumn move to Los Baños, covered herself in a shower of evil-smelling scent, put on her brightest lipstick, a brilliant yellow blouse and stalked off to see who she could find to burden with her problem.

As she went out of the room Isla could not help thinking: "What an *enormous* bottom that woman's getting!"

Thelma decided Tommy Pratt was her man. Flushed with

excitement she burst into his shanty just as he was brewing his afternoon coffee. "What are you doing about contraceptives?" she demanded without preamble.

It was a matter in which Mr Pratt had little interest. He blinked, amazed at the sudden appearance of this Jezebel in jasmine.

"I beg your pardon," he stumbled. "What do you *want* me to do?" Surely, he thought with great alarm, he had not in a moment of total mental aberration made some sort of advance to this virago among women. People were going crazy all the time in this place. Perhaps it was catching.

"Well, order some, of course. We're going to need them when we get to Los Baños. You ought to *know* about these things."

"Oh, really? Why me particularly? I've no idea if I can get them," answered Pratt now concerned.

"Well, you worked for Dunlops, didn't you?" snorted the exasperated Thelma.

Mr Pratt may not have had any contraceptives but there was plenty of evidence that others had been more resourceful. The array behind the Education Building each morning caused the sweepers to call a strike. Isla found it hard to believe that that swampy part of the grounds could be chosen for romance. It was so very public.

She herself was in two minds about Los Baños. With all the old people coming in from Manila STIC had begun to look like a home for the aged, the sick and the indigent. It gave her the creeps. At Los Baños they could live in a mixed community of younger, healthier people. But all the energy and pioneer spirit she had prided herself on had gone. She decided not to volunteer.

She was thankful for her uncharacteristic timidity when Miss McWatt came running in from the rain one July day saying a repatriation list was being drawn up. It was to be wired to Tokyo in the morning.

"Och, I'm soaked to the skin," exclaimed Margaret McWatt wringing out her ample skirt all over the floor of Room Five and kicking off her soaking bakias whose loud flip-flop up the passage had proclaimed her arriving presence minutes in advance. "Mr Stanley has jist been askin' me if I want to gae home because E'm on the sick list. I told him I'll nae be leaving here without the war ends and it's safe."

"Dear God, you must be out of your mind," cried Isla who would have given anything for the chance. "Where can I sign on?"

"Ye'll be needing a sickness note furst," advised Miss McWatt. "But they'll no be splitting up families. You'd like as get one for your wee lassie. Ye wudnae have a chance wi'out it. . . ."

Isla was off in a flash. She ran every inch of the 300 or so yards to the hospital. There was not a second to lose. Why had not someone told her of this before?

She found Dr Fletcher in the surgery. "You know how ill Gill's been," she said breathless and trembling from her dash for freedom. "Can you give her a sickness chit so we can be repatriated?"

Doc Fletcher looked up wearily. "Sorry, Isla, that's not my pigeon. You'll have to see Robby.'

She turned round to Doc Robinson's desk. The throng was as thick as a rugger scrum. Obviously others had had the same idea.

Finally it was Isla's turn.

"Yes, little Gill," said the Doctor kindly. He was grey and gaunt with overwork. "Yes, I think we can give her a chit." And he turned to look up Gill's file. "Hm, ten, no eleven times in hospital since she came here . . . amoebic dysentery, bacillary . . . avitamosis B . . . eye trouble." He wrote his report and handed it to Isla. "Good luck," he said.

Isla's heart was pounding as she carried the medical certificate over to the Commandant's office. Mr Stanley took it.

"What are the chances?" asked Isla hardly daring to hear the answer.

"Same as anyone else," replied Stanley. "Next, please."

That night Isla did not sleep a wink. She envied Molly and Mrs Baldwin their "graceful" snores.

"Oh God, I want to go home," she prayed, wondering what an agnostic was doing praying. At least this time repatriation seemed more than just a rumour. Jokes about the three Swedish ships, the *Walkholm*, the *Swimholm* and the *Goholm*, piloted by Captain Stayholm, were wearing exceedingly threadbare.

Next morning Doc Robinson confirmed that Gill's name *had* been on the list wired to Tokyo.

Isla took her diary out from behind the charcoal bin in the cabana where it was now hidden. She wrote: "I'm all pale green and can hardly write this. Please God we get on the ship."

Everything suddenly seemed brighter. Isla went round collecting the addresses of people who had lent her money. She took the names of others who had been kind and to whom she wanted to send presents when she got back to England. She asked Ansie to do her a drawing of the room.

She was confident and desperate by turns. She decided to play her trump card.

Her appointment to see Commandant Karoda was easier than she had expected. He stood up as she came into the room and offered her a chair.

"What can I do for you?" he asked kindly.

Isla drew a deep breath. Surely this would set the seal on their chances of repatriation?

"Mr Commandant," she began briskly. "I am the only woman in here whose husband has been repatriated. I would have gone with him if I'd stayed in Shanghai. For this reason I feel my daughter and myself should have priority on the list."

She waited for the longed-for confirmation.

"Mrs Corfield. Me, I am powerless," answered Karoda who always had to think long and hard about his English sentences. "The British government, they make their own list. The sick and infirm. If we, the Japanese, make it, British government say 'You try to foist off ones you don't want.' Is better this way."

Isla felt deflated: "When will you get the list?"

"Soon, I hope. You, I expect, will be on it."

"I suppose so," said Isla dejectedly. She made one last bid: "I'm sure I'm entitled to repatriation according to international law."

"Maybe, maybe," pondered Karoda. "Is best you send a letter to this office explaining your position. We do what we can."

Isla thanked Karoda. There was no doubt he was the best of the bunch. He was a thoroughly decent fellow, without prejudice, who would do a good turn if he could. She dreaded to think who would replace him when he left, as seemed certain, before the end of the year.

That night she wrote:

"Sir:
I have the honour to request consideration of the following

90

request for repatriation of myself and daughter in the event of transportation becoming available.

The grounds for this request are that I am a transient and my husband, Gerald Frederick Conyngham Corfield, was repatriated from Shanghai in September, 1942, and had my daughter and I been in Shanghai we should, doubtless, have accompanied him. Whilst I myself am in reasonably good health, the same cannot be said of my daughter Gillian, aged 16, who is not in good health as evidenced by Camp Medical authorities.

My daughter and I hold British passports and I can produce a cable from my husband dispatched from Lourenço Marques in support of my statement that he was repatriated – he having been an official in the Chinese Maritime Customs.

Trusting you will give this petition your prompt and kind attention,

I have the honour to be,
Yours respectfully,
Isla Corfield."

Don would probably have qualified for repatriation on grounds of age and health but he dared not put his name forward for the list. Already he had had a few nasty shocks with internees coming up to him saying they had recognized his picture in library books. One day a man from Shanghai told Don he had been questioned by the Japs as to whether he knew a Mr Donald from Chungking. And some indiscreet Chinese from outside had tried to contact him.

Isla was one of the few who knew what a marked man William Donald was. She put her name down at the library to buy *Inside Asia* and warned Caroline Wolff not to circulate an omnibook she had with a story about Don in it. Don assured her he had no written word of identification with him – even his passport had been hidden by a trusted internee friend. But it upset Isla that he – and Ansie too – could not try for repatriation.

A month went by, six weeks. Finally on 31 August a notice was posted on the bulletin board announcing that the repatriation ship *Teia Maru* would sail in the last week of September. There would be 150 Americans, all transients, the same number of Canadians and British and 30 Dutch. But the names of the lucky repatriates were still a mystery.

Every day they watched the bulletin board. On 20 September a notice went up. At first they could not take in the news.

"British repatriation cancelled," the notice read. "The Commandant today informed the Executive Committee that the 150 British will not now be among the repatriates sailing on the *Teia Maru*. He apologized to the Committee for the premature announcement regarding these nationals . . ."

Gill and Isla could read no more. They were stunned. But Isla would not let all their hopes be dashed by this bit of paper. She ran to the office.

"I must see Karoda, please, I must," she begged. Stanley barred the way. "Sorry, he's not seeing anyone. If it's about repatriation there are definitely no British."

Meanwhile the lucky ones whose names had been listed prepared to leave. Ewald and Flora Selph were going, Doc Robinson, Mitch, Jack Peoples and Tuck. Somehow Soeurette Perkins had managed to get herself listed. It must have been all those euphemistic "whisky sodas" she had with Commandant Kodaki, Isla thought bitterly. Karoda's protégée, Mary Reece, was also included on the list. She was reported to have told a woman friend: "I didn't know you wanted to go or I'd have arranged it."

"Ah well," philosophized Margot Ewing, "I suppose ten minutes with the two K's is better than two years in here."

The repatriates were given their orders. They were to take no diaries, books, magazines, newspapers, drawings or photographs, except personal family pictures, and no bedding. Any infringement of the rules would result in cancellation of repatriation. Isla thought dismally that the one consolation for not going was that she would not have to abandon her diary, now in its nineteenth book, or the collection of drawings of the camp made for her by Teedie Cowie, Poppy Lyman and Ansie.

On 23 September the repatriates from Los Baños assembled at Santo Tomas. Isla could hardly bear to speak to Mitch, she was so afraid of breaking down and howling. He promised he would contact T.D. for her and give him a message but he could not afford the risk of taking a note. Doc Robinson promised to see the British Ambassador in Washington for them.

Ewald was chosen as the official spokesman for the camp. He had to memorize everything and was up for hours the night before they all left going over and over the points the Committee had drafted.

The camp gave their comrades a resounding send-off in traditional STIC style with a special farewell production by Dave Harvey entitled *The Lost Tribes of the Philippines*.

All the STIC songs were recalled and new ones added. It was cheerful but tinged with the sadness of homesickness that had to be endured.

The script went: "Those lost tribes of the Philippines who, decades ago, were known as the Santo Tomas Internees . . .

"Arriving at the gate, we see before us the first evidences of the reputed engineering skill of these little-known people. We are faced by a seemingly endless wall made of a rare, matted material, which we later learn bears the quaint name, sawali, and which is celebrated in the songs and the legends of these lost internee tribes. Beside the gate we notice a shrine-like edifice made of this same sawali in which is seated, in Buddha-like immobility, one of the native internee guards.

"We learn that this guard's mission in life is to see that all lesser folk are completely cut off from any communication with the outside world. A strange and colourful band which he wears upon his arm denotes his higher caste. Bowing respectfully to this compelling figure, we pass through the gate and, through the leafy foliage, catch our first glimpse of the enormous box-like structure in which these people lead their strange existence. . . ."

The programme showed pictures of the "tribesmen" carrying great cauldrons of steaming mush, their fellows standing expectantly round crying "Hot stuff!" The expressions evoked by the passing of the basoura wagons were less genial.

"Farewell, Interneeland, thou strange and exotic community, harbouring behind your walls of sawali your little-known and wellnigh forgotten peoples. . . ."

Farewell. Isla decided she must shake off her gloom. It was both pointless and boring to go into a decline. They were not the only ones who had been disappointed. She threw a party in her cabana for her friends who were leaving. It was the least she could do after all their kindness. Somehow Mitch managed to produce a bottle of gin to liven up the calamencie juice. Flora brought hot cakes and yet another parcel of clothes for Gill and Isla. She would miss Flora. They all would. She, above all, had been the voice of reason in Room Five.

The repatriates left at 5 am on 26 September. It had been one thing seeing them all at a party. It was quite another to wave them goodbye. *That* Isla could not bear. The noise and bustle of departure preparations woke her at 3 am but she willed herself to go to sleep again and when morning call came they had all gone.

The baggage search had been thorough. Even the newspapers the repatriates had used to wrap their shoes were thrown out.

Don told her about Karoda's farewell speech. He had impressed upon the departing internees that the camps at STIC and Los Baños were the best available. The Japanese Military Authority, he stressed, were kind and thoughtful but they did not like criticism. He hoped the exchangeites would remember this and think of the ones who were left behind.

"It's more or less what I expected," said Don. "They don't want anyone spreading stories about the three boys who were shot or letting on about the conditions in the P.O.W. camps and the barbaric treatment at Fort Santiago. It's the usual thing — if any of these stories get back it will be the worse for us. But governments ought to know about these things. We must hope Ewald gets through."

Later Karoda had got into deep waters trying to explain the list. He said it had come from Washington but that some on the list had refused to leave and substitutes had been selected by the Executive Committee. The Committee denied having had any say in compiling the list. With a few notable exceptions, they maintained, it had come from Washington.

There was little doubt that Soeurette and Mary Reece had got their permits through the two Commandants. As for the rest of the list there seemed neither rhyme nor reason to it. The sick and the aged were scarcely represented, the poor not at all. The only semblance of uniformity was that the majority were not Philippine residents but transients.

Soon the rumour was going about that passages on the *Teia Maru* could have been bought for 1,000 pesos.

As usual speculation was best expressed in verse:

"Little George Washington told no lies
At least so the story goes
But 'out from Washington' comes a list
Its origin? No one knows!

You'd imagine the aged upon that list
And babes in their cribs – but no!
But the friends of the friends of the Chairman's friends
Are the first on that list to go!

So here's to whoever makes George's list
And here's to the new survey
For nobody knows why one of us goes
Nor why the rest of us stay."

CHAPTER FIVE

One down, two to go

(*Summer, 1943–March, 1944*)

THE repatriation blow would have been easier to bear if Isla and Gill had not felt so ill all the time. Lack of Vitamin B1 affected their eyes and gave them almost permanent headaches. Often Isla found herself helpless with the most agonizing cramps.

Doc Stevenson advised a diet of steak and liver for Gill. "Though God knows how you'll find it." And he gave her a chit for the Philippine General Hospital to have her eyes examined.

There was little the hospital could do in face of the poor diet but the atrophin drops prescribed went some way to relieve the scorching pain. Some glasses were promised as soon as the overworked opticians could get the order through. And, after desperate negotiations, Isla solved at least part of the diet problem. She arranged for Gill to eat her evening meal at Hunter's restaurant for 36 pesos a month – a bargain at current prices. John Hunter, though almost twice Gill's age, had a soft spot for the girl. He must have cut his profit to practically nothing to feed Gill at that rate.

John Hunter was not the only one to spoil Gill. On her trips to see the eye specialist she was lavishly entertained by her Japanese guard, a tiny flat-footed man nicknamed "Kokobun", and the interpreter who both insisted on buying her whisky and coke.

On one occasion she excelled herself and came back with a bottle of rum "guaranteed six years old". She had been having a steak with her "guards" in a restaurant and, knowing booze was dispensed there, she boldly went up and asked for a bottle. After some haggling the man behind the counter got out a large medicine bottle, filled it with rum and presented it to Gill.

Gill smuggled "the baby" successfully back into camp and produced it at supper that night much to Isla's astonishment and delight.

Gill reckoned she had broken almost every rule of the day pass:

1. You must not go to bars or other public places
2. You must not consume alcohol in any form
3. You must not spread rumours
4. You should make yourself as inconspicuous as possible
5. You should go directly to your destination, fulfil your mission and return directly to Santo Tomas arriving before the time on your pass.

Actually to return with a bottle secreted about your person was a crime of such gravity that its inclusion on the sick pass rules was not thought expedient – especially when the pass holder was a blue-eyed 16-year-old girl!

Isla got frantically worried about her daughter's adventures in town. She kept warning her about breaking the rules but Gill took not the slightest notice and looked forward with unconcealed glee to her expeditions. But every skive has its day and eventually Gill's escapades were discovered by Miss Adams, the head of the hospital, and her pass instantly withdrawn.

Isla was less fortunate in her complaints. Whisky was not given to patients having their tonsils out. Neither was anaesthetic.

She walked into Doc Fletcher's surgery.

"Are you going to make a fuss?" asked the Army nurse brusquely with what seemed to Isla something of a threat in her voice.

"No, I'm all right," answered Isla who always managed to be fairly matter-of-fact about pain. Anyway, she thought, whatever the agony, she could not stand much more of these terrible throats. She determined to bear whatever agony was in store with stoicism. She could not endure the humiliation of being strapped down as some poor wretches having surgery without anaesthetic had to be.

She was shown to an iron chair.

"Open up," said Doc Fletcher cheerfully. He now spent most of his day doing minor operations of one sort or another. "It won't take long."

The man who ran the projector in the cinema came over and held her tongue; the nurse stood by with the instruments. Soon Doc Fletcher was digging down her throat.

"Isn't she a peach?" he murmured as his knife busily cut away at the inflamed flesh. "Isn't she a peach?"

At last it was over. Isla was given an aspirin to suck and walked out of the surgery and upstairs to her bed in the ward. But Isla's throat was unmitigated hell. She would have done anything for a shot of morphine. If only she were a drunk, she thought ruefully, she would have no trouble. *They* were the only ones these days to be rewarded with knock-out shots.

Few internees passed a day without stomach pains or giddy spells but Mrs Gates seemed to suffer more than most. Often her daughter, Wendy, would wake in the night to hear her moaning with pain. She looked gaunt and drawn and grey. Finally Wendy and her sister Barbara, now over in the Annex with her new baby girl, persuaded her to go and see Doc Fletcher. It was cancer. Her only chance was an immediate operation. Doc Fletcher offered to perform the surgery for nothing but obviously Mrs Gates could not stay in the tiny camp hospital with its inadequate operating facilities and would have to pay for a bed in the General Hospital.

Like the Corfields the Gates family had very little money with them in the Philippines. Wendy, always a highly-strung and emotional girl, told Gill between sobs that her mother would die because they had no funds. But STIC, for all its drawbacks, did not lack charity when it came to the crunch. Horace Whittall, head of the British Red Cross, managed to fix up a payment guarantee for the hospital fees and a date was set for the operation.

"The op. is about equal to putting her against a wall and shooting her," Doc Fletcher confided to Isla. "Her condition's low, she's suffering from anaemia and has a weak heart as well. But if we don't try now she'll be dead in six months. If only she'd come to see me earlier. Sometimes it's foolish to be brave."

Isla thought how terrible it would be if Mrs Gates died without a word to her husband who, as far as she knew, was still in Shanghai. She remembered the time she had had a serious operation and how she had written to T.D. and entrusted the letter to a friend to keep and give to him were she to die before regaining consciousness. Years later she gave him the letter herself and he had been most touched.

Isla persuaded Mrs Gates to write. She made a solemn promise that if anything did go wrong and she did not recover she would do everything in her power to get the letter to her husband.

One thing at least poor Mrs Gates was happy about was Barbara's baby, now just one year old, whom she idolized. Somehow Barbara had managed to get the news to the father in Cabanatuan P.O.W. camp and he had sent back a message saying he would leave the baby everything. Meanwhile, however, Barbara, wishing to give the baby a name and a father, had secretly married a man in STIC and was now Mrs Weiser. When Isla expressed surprise at her new signature Barbara explained, "Yes, a sadder and a Weiser woman."

Life at STIC seemed to revolve around hospitals and disease. There had been a couple of diphtheria cases in the children's Annex. Isla prayed Gill would be safe. Next came a polio scare. A young man of 27, a good athlete of strong constitution, was taken to hospital and put in the iron lung. In two days he was dead. August '43 brought a cholera epidemic in the city. In three weeks 140 cases were reported. STIC's hospital had never been so busy and overworked doctors and nurses took rota duty on the injection line.

Isla felt the least contribution she could make was to sign up for a First Aid course. She qualified with distinction. If nothing else she could do some auxiliary medical work in the hospital.

With measles, whooping cough, trench mouth, dysentery and skin infections competing for attention with T.B., malnutrition and madness, every extra hand was needed. The situation became alarming at the beginning of 1944 when the Filipino doctors were ordered to get out. "Three men and three women doctors are quite enough for this camp", the military ruled.

The lack of isolation facilities was frightening. Gloomily Docs Fletcher and Stevenson would speculate what percentage of STICites would have tuberculosis in ten years' time as a result of the contaminating conditions.

Isla got an infection in her ankle and a high fever. Next a cut on the knuckles of her right hand went septic. It seemed as if her whole body was gradually turning bad. She wrote in her diary: "My nerves are on the twitch, nothing seems funny any more. I've got cramps all the time and headache and my joints go to sleep. My kidneys are all haywire. I want to go home. I'm a walking biped with a perpetual backache. Am sick and tired of writing this diary but can't turn back when things are getting interesting – and grim."

Grim it certainly was. By the end of 1943 shots of thiamin to counteract Vitamin B1 deficiency were limited to "advanced cases of beri-beri". Liver could only be given to those with a red blood cell count below three million, in medical opinion "just enough to tick over", the normal count being five million. Isla's and Gill's, though only slightly above the minimum, were average for the camp.

Doc Fletcher warned the internees they had better hurry up planting vegetables or they would be planting each other.

The rumour was that Wall Street were betting 16–1 against the STIC internees coming out alive. Already, they heard, 48 per cent of P.O.W.'s in the Philippines had died from dysentery and malaria, starvation and ill-treatment.

The one patient to recover, against all expectations, was Mrs Gates. After three months in the Philippine General Hospital she returned to STIC weak but with no trace of the malignant cancer.

By Christmas deaths at the camp hospital were running to three and four a week. A Burial Committee was started. Old Mrs Wolfson, who had once covered herself in glory by throwing two fried eggs out of the window on top of a Jap officer, was one of the first to go. As the poor coffin, made up out of bits of packing cases, was carried through the hallway Isla thought of how they had all laughed over the incident in the early days when hopes of release were so high. They had called the eggs "the Falling Sun".

Most of the deaths in the camp hospital were T.B. cases. Miss Adams, who ran the hospital, asked Isla one morning to go round the wards finding out the religion of the different patients. "There are going to be a lot of deaths," she told her. "We ought to know which ones will want to see the padre."

The deaths of the old and infirm were sad but expected. But when Peggy McAvoy, the young Australian who had given such good lectures on European history and culture, died in the General Hospital after a minor operation, the camp was stunned. Peggy had been one of the most popular members of STIC.

Even the most hardened thugs would flock to hear her talks on the Byzantine Empire, Peter the Great, Irish literature, Celtic art, Monasticism, the Italian Renaissance. She had been pretty and full of fun. Her husband Dennis, also in STIC, was desolate. Peggy had died of septicaemia, a victim of the chaos of war that had let germs invade the operating theatres and held at bay the vital supplies of sulphonamides and other powerful drugs which might have saved her.

Isla was among the few close friends allowed out to the funeral. She had to borrow a dress from Gill since hers had all long since become rags or bandages. It seemed to be up round her neck and her starch stomach strained quite disgustingly at the seams but she was too distressed to care.

Peggy's funeral was the first time Isla had been out since the early days of internment when she had made that dash to Pasay and unwillingly sipped tea with Commandant Yamaguchi and the interpreter. The sides of the bus taking them to the cathedral where the service was to be held were all boarded up so it was difficult to see much, but through the chinks Manila looked a pitiful sight, all bombed-out ruins and barricades and soldiers with guns. The drunken lurchings of the old bus bore witness to the state of the roads. It must be like driving across the craters of the moon, Isla thought, jaggedly pitted and totally desolate.

Back at STIC the gloom was as thick as a gluepot. Supplies of everything from toilet paper to tinned milk became more and more difficult to obtain and as supplies dwindled prices soared.

Toilet paper was cut from five sheets a day per person to three and then to one. Ida, the Issuer of Tissue for the ground floor, used to spend hours working out how many sheets to a roll and therefore how many rolls she would need for 285 women for a week. Finally the toilet paper ran out altogether and the Issuers of Tissue had to resort to cutting up the inner cardboard into little squares.

Isla was glad she had got in a supply of exercise books for her diary. Soon they would be impossible to find.

For the women the sanitary towel situation was acute. Kotex, if anyone was lucky enough to find them, sold for 5 pesos a box, almost a pound. Obviously an alternative had to be found and the Sewing Department rallied to the business of making S.T.'s out of rags. Another committee took on the task of washing them out for further use. There was no room for the niceties of life in STIC now.

There was no shame either. To show the world that she at least was not short of a pound or two, Winnie the Bitch left her four new boxes of Kotex on display on her cabana table. In Isla's opinion the whole tasteless exhibition was pure boast – she must have been well past the needs of such articles.

Shampoo was impossible to find and Isla and her friends adopted the Filipino method of washing their hair with "gogo", powder made from the bark of a tree. As the Filipina women were renowned for their beautiful, thick hair it seemed the gogo might even be an improvement on conventional shampoos.

A woman in Room Ten had a particularly unsavoury shampoo habit. She washed her hair in her own urine vowing, when she was cursed by her room-mates for her disgusting behaviour, that the urine was full of hormones and would therefore strengthen and revitalize her lank, and exceedingly gamy, locks.

She was not the only one whom shortage drove to desperate and revolting extremes. Constantly the Health Committee had to issue orders over the tannoy that internees should *not* blow their noses into the wash bowls, throw the contents of their potties out of the windows, clean their teeth under the showers or wash their clothes in the toilet bowls. Ida Lennox nearly resigned in desperation her job as bathroom monitor after repeated attempts to try and stop women substituting the meagre curtaining for toilet paper had failed.

By the summer of '43 clothes were getting embarrassingly threadbare. The Sewing Department, with its usual genius, had resorted to making pants out of chair covers and sheets, but its raw materials were limited. Socks were doubled by unwinding the complete article, separating the strands of wool and re-knitting.

Finally the Commandant announced that each internee would be allotted 80 clothing points or coupons for the year ending May, 1944 – enough, in fact, to get a man a pair of Japanese shorts, a short-sleeved shirt and a pair of socks.

The Textile Department suggested that internees might prefer to pool their coupons so that buying could be done by the Department wholesale rather than individuals trying to buy through their own outside contacts and the majority of STICites agreed thankfully to this scheme. From what Isla had heard of the great queues outside the clothes shops in town she was quite prepared to take pot luck with the general buying rather than risk waiting for what could be months for clothes bought under her own steam. Appearances had ceased to matter and anything that went on or round the body with reasonable comfort and modesty was acceptable.

The Department published a stock list of items "probably obtainable". A pair of denim men's shorts was listed at 25 points, price six pesos, thirty-six cents – over a pound. Trousers took an extra 10 points and cost 10.20 pesos. Socks, inferior quality, surprisingly demanded 25 precious points though the price was only 85 cts. For the women one yard of cotton print material, 36 inches wide, cost 10 points and pesos 1.38. Handkerchiefs took 5 points, bath towels 30 and, with only 80 points in all to spare, pyjamas and nightgowns at 50 were hardly worth the trouble.

The Department made a special appeal to those who had ample clothing for a year to donate part or all of their 80 points to the camp. These points were to be used by the Department to provide extra clothing for internees whose camp jobs wore out their normal clothing.

The buyers did extraordinarily well rounding up garments of all shapes and sizes for nearly 3,000 people. Even so, the internees felt the irony of a *Tribune* report on Jap repatriates from California. "Most of the passengers," the article claimed, "especially the women and girls, were neatly attired, some of them wearing the latest styles in footwear." Isla thought if ever they got home it would be in rags and bakias.

And these repatriates, it seemed, had rather more than stylish footwear. "On one ship three baby girls were born," announced the *Tribune*, "and on another three boys. It was said several more were expected."

One concession clothes rationing brought the women was that they were allowed to wear shorts, previously banned by the authority, so long as they were not more than four inches above the knee. Thelma took immediate advantage of this opportunity to display what she considered a shapely leg regardless of the elephantine bottom. But Isla, though she had four pairs in the bodega, felt pride even in poverty. Her shorts were *not* for the public gaze. After all her legs were not her strong point – racehorse top and carthorse bottom. She presented Gill with the collection.

Over the year the food situation, never bright, grew more and more depressing. In the spring Konichi gleefully cut the sugar allowance to two spoons a day. By June one teaspoon was the limit. On the market a kilo of disgusting white watery stuff sold at pesos 2.70. It seemed incredible that such a serious shortage could exist in a country where sugar was the main product.

By the summer meat was a rarity. The Filipinos refused to sell at the prices the Japs offered and drove their cattle into the hills. Fish was similarly scarce as the local fishermen were too scared to risk taking out their boats in the torpedo-infested seas.

The Executive Committee pressed Commandant Karoda to make urgent representations to the military for more meat. He tried but got nowhere. Finally he agreed that Grinnell could see the Colonel at military headquarters himself to put the internees' case. The Colonel's reply was depressingly to the point. "No," he told Grinnell, "the Americans can go without. The Jap Army comes first and it is no use trying again. My answer is 'No' and I will not change my mind."

Obviously what little meat supplies got through had to be given to the children – that is the under-11's – and their allocation worked out at 200 grams a day, a meagre enough amount. As for the adults they had to make do with egg plant, camotes, the ubiquitous talinum and foul-smelling duck eggs. The canteen billed the evening meal "Chile sine Carne!"

When they were lucky enough to get chicken sauce with the peanut loaf it was a case of sharing 35 chickens between 3,000 people.

But the most disgusting dish of all was the baluts George Bridgewater, the head of the Food Department, tried to persuade the internees to swallow down. Baluts were raw duck eggs containing embryo ducks. According to Bridgewater, the albumen tasted like sherry and the whole thing was full of vitamins and nourishment. The camp joke was that if he ate and enjoyed such things Bridgewater was in the wrong job!

Lack of food made everyone edgy and disgruntled. The hospital orderlies and stretcher bearers went on strike saying they wanted more sugar. Then the kitchen staff, riled at complaints that their vegetables were badly cooked, also threatened to down tools. Defiantly the chief cook put a notice on the board: "See if you can do better."

At a monitors' meeting it was suggested that each internee cook his own meat and vegetables but the kitchen supervisor, with satisfied sarcasm, rightly pointed out that you could not divide up and hand out portions of a ninth of an ounce of meat per person and a fractional bit of vegetable. There was nothing for it but to leave the eking out in the experienced hands of the long-suffering kitchen staff and be thankful for mercies, be they exceedingly small.

Ready cash was increasingly difficult to come by. A commission of 40 per cent was the going rate by mid-1943 and still Isla's sterling traveller's cheques were viewed with suspicion. Lenders insisted on drafts in U.S. dollars backed by firms in the States. Still all Isla could do was rely on her friends to help out, letting them trust her to pay her mounting war debt A.D.

Even the rich in STIC now had money worries. The Japs had changed the currency from the Filipino to the Japanese peso and were minting the stuff at such a rate inflation was running wild. The internees disparagingly called the new money "Mickey Mouse pesos".

Isla put whatever cash she could get towards stores for herself and Gill. Eggs seemed the only savable commodity available and she queued for hours to get her quota of one hundred to preserve or "intern" in lime.

Later she found a locally cured ham at a bargain price of pesos 117.50 (about £19) for four and a half kilos and hung it on the ceiling of the cabana in a mosquito bag resolving not to touch it "until the fireworks start".

As the year progressed prices became more and more outlandish. The value of the peso was still, allegedly, six to the pound sterling and two to the American gold dollar but a bar of soap now cost 50 cts, bread was 60 cts a loaf and bully beef was almost pesos 1.50 a pound. Bananas sold at 20 cts a piece and carrots were well over £1 a pound. Cabbage was 16 pesos a kilo, rice – if you were lucky enough to find it – cost 72 pesos a sack and matches were 40 cts a box. Even coconuts – with sugar the main food product of the islands – were 70 cts each. Charcoal could not be got for under £1 a sack.

The local paper captured the desperate situation in a cartoon:

"The city housewife gathers firewood" depicting a determined Filipina chopping up the household furniture.

A toothbrush made in the United States cost £2 and when Don presented Isla with this luxury she protested it was like accepting jewellery from a man and should not be done. But necessity got the better of convention and she gratefully took the fine bristle gem and substituted it for the locally-made horror she had been using.

With Kleenex at pesos 3.50 for a small packet, having a cold was an expensive business. Shoes that in 1941 had cost 9 pesos were selling two years later at 60 pesos. The internees reckoned the peso had devalued to about a tenth of a centavo since the outbreak of war.

Lines for cigarettes stretched as far as the front gate. Isla looked forward with desperation to the day the cigarette machine on the roof went into full production. Provided the raw materials could be got through the gate, the inventors reckoned one woman working a full day could roll as many as 1,600 cigarettes. At 13 cts for every hundred rolled the wages were good and fortunately so far the Commandant had turned a blind eye to the whole process.

Often as Isla waited, mute and aching, in these endless lines she wished she had bought herself a camp stool at the beginning when such things were plentiful.

On 22 November she wrote in her diary: "It's horrible to be without even this rice bread. Price up today to 1.20 per large loaf, 40 cts a little one. Peanuts are gold, a small cup now 85 cts, before 25–40. Hear there'll be no meat for days. Chickens are 9.50 per kilo (nearly £2) and eggs 50 cts each! Everything is exorbitant. We want cheese and milk so badly. Bought a Red Cross can of klim for £5. Glad to have it so cheaply!"

And on 30 November: "St Andrew's Day. Oh for some haggis and Prince Charles's own with it but not this year I fear. The Xmas kits are coming in, thank God. Line chow is squash and rice. No more bananas."

By Christmas it was costing Isla £1 a day in eggs and vegetables for herself and Gill.

Sadly Ida Lennox recalled the time she and Flora had bought a 5 lb can of margarine for pesos 12.50 exclaiming what a terrible price. Now the same size can cost pesos 77.50.

In such dismal circumstances there was but one consolation –

"bombing lotion". This was Isla's name for her home-made brew specially designed to soothe the nerves in times of crisis.

As before, the basic ingredient was comfort kit raisins, to which Isla and fellow-brewer, Margot Ewing, added orange and pineapple juice and sugar to effect fermentation.

"If I'm caught I'll say it's medicine for my bowels," joked Isla.

"Well no one should grudge you that!" said May whose stomach had taken a severe beating over the past few weeks.

The raisin brew, which Isla called "Port" since, as she explained to May and Margot, it represented "a port in a storm" turned out rather more medicinal than they had bargained for. After finishing the first bottle, which tasted like rather fiery cider, all three were on the trot all night.

"I suppose things might have been worse," said a pale Margot the following morning. "A woman on the third floor who drank fermented raisin juice had a frightful nightmare and fell out of the top bunk catching her foot on a shelf and sent a large bottle of eau de Cologne flying across the floor. The woman below woke up, lit a match and her mosquito net caught fire."

"Well, we'll just have to try a different recipe," said Isla practically. "What about starting with currants not raisins this time? Or mashed banana? It's important to have *something*. After all we don't want to impair our elbow action through disuse."

They decided that the cellarage behind Isla's "wardrobe" in Room Five might have been at fault and voted that "the baby" should be moved from the hot room to the slightly cooler patio.

A new cellar was created on top of Isla's cupboard in the cabana and the serious business of brewing started again. The currant wine turned out a great improvement on the raisin. But the banana brew with yeast, sugar and salt was the best yet. Everyone, including Gill, agreed it gave a real boost. Even Don, who was a teetotaller, voted it delicious and Isla brewed up a fresh bottle for him and another for Ansie.

The real McKoy was still possible to get – though difficult and, of course, illegal. Gin was known as "white" and sold at 15 pesos a bottle and rum or "brown" cost 25.

Isla never negotiated with a bootlegger direct but occasionally one of their friends – John Hunter or someone else in the know – would turn up with a bottle. Swift decanting action was then required to transfer the stuff to some innocuous-looking receptacle and, this done ,"the body" was wrapped in a paper bag and discreetly deposited in a distant garbage can.

Gill was, in fact, considerably bolder than her mother in the pursuit of liquor. Her return from the Philippine General Hospital with a bottle of "brown" had astounded Isla earlier in the year and when she produced a second "brown" for her mother's birthday just before Christmas Isla knew she had a daughter of talent even though she might lack a formal education.

Booze continued to get through the gate in spite of strict inspections and severe penalties for bootlegging and drunkenness. Rum runners, who tried to smuggle the stuff through concealed under a layer of eggs, got sixty days in the clink.

But, ironically enough, if you wanted a drink jail was the best place to be. As artist Teedie Cowie aptly put it: "The customer's always tight." One jailbird, it was rumoured, had been out every night collecting supplies of "brown" and "white". Another was so tight he tried to trip the guards on either side of him by raising both feet at once forgetting the manoeuvre left him nothing to stand on and fell flat on his face!

Catching up with the big bootleggers was still an impossible task for the patrols. To start with they were not especially anxious to enforce a clampdown. Secondly, if they got their man, he was all too often in the pay of someone on the Executive Committee who would try to get him off his punishment. Rumour had it that "the protector" would take three out of every ten bottles smuggled through the gate as his rake off. Naturally when the bootlegger was brought to book he wanted his money's worth from the "protector" or he would squeal to the Commandant.

The Japs at the gate and some in the Commandant's office were bribable too. Hartnell, a notorious bootlegger, had been allowed to use the same pass for six months. It was his arrest, in January, 1944, that led to another show-down on the Jim Tullock lines in the early days of STIC. Once again the police chief, this time Gordon McKay, Sister Fairchild's husband, threatened to resign if the Executive Committee refused to back him and enforce the sentence on Hartnell. It was only the Commandant's threat to bring in the military police if order was not restored that saved the situation.

The system whereby some were severely punished and favourites got off scot-free infuriated Isla. The attitude of the Executive Committee towards the misdemeanours of its own members incensed her particularly. Both Earl Carroll and Stan Lennox were known for their heavy drinking. Ida was often in despair at Stan's addiction to the bottle and Isla wished, for her sake, that he would get hauled before the Court of Order. But while others were tried and punished for minor drinking offences Stan and Earl continued to drink without ever seeming to run the risk of censure.

One particularly boozy night in February a group of quieter-living internees complained to the patrols about Stan's behaviour. Once again no charges were preferred.

Isla had had just about as much as she could take of injustice. She challenged Chairman Grinnell with the situation: "You make all these rules about bootlegging and drunkenness but what are you doing about your committeeman being drunk? If I'd been a witness I would have forced the police to take him to court."

"I must see what *my* police were doing," replied Grinnell loftily.

"*Your* police!" exploded Isla. The megalomania was insufferable.

On 14 February, 1944, she resigned from the Court of Order giving as her reason, "I am not in sympathy with the policy which shows partiality to some internees and not to others in the enforcement of camp regulations."

Looking back over the two years she had served as a member of the Court Isla felt the experience had been worth while. The funniest cases had been the prostitutes – Housecoat Lil, Volga Olga, Queenie, who was said to have gone back to Shanghai with a load of jewels, Princess Papaya, celebrated for her amorous encounters in the talinum patch, and Diana who called a bayonet a "baronet". The usual reason for their appearance in court was fighting. Battles would constantly break out between the ladies over client pinching and price cutting. They would continue or renew their arguments in the courtroom much to Isla's amusement.

One day Queenie had come to blows with a mestiza co-professional, Josepha. In a mood of unusual benignity Queenie had commiserated with the mestiza over her attack of V.D.

"It's an occupational hazard. Can't avoid it really," she consoled Josepha. Then Queenie, unable to resist a jibe, went too far. "Of course with the lot you have I wonder you're not . . . "

Josepha took one leap at Queenie whose top-heavy form went over like a ninepin. They kicked, scratched, pulled at each other's hair. Finally Josepha got Queenie's first finger between her teeth. She bit mercilessly. The police had to prise her jaws open before poor Queenie could be released.

In court it was as much as four stalwart patrolmen could do to keep them from one another's throats. Their language would have amazed even the proverbial trooper.

"I didn't know she lay on her back for two pesos," yelled Queenie. "No f...ing wonder she's got what she got."

In fact, as Isla knew from her hospital work, Queenie was being treated for V.D. too. They all were.

"She," spat Josepha. "She do anything for two pesos. If she have as many pricks outside as in she be a porcupine!"

"I may be a whore," retorted the honest Queenie cut to the quick. "But I don't go with niggers. She . . . "

The men in court looked embarrassed by this exchange but Isla could scarcely contain her laughter.

Housecoat Lil was the champion fighter of her number and a great troublemaker. She resolved that one of the women in her room, a Mrs Judy Scott, was a spy and for eight months went about making her life a misery. Housecoat Lil, in spite of her appearance, was the most plausible of sluts and everyone believed her scurrilous stories and refused to have anything to do with poor Mrs Scott.

Then one day, leafing through a copy of *True Detective* in the library, Mrs Scott's eye caught a lurid headline. "Lil, the woman who killed for love." Sure enough, it was Housecoat's true story. She had shot her husband in Chicago – basically because he was hampering her "career" – and had revealed all to the journalistic sleuths of *True Detective*. Now Mrs Scott could get her own back. She lost no time in spreading the amazing tale and every time she saw Housecoat jeered, "Here comes two-gun moll!"

Strangely enough, Housecoat complained to the police that she was being slandered and it was at this stage that the case came to court. In the event the ending was tame. The case against Mrs Scott was dismissed and Housecoat was told to go away and not make any more trouble. As for Isla she put herself straight down on the waiting list for *True Detective*.

The case of the British Oliver girls was less amusing. Both sisters, Olly, aged 18 and Chris, who was 20, were strikingly pretty but because of their endless boyfriend troubles, their noisiness and their lazy and untidy ways, no one wanted them as room-mates. Chris was in fact married to a pleasant enough man, Henry Sperry, but the marriage was a disaster and her boyfriend was Earl Carroll. Olly had more boyfriends than even the most enthusiastic gossips could keep pace with.

Room 49 had put up with the two of them for almost a year but at last the monitor complained she could stand no more of it and Olly was ordered to transfer to Room 42. But when she arrived with her belongings Room 42 was having none of her. The inmates barred the door booing and jeering. The patrolmen tried to push Olly and her things through the crowd but the harder they pushed the more incensed the affronted inhabitants became. Never was there such fury as the scorn of these righteous women.

In the end Olly got hysterical and had to be taken off to hospital, sobbing uncontrollably. It was obviously impossible to place her in any room in the charged atmosphere so in the hospital she stayed.

If the Oliver girls had been unpopular before, the camp's indignation knew no bounds when Chris went to the Commandant to complain about her sister's treatment – the unforgivable sin. Tersely the Commandant told her that the two of them should obey the rules. He had no doubt justice would be done in the end.

Stan Lennox agreed to represent Olly in court. He based his case on the original STIC housing rule that "no room could vote on the acceptability of a room-mate assigned there". In the end she was grudgingly taken in though after a stream of protestations and petitions.

Shapiro and Sniffen were STIC's blackmarket kings. They were a thoroughly unpleasant pair, both of them Americans though Shapiro's swarthy looks showed his Italian descent. The Sniffens had originated somewhere in Eastern Europe. One or the other was sure to be behind any shady enterprise that was on the go.

In Manila Shapiro had been known as a great gambler. In STIC he was making a fortune out of poker, fleecing the unwary of their meagre possessions. He boasted there was nothing he could not get if the price was right and in this at least he kept his word. He bribed the guards to get special supplies through the gate. He and Sniffen bought Red Cross kits from foolish old men who thought ready cash was better than saving their rations for a rainy day. When the cloudburst came and they were hungry they found Shapiro a true fair-weather friend. He would offer to re-sell goods at 70 pesos an item when he had paid no more for an entire kit. He also acted as a fence for stolen property. After several abortive attempts the police eventually brought him to book for selling ice-cream, an activity forbidden by the Commandant. In court Shapiro denied the accusation saying he had only sold "cold custard" and witnesses came forward to back him. It seemed as if, once again, Shapiro was to wriggle, maggot-like, from under the long arm of the law until one member of the Court had the bright idea of looking up the definition of ice-cream in the dictionary. Sure enough, ice-cream was cold custard. Shapiro had looked too. He got thirty days confined to barracks, sixty barred from the shanties and for ninety days he was ordered to do no business deals.

Still believing himself immune from punishment – naturally there were several people in positions of prominence who, he considered, owed him favours – Shapiro broke his bounds. But the patrols were not so easily fooled. Shapiro was hauled before the justices once more and sentenced to thirty days in jail. Before the sentence was broadcast – and therefore put into effect – Shapiro showed his true yellow colours and went squealing to the Commandant. He gave the names of those for whom he had done deals, selling their effects and getting money from outside. No denunciation was too low for him. But Commandant Karoda was disgusted by this archetype of treachery.

"I am very disturbed you can talk against your own people this way," he told Shapiro. "If I were hostile to the internees which I am not I might make great trouble. You are the kind that could turn to any side. *You* are the wrongdoer. What good does it do you to implicate your fellows? You disgust me. Out."

And Karoda ordered the Court to give Shapiro an indefinite

sentence.

"If you do not," he told Grinnell, "I will see to it myself."

Shapiro's disclosures provoked an inquiry as Owens' had earlier but the camp breathed sighs of relief that Karoda was the man he was. He kept investigations at an internal level, not handing the matter over to the military.

"That man has saved our bacon," commented Jim Tullock wryly. "It's just the sort of thing the M.P.'s would love to get hold of."

It had been a great relief for Jim when Gordon McKay took over as chief of police. For discipline was getting more and more difficult to maintain.

Gordon confessed he was being driven frantic by the thieving. Nothing was safe. A woman in the Sewing Department left a reel of cotton threaded on her machine while she turned to pick up her pattern. When she looked back the reel had vanished. Another woman left her half knitted sock on a bench while she went to get a cigarette. It disappeared.

Isla was careful not to risk hanging anything to dry on the public lines after she heard of one poor woman who returned to find all that remained of her best sheet was the name tape! A thief who was caught was found to have fifty-five sheets stuffed into one bag! The cartoon in the *Tribune* was apt. It showed a Filipina guarding her precious washing with scythe and axe. "Wash day is also watch day" read the caption.

Food was stolen all the time. And clothes. And the precious tin cans the internees used for their baking tins and saucepans. Vegetables growing in the garden, destined to supplement diets in the children's Annex and the hospital, disappeared over-night. Chairs, umbrellas, blankets, soap, matches, charcoal – nothing was sacred. One day the patrols uncovered a cache of stolen ladies' underwear. Isla had not been among those deprived of their lingerie. "Mine's so frightful not even a STIC thief would want it," she thought.

STIC thieves were not the only problem. Often Filipinos broke in from outside to loot the bodegas and rob the shanties. The few warm clothes that Isla and Gill had managed to bring with them disappeared in one of the bodega raids.

But penalties for looting were stern. Two Filipinos who were caught robbing the shanties were made by the Japs to stand outside the front gate with placards on their chests saying: "I am a thief. I have been robbing STIC." When their heads drooped they were given a sharp biff under the chin.

In many ways the Filipinos could not be blamed for looting. By the summer of '43 conditions in Manila were appalling. Lines at the rice stores stretched to over a mile long and the markets were almost bare.

Throughout the year the carrot of Independence was dangled before the noses of the hungry Filipinos. In vain did ex-President Quezon broadcast to his people from his exile in Washington: "Do not believe the Jap propaganda. You will get your independence from the United States in 1946. Any independence the Japs offer you will be on the lines of Korea or Manchuria, a subject people, free in name only."

No doubt the majority of the Filipinos were pro-American but as the saying in the islands went: "Our hearts are with the U.S. but our stomachs with Japan."

It was also said the the Spanish had brought civilization to the Philippine Islands, the United States education and the Japs sampalitation, a Tagalog word meaning prostitution.

In May Japanese Premier Tojo came to do his wooing. Don had always admired the diplomacy of this elder statesman of the empire and his handling of the Filipino situation showed he had lost none of his skills.

Preparations for independence forged ahead and the papers continued to report popular enthusiasm for the project, though no great delight seemed to be in evidence.

Parades were well attended simply because if a Filipino did not appear his food card was taken away. Only a handful of doctors and nurses were granted exemptions. Those not listed had to appear with Jap flags or "drastic measures would be taken".

At last it came. Independence Day, 14 October, 1943. Filipinos were warned that failure to attend the celebrations would incur a heavy fine.

So they came in their thousands.

"Independence?" snorted Isla. "Sold down the river more like." And she thought of the poem by Ogden Nash.

> "How courteous is the Japanese,
> He always says 'Excuse me please'
> He climbs into his neighbour's garden

And smiles, and says, 'I beg your pardon.'
He bows and grins a friendly grin,
And calls his hungry family in;
He grins and bows a friendly bow;
'So sorry, this my garden now.' "

The Japs may well have intended to give co-prosperity to
the peoples of South-East Asia but that was not the way it
worked out. Food became scarcer and scarcer and it went hard
for anyone who was known to sympathize with the Americans.

The local rag ran a headline "Bad news for Bow-wows".
According to the article many residents of Bacolor, Pampaya,
were finding that dog's meat possessed "a more superior taste
than any other kind of meat with the exception of ham and
bacon".

It was bad news for cats too. A correspondent to the *Tribune*
alleged that kittens in his district were being bought up at one
peso a head by restaurant agents. Another correspondent was
concerned on a different point: "Cat butchers", he complained,
"are not only making some downtown restaurants' customers
contented but are threatening the city with a large-scale influx
of rats. Unless the health authorities do something drastic,
the cats are in for fewer lives!"

And an editorial took the balanced view: "While there is
no harm in eating cat meat the restaurant operators should let
their customers know they are being served with such meat and
not try to pass the meals for other meats."

Indeed the starving Filipinos counted themselves lucky to
find a tasty cat or dog steak. Pictures in the *Tribune* of a banquet
at the Manila Hotel captioned: "Food problem was discussed
at a conference called by the Food Administrator" did nothing
to inspire confidence in their new rulers' desire to help. And
the paper's advice: "Filipinos should learn to suffer as suffering
is a precious investment" just rubbed salt in hungry wounds.

Natural Filipino resilience was being smothered by starvation. Even the war jargon to which the *Tribune* devoted an
entire column did not seem amusing any more.

"To Blitzkrieg" meant to do fast work in the buy and sell
business or in love-making. A man who married a rich girl was
said to have found an "air-raid shelter". A suitor who went on
his bicycle to escort a girl was called "a convoy" and a woman

with many admirers was described as "heavily convoyed". "Occupied territory" spoke for itself.

It was difficult to separate propaganda and rumour from genuine news. But by the New Year of '43 the tide had definitely turned in the Allies' favour.

In February, 1943, the internees heard that the Japs had evacuated Guadalcanal. In April MacArthur warned the Filipinos to keep away from military objectives such as piers, wharfs, airfields and railways. It was said he would eat Christmas dinner at the Manila Hotel but Manila itself would be "like a scrambled egg".

In July MacArthur broadcast that the Allied successes in the Solomons were tremendous and the losses less than their wildest expectations. Rabaul was their next objective and after that the Philippines. Isla bet Margot a bottle of whisky it would be all over by the end of the year.

She knew her journalist friend Clark Lee had been grossly misquoted when the *Tribune* reported him as having written in *Collier's Magazine* for 26 May: "Some American public leaders are stressing the importance of wearing Nippon down by attrition, but the truth is that Nippon has already won her war."

There were, of course, some Jap successes. In terms of ships and men lost, the Battle of Kula Gulf, 5–6 July, was a Jap victory though the Americans claimed it as theirs.

But all the time the American advantage was growing. They had radar; the Japs did not. They were mastering the tactics of night fighting which had earlier baffled them. And in the Central Pacific a fleet more powerful than the world had ever seen was being built up under the command of Vice-Admiral R. A. Spruance, the victor of Midway.

For the Japs the main difficulty was keeping up reinforcements and supplies – "The Tokyo Express" – to the isolated island chains which they had hoped to make their empire.

By October the New Georgia group of islands were in Allied hands. By Christmas the Solomon Sea was an Allied lake, the Gilbert Islands were secured.

The news that filtered in from Europe was grim but encouraging. The Ruhr was now called "Happy Valley" it was so flattened. Hitler had appealed to the Pope to beg Britain and the U.S. to stop the bombing "for humanity's sake" and the Allies had replied they would continue for that very reason.

An American in STIC, whose German wife was living out in Manila with her parents, told how his father-in-law listened to the radio all day and often the news commentators would break down and cry. Other Germans in Manila were speaking in the past tense of their cities.

The story went that some Germans from a submarine had gone to the Manila Club and been greeted by the Manilan Germans: "Heil Hitler." Their answer had been the equivalent of "Goddam Hitler".

In May the internees heard of the fall of Tunis and Bizerta to the Allies. But the big news of '43 was the surrender of Italy in September. "Keep smiling. One down and two to go", proclaimed STIC's menu board. And the Filipinos went wild with their celebrations.

As Christmas approached there was a lot more air activity. The internees were warned they should be prepared for black-outs. For almost two years there had been nothing – no bombs, no planes, no sign that help was on the way. Now, as the Filipinos at the gate reported, the Americans were becoming "so offensive".

Isla felt she could stand anything so long as the end was in sight. She hoped against hope that the good news she had logged in her diary was not just another product of well-meaning newsmongers. A Filipino who had been supplying cheerful news for five pesos a week had recently been exposed as a fraud.

Home news was as precious as war news – and even more scarce. Isla had to wait five months for a reply to her cable to T.D. When it came, in April, 1943, she felt she was the luckiest woman in camp. In May she heard from her mother and an aunt. Their letters were nearly a year old but they told her of Richard's commission in the anti-tank battalion. She was thrilled he had passed through all his exams and kept saying to herself: "He'll be all right. Some have to come through it all."

She got permission to send a reply to T.D. in August. Censorship ruled out a quantity of comments but she told him: "It's not a bowl of cherries but this is internment. So far my impression of the Philippines is not high. The fauna is varied and bothersome and flora I've seen none. July was perfectly frightful – 36 inches of rain when the average is 19. Gillian is now my height but I'm afraid her education is sadly lacking. She and I

sleep under one net with twenty-one others in the room including two snorers. Prices are frightful and soap, sugar and toilet
paper a rarity. Had my tonsils out – surgery first class but
trappings primitive. But I feel better for the loss. Hope to be
with the family soon."

It was a good month. A few days later a second letter arrived
from T.D. and a third. It seemed he was back in the army.
No doubt by now he would be in India with Richard.

He was frantic for news of her and Gill. Nothing seemed
to have got through since Isla's first cable and the Foreign
Office and the Red Cross could shed no light on the situation.
All they could say was that medical supplies and food had
reached Hong Kong and Singapore so they assumed they had
reached Manila.

There was a letter from Richard too and Aunt Lucy whom
Isla had only met once in her life.

"I do hope you have some needlework and some books there",
Aunt Lucy wrote. "It must be awful having nothing to do."

Nothing to do! Bless her, thought Isla, the struggle against
bugs is exhausting enough in itself!

The letters were tremendously cheering. She only wished her
American and Canadian friends could have shared her happiness. But, for the Japs, the Americans were the real enemies
and, although some mail got through, they were cruelly dis-
criminated against.

July's 36 inches of rain were drops in the ocean compared to
November's effort. It was the dry season, supposedly one of the
best months of the year. But on 15 November the barometer
fell lower than it had been for ten years. A typhoon was on its
way. It broke at 11.30 in the morning. Ironically as the raging
winds reached the little camp they veered sharply and dangerously to the east as if to show the wretched internees the Orient
was master. Shanties collapsed like houses of cards against the
storm, trees snapped at the pressure, papaya and banana plants
that the internees had cultivated with such loving and expectant
care were flattened by the wind. The rain was like a spiked
waterfall. It cut through every chink, flooding passages, bed-
rooms and hospital wards. The water in the buildings swirled
four inches deep. In Glamorville it came waist high. Once again
the shanty dwellers crowded into the main buildings salvaging
what they could of their possessions. Tin cans bobbed mockingly

on the torrid muddy waters.

Isla had rushed over to the hospital to be with Gill who was smitten yet again with amoebic dysentery. Looking out of the rain-lashed window she noticed that the sawali fence had blown down. They could walk out – if there was anywhere to go. The sky was yellow-black. Like the end of the world. At midnight the electricity was cut. All night the wind moaned and battered like an angry ghost. The rain was frightening in its intensity.

In her diary for 16 November Isla wrote: "The situation beggars description – the horror, the misery and squalor. No lights and no candles allowed. The evening seemed interminable and most of us were in bed by 9 pm. No reading and no cards. A pipe burst on our floor and there was a huge fire somewhere in Manila. Got my boots from the cabana but the water came over the top. Sat up in the passage till 3.30 am. In the hospital there's water everywhere, road very difficult to manoeuvre as the water's running in strong currents. The clinic, the doctor's office and the dispensary over a foot deep in water. Things swirling all over the place in the current from the main gate and hospital gate. I hear there's a gang of boys out looting and the Filipinos have come in to loot. The Gym's under water and the paths are useless. Children's hospital evacuated. Toilets out of order – no pressure. Only pull plug for major operation and then buckets have to be used. Clean teeth with rain-water and shower when the sun comes out!

"Notices everywhere 'Boil your water', 'Rainwater is safe'. Line all day for the canteen. Garbage cans all full but by wading up to my hips I found a half-empty one. If we come out of this without an epidemic we'll be lucky. Everyone is worried about the Christmas kits and the luggage in the bodega not to mention the food in the Red Cross bodega. Still raining heavily. It could go on for ten days. Some say it could be forty-two days and forty-two nights – hellish Philippines!

"This defeats all. If such a situation arose anywhere civilized there'd be ships and trains, nurses and doctors rushing to relief. Shanty Town nearly up to the roofs. Charcoal men had to wade up to their necks to get charcoal. No place to hang wet clothes, just keep 'em on and hope for the best. The animals floating on the water are horrible. Boots protect a bit but if they get inside . . . "

All through the storm the kitchen staff worked gallantly

providing jugs of hot coffee. Gordon McKay and his patrols toured the shanties to make sure no one was trapped. Gill's friend Doug, just back from Los Baños, kept the children's canteen going in spite of power cuts. Father McMullin, the Roman Catholic padre, organized a group to fetch buckets of water up to the toilets. Isla did what she could in the hospital. Though many of the Japs seemed to disappear in the crisis Kato, the new Commandant who had taken over from Karoda in October, never left the scene. Elderly, bald and bespectacled he stayed night and day with the internees and kept saying: "Sorry, so sorry", as if he felt a personal responsibility for the disaster.

On the 17th the rains abated. The lights came on and the loudspeaker played: "Happy days are here again!" It was a week before the gas was working.

The following day the sun came wanly out through the clouds. There were clothes-lines everywhere and mattresses, pillows and beds steamed in the pale heat.

Thoughtfully Commandant Kato arranged for shanty dwellers to buy sawali and bamboo at controlled prices so they could rebuild their homes.

The typhoon had also hit Los Baños and much of the work the men had put in during the last six months was undone. Some of the barracks were blown down and would have to be rebuilt. The summer rains had already caused enough delays to the building programme and the wives began to wonder whether they would ever be transferred.

Christmas loomed depressingly ahead. MacArthur had not booked his suite at the Manila Hotel nor put in an order for turkey and plum pudding. The internees would simply have to make the best of their second Christmas "inside".

Gill announced that all she wanted this year was to have her ears pierced. Isla told her she must wait at least until her seventeenth birthday in January. She seemed to be growing up so quickly. Isla was plunged in depression when she found nicotine stains on her fingers. Gill swore she had just been trying out a cigarette and would not do it again but a few weeks later there were the tell-tale signs. Isla was furious. "At least I thought you were honest if uneducated," she stormed. "What you need is a strict school . . ."

Soon Gill was in tears again. It was not fair. Her mother

didn't understand. *She* hadn't been shut up in an internment camp when she was 16 doing an adult's job.

It was always the same these days. Isla seemed to have no control over her daughter. It was quite impossible to get her to do any of the chores in the bedroom or little cabana. Mending had been lying in the sewing basket for weeks but Gill always had some splendid excuse why it should not be done.

Her only interest seemed to be her work at the Children's Hospital, where in October she had been promoted from the canteen to the wards, and in cooking. As Isla thought about her disobedient daughter her anger simmered down. She was infuriating and undisciplined – but she could have been a great deal worse. At least this miserable dump had provided her with a job she loved. She had made some good friends too – Doug and Bill Slingsby and Betty-Lou Gewald, herself a more cheerful companion since the good news that her fiancé was safe in Cabanatuan.

Virginia Hewlett, an American woman in her late 20's, was one of the many sad cases in STIC whose mind had been temporarily unhinged by the horrors of war. Her husband was United Press correspondent Frank Hewlett and on New Year's Eve 1941 he had gone to join MacArthur in Corregidor leaving Virginia, who was a qualified nurse, working at a hospital in Manila. Somehow his message to his wife had never got through and Virginia had a complete nervous breakdown. She would not eat, she would not wash. When Isla first met her in STIC's hospital she just sat staring into space picking at her face and nails and murmuring: "He's gone, he's gone. I didn't know."

By Christmas, 1943, encouraged by Isla's care and interest, Virginia, though still painfully thin – she was five feet five inches and under six stone – was beginning to live again. She was even well enough to join Isla for a pre-Christmas lunch in the cabana.

Though the Christmas spirit was not exactly flourishing in STIC, the wives were considerably cheered by Commandant Kato's announcement that in the New Year they were to be allowed to sleep out in the shanties. Those with husbands at Los Baños were to join them in time for Christmas. Obviously the boys had done a splendid job on repairing the barracks.

Thelma was in her element.

"Would you like my space, Ida, when I move to Los Baños?"

she asked generously.

"No thanks, Thelma," Ida replied. "I'll be moving out to our shanty, I hope."

"Good heavens, Ida, have you gone off your nut? No one will be allowed to sleep in the shanties without contraceptives. You haven't a hope unless a supply comes in with the kits. Of course, as a Filipina told me, cocoa butter and . . . "

Ida cut her short. She could not stand any more sex instruction from Thelma. "I don't see that's got anything to do with it," she answered stiffly giving what she hoped was a withering glance.

"It will be a real orgy at Los Baños," continued Thelma unabashed. "I can't wait . . . " and she rushed off to try and find someone who would discuss the forthcoming happy events with her.

The Los Baños crowd, including Margot Ewing, Jean Mackay, Thelma and a number of unmarried girls left STIC on the morning of 10 December to the strains of "The Wedding March" and "Happy days are here again".

A few days later the internees heard their Christmas comfort kits had arrived. They may have been short in the contraceptive line, but, for all save Thelma, food was the priority. They awaited the distribution of the kits like hungry wolves prowling wide-eyed and alert for the first sign of prey and licking their chops in hungry anticipation.

The kit inspection news aroused fiercer emotions than had been witnessed in STIC for many a month. "Me, I'm disgusted," wrote Isla. "But what's the use of using energy and being angry? The kits are all out on the road being examined by the military police. They're opening cans of food and pouring out the contents. The road is running with butter, cheese and milk. They've broken into the raisins and torn all the Old Gold cigarettes out of their packets."

At least Kodaki had been honest in his valedictory speech – "while Japan is winning we can afford to be magnanimous" – thought Isla hotly. Carrying through that argument the cruel mess of the kits could be the best news yet.

Isla made the only appropriate comment on the situation: "What can you expect from pigs but grunts!"

But the kits did get through in the end. Isla had never seen so many cans. The little cabana was bursting its seams. There were thirty cans of jam each, tins of cocoa, eight cakes of soap each, butter, klim, large slabs of chocolate and, of course, cigarettes.

Warnings against eating the food too quickly were broadcast over the tannoy. One small boy had to be rushed to hospital after wolfing his slab of chocolate in one go. His shrunken stomach simply could not cope with the unaccustomed feast. Craig Stopford, not to be outdone, ate his way, with his three-year-old girlfriend, through an entire packet of prunes and one hundred calcium tablets – and ended the day looking like a million! Internees were also advised how best to preserve their cans and instructions were given on what to eat first. With the kits came sacks of sorely needed medical supplies – bandages which, of course, had to be inspected at Fort Santiago; thiamin, though not much of it; and vitamin pills.

Commandant Kato, though a considerate man, was under the strict eye of the military. Anxious at 60 to win for himself an honourable retirement, Kato sought to bring STIC more into line with military discipline. As with former Commandants the freedom of the Shanty area struck him as a major sore thumb in a regulated community. Of an egalitarian turn of mind, he maintained that all internees should eat the same food. He resented the shanty dwellers' habit of mixing their line food with some private supply to make it more palatable and still more he hated to see them cook their own – for he had a phobia about fires. To Commandant Kato Christmas, with all the extra food coming through the gate and the endless cooking in the little shanties, represented unsocialistic chaos and a terrifying fire hazard. On New Year's Eve he ordered the gate closed. Next cooking in the shanties was banned in spite of Grinnell's protests that there had been only two small fires in the two years they had been in STIC. Shantyites were forced to feed on the line or cook in the open – a choking, messy job for which the booming tannoy offered the doubtful consolation of "Smoke gets in your eyes".

Oddly enough, though Kato did not like fires he had no objection to "co-mingling". On 1 February the sleeping-out promise was fulfilled and wives were told they could join their husbands in the shanties. Immediately the gramophone, never at a loss, struck up with "I've been alone too long" and the inevitable "Happy days are here again".

Gill's 17th birthday on 31 January was hardly the gay affair it should have been, although she wore some of her new clothes from the U.S. kits which had arrived just five days earlier. Each woman had been issued with a bra, a pair of pants, a pair of lace-up shoes plus polish, a toothbrush, tooth powder, nice smelly soap, wash soap and a comb. When it came to night-dresses – one each – the outsizes were in great demand for something else could be made with the extra material. Isla and Gill were too late for the really voluminous garments which had been snapped up immediately, but they decided they could with decency take enough off the hems of their own unromantic, sacklike objects to make at least one blouse.

On 17 February it was announced that Commandant Kato was leaving to be replaced by a full military commandant. The stranded internees feared the gate would close for ever. Isla bought while the going was still good. She managed to get four kilos of sugar at 6.50 pesos a kilo the day before sugar supplies were banned at the gate and two packets of Kleenex at the exorbitant price of 22 pesos (nearly £4). Gill bought a kilo of cassava flour – which helped to thicken the watery rice they got from the line – for 6 pesos. A final triumphant purchase was a quarter of a pound of bicarbonate of soda for 6.05 pesos, over £1!

Charcoal was the next commodity to come under a ban. Isla had six weeks' supply. Peanut butter, now classified as a luxury, followed in the list of prohibited goods. Konichi was working hard.

By the end of the month milk cost 1 peso a half pint, a small tin of margarine was up from the pre-war price of 5 pesos to 275, eggs cost 80 cts each, mangoes 7 pesos a piece, and a box of matches was £1. A pair of American shoes was advertised at 750 pesos – £125! Vinegar was out of the question and Isla took to making it out of banana yeast – when she could get the bananas. The *Tribune* suggested the common water-lily as being full of nutritives.

Isla wrote in her diary: "Sure enough they're going to slowly twist our tails, first one little wring, then another, but we've got to take it. It can't go on for long."

In defiance of Konichi the tannoy blared out "Who's afraid of the big, bad wolf?" and the latest song from the States, "I'm waiting for the Rising Sun to go down".

The Rising Sun *was* setting – but slowly. Having ousted the Japs from the Solomons and the Gilberts, the Allies' New Year target was the Marshall Islands. By February, 1944, they were in Allied hands. New Britain and the Admiralty Islands followed.

In two years 8,000 Japanese naval aircraft had been destroyed and few of the country's experienced pilots were left. As Saburo Sakai, the ace pilot, later wrote in his book *Samurai*: "The Navy was frantic for pilots . . . Men who could never have dreamed even of getting near a fighter plane before the war were now thrown into battle."

Yet the *Tribune* continued to report high Allied losses. "Enemy is cracking", declared a December editorial. "Stalemated at Bougainville and decimated at Gilberts the Americans are getting really desperate."

Don's explanation of the disaster figures was the only one that seemed to make sense. He told how after a raid in China the Japs all lined up in front of their planes and held up their fingers to denote the number of enemy planes they had shot down. It was a brave man that put up his clenched fist denoting none. The fingers were tallied and the total given but there was no proof.

By February the papers were less optimistic forecasting "Anglo-Saxon bombing raids" on the Philippines. Manilans would have to prepare themselves for blackout practice. Yet in the same issue, 2 February, 1944, Don Juan de la Cruz declared the Axis powers ready to fight to the end until victory was attained.

The Japs were getting touchier every day. There had been a great purge on the guerrillas. In the summer a group of some 40 men, Filipinos and Americans, under a Colonel Noble, had been captured in Northern Luzon and taken to Fort Santiago. Their wrists had been tied with wire and they had been given the water torture – filled up with water with a hose pipe to their mouths and then beaten over the kidneys. When they were released to the P.O.W. camps their hands were paralysed. Many had damaged kidneys.

In December seven priests came to STIC from Fort Santiago. They were suspected of having contact with the guerrillas and had been thrown naked into a dungeon with eighteen others with only a hole for a lavatory. One had a broken arm, another had his head bandaged. It must have been the nearest approach to hell the fathers ever expected to see.

Any suggestion of criticism of Nippon was severely punished. A show in Manila which included jokes about the Japs was closed down and the two comedians, Togo and Pogo, taken to Fort Santiago.

At Los Baños Geoff Morrison was warned not to play *The Mikado* on his tannoy programmes and in STIC a man was called up before the Commandant for talking about "the cock-eyed Jap navy". What did he mean by that? "Oh it's a very common term in the States," explained the terrified little clerk, "it's cock-eyed this and cock-eyed that all the time."

Cassy the Ratcatcher had his shanty turned inside out and all his arsenic confiscated. "We'll have a plague of rats now as well as yellow vermin," commented Isla.

When she heard these stories of questioning and searches Isla went hot and cold with fear. If the Visiting Vermin found her diary, now in its twenty-fifth book, full of illicit news, rude comments and jokes about the Japanese, it would almost certainly mean Fort Santiago, the water torture and probably the death sentence.

She got an old box, piled in the eight by six inch exercise books, together with all the cartoons, drawings and newspaper clippings she had collected, bundled some dirty clothes on top and hid the box in the cabana. "It's better to have them mobile," she said to herself. "I can't bear to tear them up after all these months of writing every day. Unless I'm suspect, and I can't see why, I should be O.K."

22 February: "George Washington's birthday. The dear, dead days beyond recall, good parties and plenty drinks and drunks. Never mind I'm told I'll be able to celebrate next year."

23 February: "I'm so tired, need meat badly, low blood pressure. I want to open something but Gill says wait."

March, 1944: "They've sealed up the electric room and stopped the tannoy. Suppose we'll have to rely on a town crier. No more lines – the egg and bread rations to be doled out by monitors. No library in the morning. They're taking away the extension lights, only dim lights in the hall. Won't be able to play cards or read, ruin our eyesight. They're making us as miserable as possible."

Line food was limited to radishes, pechay, fish, rice or mush and the inevitable mungo bean. When the Executive Committee complained to the new almighty, High Commandant Kuroda, a grim-faced man with a mass of medals on his chest and the droopiest drawers Isla had ever seen – just like an elephant's bottom – his answer was unsympathetic in the extreme.

"I have personally inspected the garbage bins," he told the exasperated delegates, "and have seen there scrapings of rice. Evidently you are not hungry yet."

In the stifling, humid air the stench of the food mingled with the pungent odour of sea algae which rose from the steaming beaches – another Manila speciality. Could Los Baños be worse than this? Could *anything* be worse than this?

Margot sounded happy at Los Baños. There was meat three times a week, she said, cigarettes at 2 pesos a packet and milk for 40 cts a pint. There were coffee parties every night and dancing. Five pregnancies already, one wedding and thirty more couples asking for trouble.

In STIC it was announced that another 500 would leave next month. Gill was all for going. But if they left would they lose all chance of being repatriated? At least STIC was near the centre of things and when the end came – and it could not be long now – the Santo Tomas internees would be sure to be on the first ship out. Then there were all the eggs Isla had "interned" and the charcoal stove. She could not take *them* with her. And the cabana she had fought so hard to win. She was in turmoil. Should she go or should she stay for the ship in the bay?

CHAPTER SIX

Paradise lost

(*28 March–14 September, 1944*)

28 MARCH, 1944: "I need a sign from heaven and I need it quickly and badly. A bombardment too. Gill has finally talked me into volunteering for Los Baños. I talked to Doctor Thorsen and he thinks the place has more advantages than here and he doesn't think we'll get out until the war is over. I think it's the optimists staying and the pessimists going . . .

"The thought of the move is making me ill and I haven't the energy for it . . . I am unattached to this place but I am tied to it."

STIC bound Isla by habit, by hope, by the little cabana that was home. The bucket of eggs, worth their weight in gold, was one link in the heavy chain. Her small store of charcoal was another. For the removal men of Interneeland made no provision for shifting bulky possessions. But the die was cast. She had volunteered and there was nothing for it but to pack and look forward to the future – whatever that might be.

In fact Isla and Gill had over a fortnight in which to brood on whether they had made the right decision. In Gill's mind there was no doubt. Several of her friends – Betty-Lou, Bill Slingsby, John Hunter – were either already there or had volunteered. There would be more space in Los Baños, beautiful views of the mountains and cool air. And, above all, it would be a change. To the eager 17-year-old two years in the same camp, in the same room, with the same people, seemed a lifetime.

Isla's misgivings centred mostly on the conviction that STIC would be first in the liberation stakes, but, having once made her decision, she began to see the advantages of a move.

STIC was getting more and more unbearable. A new disease

was sweeping the camp – nasal diphtheria – and Isla prayed that Gill, who was in hospital for the twelfth time, on this occasion with bacillary dysentery, would escape infection.

Cooking in the open was hell. The whole camp seemed to be an inferno of smoke and the ragged, emaciated internees, banned indefinitely from cooking in their shanties, looked like the tortured devils of some medieval painting as they crouched painfully over their little charcoal stoves desperately fanning the fading flame, their eyes sore and streaming from the grimy clouds. Every time a fire failed to kindle the cook would have to run to a fellow stoker for a light – for no match was lightly struck in STIC now with boxes at 60 cents and upwards a go. All over the charred lawn, once the pride of the University, they gathered in small groups to cheat the wind. And as they coaxed the obstinate embers the sun mocked their puny efforts, beating down on aching backs, tense shoulders, bare heads. It seemed fire was everywhere except the one place it was needed.

At night smoke gave way to pitch dark as blackouts were enforced. Even smoking was forbidden after dark. The final blow to the shantyites came when they were told that henceforth all shanties within 20 metres of the wall would be out of bounds. They would have to move out fast before another sawali barrier cut them off. Although the ban did not directly affect Isla she felt the claustrophobia of the encroaching sawali. Los Baños would surely be a paradise of space and freedom after this.

In the event, paradise expected was paradise postponed and Isla and Gill sat for nearly a week with their luggage packed waiting for the "all clear".

If Isla had wanted to do a sharp deal this was the time. For with the announcement of the 20-metre ban, demand for new accommodation had risen out of all proportion and shanties and cabanas were selling at fantastically inflated prices. One miserable 12 ft by 10 ft shack went for the promise of a new Ford coupé after the war. Another sold for 500 Filipino pesos and a patio space near Isla's was knocked down at 500 Mickey Mouse pesos. Isla knew she could get at least that for their corner site cabana but she could not bring herself to make money out of adversity. She promised it to the Gates family for nothing. "Let someone who needs it have it," she thought to herself. "We'll be all right at Los Baños."

On the same basis she gave her 150 "interned" eggs, now selling at three gold dollars a piece, to Sister Fairchild for her old, sick father in exchange for half a bottle of Blue Grass scent.

It was 12 April before the Corfields were told they could leave. Don and Ansie had already gone in an earlier batch. So had the Gewalds. Ida and Stan Lennox and the Stopfords opted to stay in STIC, as did Doctor and Mrs Foley, the only two missionaries Isla had ever liked. The Rich Bitches were staying and the two snorers and, as far as Isla knew, her quarrelsome neighbours, the Bisingers. However, with both Shapiro and Sniffen press-ganged into the last lap of the Easter move and Mary Warner, the singing mish, coming along to convert them, Isla and Gill considered themselves in good company. Doug, who after working his stint at Los Baños in the early days had decided to stay in STIC, helped them pack and fold up their wooden-slat beds in crate form with all the bedding inside.

Suddenly there was so much to do. Isla ran over to the hospital to say her goodbyes to the people she had worked with for so long. Gill disappeared to find the remnants of "the gang". Then it was a quick farewell lunch with Stan and Ida and line-up on the Plaza with hand baggage at 1 pm.

Isla, with her First Aid certificate, had been asked if she would take charge of a truck-load of passengers. She would have felt more confidence in her medical abilities had her kit included a bottle of brandy. "I know it's contrary to all First Aid teaching," she told supervisor Bill Williams, "but that's what I think is best – pour brandy down the victim's throat." And, if possible, down the throat of the physician too, she thought ruefully.

They piled into the trucks, seventeen to a waggon-load including two guards, and rumbled off past the sawali fence, past the sentries at their posts, through the big, iron University gates and out onto the dusty road. It was boiling hot and the heat seemed to rise in mirage waves from the arid countryside about them.

The journey was not without incident. They were hardly out of Santo Tomas when a great crack came from the corner of the Corfield truck accompanied by a surprised whimper and a flurry of clothing. A fat, female, fellow-traveller had proved too weighty a burden for the makeshift bed she had found a seat on and it had collapsed under the strain. Ponderously the distressed woman did a diagonal lurch across the truck to try her luck on Isla's seat, another internee bed, whereupon a second set of slats bit the dust with agonizing groan and splinter.

"Just stay where you are, dear," advised a worried voice. If this woman was allowed to make free with the seating there would soon be no beds at all left for Los Baños.

As First Aid attendant, Isla sat at the rear end of the truck next to one of the guards. He smelt appalling and, with the reek of stale sweat and the bumpy road, Isla feared she might be her own first case – that is if the fat lady managed to complete the journey without breaking anything more serious than a brace of beds.

Soon they were driving through Manila. Craning her neck as much as she could with a rifle butt almost next to her jaw, Isla gazed in chilled amazement at the ghost city. It was desolation and, in the buildings that still stood, pinched and grim little faces pressed noses to window panes as they passed.

After Manila they turned out into the open countryside and were soon driving due south along the shores of a great lake. At about 2.30 the convoy called a sudden halt.

"Everybody W.C.," ordered the guard. "Everybody W.C."

Isla looked round. There was not a bush, tree or rock a dog would have patronized. "Thank goodness I'm too dehydrated to have the urge," said Isla, and Gill, always rather bashful, agreed heartily.

They arrived at Los Baños at about 4 pm, having completed the 50-mile journey, "Everybody W.C." and all, in just over two and a half hours.

Two of Gill's young friends, Bill Slingsby and Owen Krauss, were waiting to welcome them. They seemed to be surrounded by buckets and, noticing no champagne lurking in the depths, Isla wondered what on earth was their purpose.

"I'm afraid you have to carry every drop of water here," explained Bill. "I'll show you later where to get it. Count the buckets as our house-warming present."

Isla's heart sank. She began to wish she had never left Santo Tomas.

"Come on," said Bill, anxious to get his charges settled. "We've fixed you up with a cubicle in Barracks 7. You've got an eastern aspect overlooking the bathroom and two wooden partitions!" Obviously the young man was delighted by what he had managed to secure for Gill and her mother.

"The wooden partitions are a stroke of real fortune," he went on to explain in case they should miss the point of his enterprise. "Most are made of that dreadful sawali stuff."

The long rows of wooden barracks stretching endlessly across the rough campus made a depressing sight. After Bill's enthusiasm Isla and Gill had difficulty in concealing their reaction to the tiny cubicle in Barracks 7 – Stable 40.

It was about 6 ft by 8 ft with two gaps for doors. One led on to a passage, about 5 ft wide, which ran the length of the 50-stable barracks, and outside the other was a rough strip of land culminating in a mound – the result of levelling off the site for building. Looking diagonally to the left Isla could see another wooden hut connected to their barracks by an intersecting passage. It was her eastern aspect – the bathroom.

Apart from their luggage in a heap on the floor, Stable 40 was completely bare – no shelves, no covering on the wooden floor. The partitions separating Isla's cubicle from its two neighbours were a uniform 5 ft high – quite seeable over the top – but, as Bill had promised, hers were made of wood and not the flimsier sawali. A mean, unshaded light hung high over each intersection. The tall roof was a covering of nipa fronds which, as Isla knew from the shanty owners' experience, had an alarming tendency to billow out in the wind, leaving the poor nipa-hut dweller more often than not without a roof over his head. The nipa also made a happy home for all manner of bugs.

"I know it looks a bit grim now," said Bill sensing the disappointment, "but wait till we've got all your stuff arranged."

"And shelves put up and a couple of sawali doors," added Owen, able for the first time to get a word in. "We'll make the back one like a stable door to give you a window."

"And we'll get a window flap for that and fix up a mediagua to stop the rain coming in. We've got a couple of months till the rainy season gets under way," said Bill, who in spite of having to sustain 6 ft 3 ins of hungry 20-year-old on a maximum of 1,800 calories a day was a fund of plans and energy. "In the good weather you'll be able to sit out under the mediagua too," he added eagerly.

Isla was impressed by their kindness. "I'm sure it will be fine," she said smiling. "At least we won't have to share it with anyone else!"

By the evening the stable had certainly improved. The two beds were in, arranged so that during the day one plus mattress would go up against the wall to make a sofa, and in the corner Bill and Owen had installed a sawali wardrobe of their own making. They planned to put in high shelves above the "back window" and promised a little folding table which could be kept by the passage door for card playing.

But even by Santo Tomas standards conditions were primitive. The water situation fulfilled Isla's worst fears. There was no running water in the lavatory cistern and to clean the lavatories internees had to hump buckets of water from a muddy hogwallow about 100 feet away from Barracks 7. There was only one small cistern to cater for the whole toilet system of a barracks of some 80 to 100 men, women and children. To flush it the internees had to lift their buckets shoulder high, pour the water into the cistern and manipulate it till it gushed down, first through the women's lavatories and then on through a drain under the sawali partition to the men's. It took twenty buckets to flush it through and was the most back-breaking task Isla had ever had to face.

As at STIC, bathroom duty was a camp detail and cistern-flushing squads were appointed. But all too often the pipeline to the hogwallow, which was outside the camp boundary, would get blocked or broken and, since internees were not allowed to go out and mend it, the camp could be days without water, waiting for the Japs to authorize a repair team. Meanwhile the lavatories became more and more congested and the stench that wafted over towards Isla's window with the "eastern aspect" was insufferable. The flies swarmed in black Catherine wheels or settled in heaving, buzzing groups on floors, walls and lavatory seats, as on a rotting carcass. When the lights failed, as they often did, the mess in the morning was indescribable.

There was some running water in the three miserable showers and few washing troughs but, here again, its availability was erratic in the extreme. The internees counted themselves lucky if they got more than a few hours' water a day.

The nearest source of drinking water was a tap by Barracks 5 and, when all else failed, there was a run on this for other purposes. For Isla the tap was about 150 yards there and back – an exhausting journey with a heavy bucket.

Not long after her arrival at Los Baños Isla was voted Barracks Monitor with the unpleasant responsibility of seeing the washroom and toilets were kept clean. Once again her day seemed to revolve round wiping seats. The mothers with small children were the worst offenders. They would splash the contents of their infants' potties all over the shed, impervious to the acute water shortage and the consequent difficulties of cleaning. Finally in desperation, Isla and another woman, Joan Smith, devised a system of one-hour bathroom watches so the culprits could be caught in the act and reprimanded. But dirty habits die hard and when one day Isla caught a woman who had made a filthy mess of a seat she had just wiped, the woman turned on her shouting abuse. Later Isla heard her regaling her friends with an account of the incident. "She accused me of making a mess of the toilet. She's just gunning for me. But I'll show her. I'll see her life's made a misery. I'll report her to Chairman Fonger then she'll be sorry she tried anything on. We'll not have *that* one long as monitor in this barracks!" Isla did not care what anybody thought of her so long as she could get some sort of cleanliness and order. With John Hodges, the men's Monitor, she went to see George Gray of the Housing Committee.

"We want soap dishes and washers for the taps which spurt all over the place and waste valuable water," Isla told George. "And I'd like the lavatory seats made removable so the potty-emptiers won't make a mess and a new tap so they can clean them out in a separate place. At present they're using our wash troughs which is disgusting and horribly unhygienic."

Gray promised to help as soon as possible but after three weeks Isla was still waiting for the extra tap and the potty business was as bad as ever. She stormed off to see Chalmers Vinson, director of Sanitation. If nothing else, her protests resulted in a stern letter to the offending barracks.

Having won one round Isla took up her second point – more disinfectant.

"I'm sorry, Mrs Corfield," explained Vinson, "there's simply nothing to spare. I've only had three pints for 1,500 people and most of that has had to go to the hospital. You'll just have to make do with the bit you've got."

Make do. That was their whole life. Make do with cardboard for toilet paper. Make do with no medicines. Make do with a couple of hours' water each morning to do the week's washing and clean out the stables.

Then one insufferably sticky and fly-ridden day in June the water system failed altogether. Even the drinking water was only a trickle and there was nothing in the hogwallow. Someone had removed the pipeline.

John Hodges did his best. He complained to the Plumbers, the Sanitation, the Housing, the Executive Committee – Los Baños government was based on the STIC pattern – but by roll call next morning there was still no pipe in the hogwallow.

Isla decided to take matters into her own hands. As the Jap guard counting his charges at evening roll call approached, she stepped boldly forward. The guard came to an abrupt halt. Isla wasted no time in coming to the point. She addressed her remarks to interpreter Ernie Cummings, a good friend of hers: "Ask them, please, when we are to have water. In two days we've had less than two hours. We've nothing to fight a fire and the dangers of epidemic are awful. The Japanese are a clean people, surely they can understand our situation? Or do they want us to die of disease?"

The eyes of her barracks were on Isla. Even in desperate circumstances it was not considered proper for a mere internee to address the Japs: the Committee were the only ones expected to have direct contact with the enemy.

In a calm, quiet voice Ernie interpreted. The guard remained impassive, fanning himself and looking neither at Ernie nor at Isla as he listened. Isla continued. Whatever the etiquette about talking to Japs she *must* get something done. The Committee might be frightened into keeping quiet but *she* was damned if she was going to be. "Our lavatories are in a frightful state, piled high. Let them go along and see for themselves and then perhaps they'll realize the seriousness of our situation. We must have our hogwallow pipe back."

The guard might have been stone deaf for all the notice he appeared to take of this confrontation. Still fanning himself, he waved Isla aside and continued his count.

"They don't feed us so at least they might give us water!" she protested as she returned to the stable.

That night Isla was convinced her efforts had been in vain and that all she had probably done was incur the wrath of the Executive Committee. She was consequently amazed the following morning to see Commandant Tannaka himself inspecting the hogwallow.

The contractor was called. Angrily Tannaka told him: "Your cement can wait but 1,500 people without water cannot. The pipe must be fixed immediately."

Later Isla had to face the music when George Gray demanded what she was doing interfering in the Housing Committee's job.

"Both John Hodges and myself tried the official way with no results," she told Gray. "One or other of us has been badgering the Committee three times a day in the last 48 hours. I felt if I didn't get a move on nobody would and we'd all die of some foul disease. You send out beautiful notices about fire, 'Take it easy, keep calm, bang a tin, tell the other fellow', and then give us no water to fight it."

She hated being pushed into the limelight like this and had no wish to fall out with George Gray whom she liked and respected. But the battle was worth it. At least she had got action. There was water again.

She sent a note to Ida Lennox in STIC: "Water situation desperate. Don't come unless forced."

About 500 more were expected from STIC and the Los Baños internees had been asked to nominate their friends. Isla thought she would nominate the people she hated. However much she might want to see Ida and Stan again she would not drag them over into this hell hole, now more aptly named Paradise Lost.

Even the food, which they had expected to be better and more plentiful out in the country, was worse than the old STIC fare. Los Baños operated the same system of line food from the kitchen to be supplemented whenever possible by internee purchases from the canteen shop. The difference now from the days of plenty two years ago, both at Los Baños and STIC, was that supplies were strictly limited, prices exorbitant and no Filipinos were allowed in to set up stalls with their wares. Those with no private means to buy extras were given Indigent Relief. It did not amount to much but was better than existing on line food alone.

Eggs were almost impossible to get and Isla bitterly regretted her "interned" supply given to Sister Fairchild. Bread was non-existent and coffee so scarce it barely coloured the water.

Commandant Tannaka suggested boiling up potato peelings; he said it made a good drink. The papers were full of the rice shortage and the internees were warned not to waste a single grain.

On 23 May Isla, as Monitor, was asked to make an appeal to the women in her barracks to volunteer for the rice detail.

"We have had a small group working there daily for several weeks," wrote Marie Janda from Women's Personnel, "but the rice is composed of a sack that was spilled at the station and another that is made up of sweepings from the bodega floor, which the kitchen authorities tell us cannot be thrown away because of the present shortage of food. The rice is so full of weevils and worms that it must be picked by hand but the present group are waging a losing war with the worms."

Isla led her troops into battle. Marie's description was mild compared to the sight that greeted their eyes. The worms were enormous and the stuff was also full of rat droppings. Even chickens would have turned up their beaks.

It was the season for bananas, avocados, mangoes, pineapples, papayas, yet none reached Los Baños. The May sugar ration failed to arrive. There was no toilet paper and precious little soap.

Jim Tullock made a survey of the situation. Taking Barracks 7, 8, 9 and 10 as typical of the condition throughout camp, he found that 91.7 per cent of the inmates were completely without sugar and 78.5 per cent without soap. In the name of humanity he appealed to Tannaka for relief.

Mush could substitute for bread, potato peelings for coffee, but there was no substitute for sugar.

Isla addressed another yellow P.O.W. postcard to Winston Churchill: "British evacuees, women and children, still awaiting repatriation. Conditions appalling: hungry, ragged, housed in huts, lacking medical supplies, no money." She did not send love.

She wondered if Churchill ever got the card. Certainly no one else at home seemed to have received their letters. She guessed, however, from one of T.D.'s cards that Mitch must have made contact with him on his repatriation from STIC, now almost a year ago. It was so depressing to write knowing, almost for certain, that the letters would never reach their destination. Her gloom was really bad on 4 August, Richard's

21st birthday. "I can't even send him a cable," she wrote miserably. "Anywhere else in the world I could get in touch with him, bless him. And 30 years ago today we got into the First World War."

Gill was hungry all the time and Isla bought what she could at exorbitant prices. By never missing a line she managed to get together another 71 eggs for "internment". Don gave her three kilos of sugar and eventually she managed to buy three more at £2 a kilo, which compared to the current STIC price of £25 a kilo was considered a bargain! Gill had a stroke of luck getting 10 cups of cassava flour for £5!

But the pair really felt like Mrs and Miss Rich Bitch when they managed to swop two ancient dresses for four cans of corned beef – eight whole meals! They felt even richer when Isla was called over to the Finance Department to be told: "Mr and Mrs Stanley Lennox have sent you 200 pesos from STIC." What good friends they had!

Precious little meat came into camp. Almost the only source was the pig farm where close on 90 miserable animals eked out an existence on garbage already picked over by starving internees. If a pig died of kidney worms there was loud rejoicing – it meant hamburgers for supper and gravy with the mush for at least three days. The internees waited almost ghoulishly for the day when the order to slaughter all pigs would come.

Meanwhile the hunger pains, the searing headaches, the cramps, continued. And the most popular song at the June show went: "She'd get very slim, On two cans of klim, I wonder who's feeding her now?"

On a more serious note, the doctors went in a deputation to the Commandant to protest about the food, saying everyone was losing weight rapidly, dangerously. Their only reply was: "What? Have you weighed each internee?"

True to their word, Bill and Owen fixed the Corfields up with some shelves, a passage door, a stable door and a folding table. Isla and Gill cleaned out the cupboard, packing away as much of their gear as they could. They scrubbed the floor and polished the rough wood with coconut oil deodorized with garlic and charcoal. Soon their little stable was the pride of the barracks and people came to look round it as though it were a stately home.

As an added and, she hoped, useful refinement Isla dug up

part of the land at the back of her stable and planted chillies, greens and eggplant. The soil was appalling but, with fresh vegetables so scarce, she thought it worth a try.

The next task was to build a cookhouse for it was too hazardous – and indeed forbidden – to burn fires in or even near the crowded barracks. One spark and the nipa roof would have gone up like a matchstick. The cookhouses were to be built 20 ft away from the barracks on the mounds "at the bottom of the garden". The idea was that in time every stable would have a cookhouse opposite its back door. In practice several internees were never able to afford one.

The problem was getting lumber. Isla reckoned there were three ways – buying it, being given it, or looting it. Naturally many, including, of course, Sniffen and Shapiro, resorted to the latter method and got 30 days in clink for their pains. Geoff Morrison, the musician, was another who fell foul of the lumber regulations and, to compensate for his 15 days' confinement, he dedicated the Sunday concert to himself, selecting for his records: "Prelude to the Thief of Baghdad", "Orpheus and his Lute", "We three", "I want to go back to my Little Brown Shack" and "The Prisoners' Song".

Isla felt if only she could spot a stray piece of sawali she would not be averse to lifting it herself. But since she came across nothing she could decently steal she had to resort to begging and borrowing. Bill and Owen, who were allowed out on the men's foraging expeditions, managed to bring back a bit of nipa and sawali. Jean Mackay made her a handsome present of a bamboo pole. But, even then, as she lugged it up to her site on the mound people called out, "Loot, loot!"

Isla was lucky. She had friends. But there were many women in her barracks, and many old people too in camp, who had no one to fetch them lumber and no money to buy with. Once again, Isla found herself confronting George Gray.

"This is a list of women and some of the sick and aged who have no one to get them lumber," she told Gray. "Can you get a volunteer squad to help?"

No doubt George Gray did his best but somehow the lumber that came in hardly ever reached the really needy. Isla had to stick her neck out again. At the Monitors' meeting she rounded on Chairman Fonger.

"The Executive Committee have assigned us stables and

done nothing else about us. There seems resentment at us coming down here but that is hardly our fault. There are dozens here, aged and friendless, who cannot help themselves. They have no means of getting lumber to make shelves, mediaguas, window flaps or doors, let alone start a cookhouse. Without mediaguas to protect them the occupants of these barracks suffer from heat and glare and in bad weather the rain pours into their wretched stables. Yet there is an unoccupied barracks in this camp full of sawali flaps which lie rotting on the floor. Surely the Committee can get the Japs to release this material for mediaguas for those who cannot afford to buy and are not prepared to loot?"

Isla paused to draw breath and Fonger, a missionary, took his chance.

"My good woman," he waved an admonitory finger in Isla's direction. "My good woman," he repeated sternly. "My committee point this situation out daily to the Japs. We cannot get the stuff released. As soon as we can mediaguas will be made available. Meanwhile . . . "

"Meanwhile," continued Isla, now well and truly on her soap box, "will no one help the old and the sick? I know one old couple aged 76 and 74 – the man has just recovered from typhus – who are eating their meals off an up-ended cardboard relief box. They have no shelves and no door to their cubicle. Yet there are masses of Red Cross packing case tops in the possession of the Committee, ten of which would make a table and shelves for these people. Surely material like this should be given to the needy and not stored away for the benefit of the more affluent members of our community? Surely Construction can provide a squad to help with the building?"

"My good woman." Fonger was at it again. Isla hated being called "My good woman".

"My good woman, these people have neighbours who should do things for them. The Construction Committee has to concern itself with the wider aspect of camp building."

"The neighbours," said Isla, not to be put down, "have their hands full trying to settle themselves, without lumber and any help from the Committee. In STIC it was quite a different story for the newcomers. There the transferees from Davao, Cebu and Iloilo got marvellous consideration."

Isla felt the mood of the meeting swaying towards her. Finally a resolution was passed that a petition, signed by the whole camp, should be sent to the Commandant requesting, among other things, that the extra sawali be released. The problems of the old and the sick were fairly speedily forgotten but at least she had gained a partial victory in the matter of mediaguas.

Her own cookhouse was more dream than reality until Jim Tullock came along one day towards the end of April saying he thought he could get enough nipa and bamboo to build a small open shack. By mid-May it was ready, nipa roof and all. Owen planted a ceremonial banana tree outside to mark the occasion.

Later Isla dug out steps in the soil leading up to the shack and laid a stone floor with her own hands – an effort which resulted in numerous painful blisters. At the bottom Bill dug a ditch so that when the rains came water running down the mound would not cascade into the stable. Finally Ansie drew a picture of the completed cookhouse for Isla to add to her collection of "internment illustrations".

All Isla's campaigning and the work that she and Gill put in on the stable and the cookhouse helped them bear the tragedy of Betty-Lou. For some time Betty-Lou had had stomach pains and Dr Dana Nance, chief surgeon, advised an appendectomy. She was young and strong and as healthy as anyone could be after two years of internment. There seemed no great cause for concern. But after an apparent recovery an infection developed. Soon Betty-Lou was running a temperature of 108°. She died at 4 pm on 25 April, 1944, aged 22.

Everyone was stunned. Gill could hardly believe the friend she had laughed and chatted with only a few days before, the pretty, vivacious girl who had shown her how to make fudge and hot cakes, was dead and cold in the poky little hospital. Her fiancé in Cabanatuan P.O.W. camp might never know. Isla tried to comfort her mother, Myrtle, but what sort of comfort was there for a woman whose husband had been killed on active service and the daughter, whom she idolized, struck down by some hideous Los Baños germ?

Jim Tullock and Jean decided to go ahead with their wedding the following week but the celebrations were tinged with sadness for the young guest who had looked forward so much to her own wedding day.

About thirty guests attended the wedding service in the little garden chapel with Dr Fonger officiating. Jean's ring was Isla's gold signet ring which she had promised for the wedding when the couple first got engaged at STIC.

Gill had insisted that Isla wear a dress and high-heeled shoes for the occasion and, since nothing more sturdy than a pair of bakias had graced her feet for nearly two years, Isla suffered the torments of the damned. She could not wait to reach the coffee and cake reception at Margot and Bud's cookhouse so she could kick off the agonizing footwear, once so fashionable and now, thought Isla, so ludicrous in this primitive country setting.

Jean and Jim were not the first bridal pair in Los Baños. Three couples had already taken the plunge, one pair of newlyweds leaving the chapel in style on an old garbage cart all decked up with banana leaves and sawali palms and "Just Married" on a placard behind.

By the end of the summer about thirty couples in all had sworn to love, honour and obey. Dr Fonger ruled that the banns should be published a week in advance. "Not much opportunity for a change of heart!" thought Isla.

Barracks 10, where there were five brides and grooms in a row, soon became known as "Honeymoon Corner".

The next thing, thought Isla, will be the patter of tiny feet. Unlike STIC, pregnancy in Los Baños was no crime.

The same eventuality had, of course, occurred to Dr Nance. With no wish to increase the numbers of his patients, Nance had procured a number of contraceptive douches and, as Women's Monitor, Isla was presented with one for their barracks. One of her duties was to take the douche to the hospital each day to be sterilized and when she was asked to think up some kind of title for the job she suggested "Dame de Ladouche" as being clean and wholesome.

It seemed to Isla that no sooner was one battle over than another started. On 17 May, scarcely a month since their arrival, the Housing Committee announced that all unattached women and mothers with daughters over 16 were to move from their present barracks to some new barracks in the lower part of the camp where they would be accommodated eight to a room. Isla was furious. It was the cabana story all over again. She had spent 500 pesos – her all – making something of their pathetic stable. She would *not* go. She rallied together four other mothers and daughters who were threatened by the move.

"The camp's policy has always been for families to live together," she told them. "The reason most of us volunteered for Los Baños was that we could have a stable of our own and some privacy. We came here to live in a mixed community, in mixed barracks, as a family unit, not to be pushed into dormitories with eight or more other women. If the order comes through we must stand our ground and fight."

"But what if we're sent to jail?" asked Mrs Lesner whose daughter was an epileptic. "I couldn't face that."

"I'd sooner go to jail than give this lot up," said Isla stoutly. "Anyway they'd *never* send us. It would be too much trouble. They think they can frighten us into anything. We've got to show them we will not be pushed around."

"I'd rather move than take the risk," Mrs Frampton, another mother, gave her vote. "I haven't your confidence, Isla."

What could Isla do with this lily-livered lot of hens? By all accounts, the women's barracks were appalling, just barns, and the water situation was even worse than at the hogwallow and yet this crowd were prepared to be shunted off without so much as a small boo to the Committee. Fortunately Jim, now Senior Monitor, took up Isla's cause and challenged Housing Manager, Hank Heichert, on his inhumane policy.

"When the hurlyburly's done, When the battle's lost and won", thought Isla recalling the opening scene of *Macbeth*. And, indeed, from her extraordinary appearance these days – long wispy hair, now mostly grey and with hardly a curl left in it, clothes full of holes, skin wrinkled and yellow from lack of vitamins and bony with starvation – she would have auditioned well for the part of chief witch.

While the battle was played out the rains started. With no mediaguas or window flaps the water poured through the open windows of the barracks, soaking beds and turning stable floors and the rough earth passage into pools of thick, evil-smelling mud. The nipa roofing billowed and flapped and, through the gaps, more rain fell in steady streams.

The rain that drove the internees to take cover had a similar effect on the insect, reptile and animal life of the camp. Big ants, little ants, red ants, black ants, swarmed into the buildings, competing for space with the assorted cockroaches and bed bugs already in hiding. Some of the flying cockroaches had a terrible sting. The flies seemed worse than ever, hissing about looking for some garbage or an open sore on which to settle. There was hardly an internee without an ugly infection on legs or arms. The very air seemed unwholesome, like a plague city.

More alarming than the insects, though not in fact poisonous, were the rat snakes that scuttled and slithered underfoot in the dark corridors or wound themselves round the nipa fronds in the ceiling. Rats and shrews completed the wild life making nests under beds and in boxes, squeaking and squealing in the humid night, their cruel pin eyes glistening blood-red in the watery moonlight. The mosquitoes never relaxed their hungry vigilance. It was more like Noah's ark than a home. And the rain went on and on.

At last Isla got her mediagua. Now at least, she thought, some of the rain would be angled off. But, to her acute annoyance, her two next-door neighbours, Snooks and Mrs Judge, though they had the sawali, refused to fix their mediaguas until the decision on the move was made known and without a continuous line of "eaves" the water still splashed in.

It was 18 June, a month after the original moving announcement, before Isla learned she had won her battle of the barracks. She and the other "family units" were not to be moved. At last her neighbours felt safe in putting up their mediaguas and Isla was given a flap of sawali to put across the window. It made the place horribly dark but at least it meant a bit more privacy and less rain.

Her next task was to get the light, which hung over the intersection between their stable and Snooks' next door, lowered so they could read better. Snooks, a quiet little plump woman with beautiful thick, dark hair who looked like a Filipina but swore she was an "American of Spanish descent", agreed, and Isla went off to tackle the Electricity Department. Once again the tape was red.

"We canna do a thing aboot that, orders from the Executive Committee," department head Mr Mackintosh, a surly dyspeptic Scot, told her without looking up from his books. And, try as Isla might, she could get no more out of him.

Once again, there was nothing for it but to take the law into her own hands. A friend of Don's fixed up an extension and for a couple of days all was well. But when the news leaked out, a Mackintosh minion, Hodges by name, with an Australian accent you could cut with a knife, came storming along to the barracks.

"Yer extension's gotta go, Commandant's orders," he announced without ceremony.

"But it's nothing to do with the Japs," protested Isla. "The lights are an internee matter. I'll go and see the Commandant myself."

"No yer don't," said Hodges, pushing his way into the stable. And with one bound he was on the bed and had taken out the light bulb.

"That'll learn yer," he shouted, leering down at her in triumph. "Until y'change y'mind."

Snooks, always plucky in the face of adversity, decided it was her turn to face Mackintosh. Isla knew if she saw him now she would probably lose her temper altogether and achieve nothing. He reminded her of that dreadful little man in the Cleansing Department at STIC who had reduced poor Ida Lennox to tears refusing to give her brushes and soap for her bathroom job "because she was not in the department".

True to type, Mackintosh gave Snooks no better reception. When she asked for the light back she was told: "My men are too tired to come messin' aboot wi' your light. They've bin workin' hard all day."

"So have I," rejoined Snooks. "Five hours in the hospital. Now please can we have that light back, Mr Mackintosh?"

But Mackintosh felt the strength of his desk and revelled in his tiny slice of power. He would show these two upstart women who was master in the Electricity Department! Snooks returned angry and defeated.

Not for long. Isla and Snooks decided to play their last trump card before the Commandant. They got Chairman and Mrs Fonger over to see the height of the lights above the partitions and they agreed they were too high. To strengthen her argument Isla pointed out that in Honeymoon Barracks several couples had put long flexes on their lights and not a word had been said. Mackintosh was ordered to restore the bulb. But Isla, Gill and Snooks had been nearly three weeks without a light. It burned Isla up to think how internees could treat their fellows.

Life in Los Baños was far from dull. STIC had originally called the camp "Paradise Lost" it was so full of jail birds, and

Isla and Gill's barracks had its share of ruffians and eccentrics.

Mr and Mrs Sniffen were four doors away on the same side, Olly was just up the corridor and directly opposite – and in full view – was Diana, "the all-American girl", a professional prostitute and former inmate of Muntinlupa women's mental hospital.

At 37 Diana, skinny with long, dark, lank hair, described herself as "getting old but not cold". Like Chicago Lil, she favoured the wearing of a kimono and nothing else. The fact that her stable had no door, nor even a curtain, inhibited her activities not a bit. Gill was profoundly shocked when one afternoon she came across Diana in a state of gay abandon.

"That woman's quite disgusting," she told her mother. For neither Diana nor her clients had the slightest discretion and, through the curtainless door, all was only too plainly revealed to anyone walking along the corridor.

"I'd use the outside door," Isla advised her daughter. "I always do. I only go into that passage for monitor duties."

At last after four months of unconcealed professional activity Diana got herself a door.

"Thank God for that," sighed Isla. "This place is just a red light district!"

But she had to admit Diana was funny. Listening to her and Mary Warner, the wispy missionary who had decided to convert her, was better than a music hall show.

In the middle of the "moving" crisis Isla heard her brash and twangy New York voice: "Oh Christ, what does it matter where we move in prison? If I had a belly full of rum it'd be O.K. anywhere."

"Now, now, Diana," remonstrated Hallelujah, as Isla called Mrs Warner, "you don't mean that and if you had Jesus in your heart you'd not want rum."

"Like hell," swore Diana. "I'd sell my soul for rum."

"Oh no, Diana, rum cannot save you, the Bible says nothing of rum . . . " Hallelujah was getting into her stride.

Rum was not the only opposition Hallelujah had to face in her "conviction" of Diana. As she explained to Isla: "That girl is full of demons. I try to tell her to stop going with men, that it's against the teaching of the Bible, but the next thing I know she's off to the R.C. church and hearing a sermon on 'Let him who is without sin cast the first stone'. And *now* she

thinks she's a saint! But I'll convict her. I've convicted worse."
And she told Isla of the time she had met a woman far gone
in drink and immediately seeing her had yelled out: "Praise
God, Hallelujah!" Whereupon the woman straight way snapped
out of her drunken stupor and was "convicted for good and all!"

"My church is the Church of God," she told Isla. "Diana
will listen to our word in the end because right is with us.
Hallelujah!"

And later Isla heard her over in the washroom with Diana
singing "Jesus never fails" and "This world is not my home"
and Diana yelling, "Swing it, Mary!"

Diana had good reason to encourage Hallelujah for no "conviction" was ever worked by bread alone and she managed to
extract endless non-spiritual supplies out of poor Hallelujah to
help with her "instruction in the faith".

Naturally none of the women were keen on sharing Diana's
stable. But George Gray, head of Housing, ruled that she could
not have the place to herself and her boyfriends and that Rodda,
an Indian woman, who had no friend to share with, should
move in. Rodda, a comfortable woman in her late 50's who
had spent nearly all her life being an ayah and who could neither
read nor write, was indignant at the decision.

"Why should I suffer?" Isla heard her wailing to no one in
particular. "I'm a good woman and I say God will punish the
Committee men who are making me move in with her."

Nevertheless, since she had nowhere else to go, Rodda took
her capacious bags and moved up to Diana's stable. It was like
Olly and the room at STIC all over again. Diana took one look
at Rodda and pushed her out, sending her possessions flying
after her. Isla and Gill were wedged in their stable by the
evicted baggage. Everyone else was out in the passage to watch
the fun.

George Gray came along to reason with the outraged Diana.
He should have known better. As he came up the passage Diana
hurled herself at him, biting, scratching and hitting, her thin
kimono flying loose, revealing all.

The next minute she had got a bottle from somewhere and
was flourishing it in George's face. She was using the foulest
language and, in between bouts, uttered the most piercing Red
Indian type war cries. George was a strong man and tall but
subduing the almost naked Diana was no easy task. Eventually

he got her arms pinned back and extracted a breathless promise of no more fighting. His face, arms and chest were a mass of scratches and he swore a chunk of hair was missing.

But the battle was by no means done. As soon as she had recovered her breath Diana girded her kimono, put on some bakias and charged off to see Commandant Tannaka, closely followed by Rodda.

Though a smaller man than George Gray, Tannaka somehow managed to reconcile the pair to their fate and Rodda, still full of injured pride, moved in.

Isla and Gill heard them quarrelling.

"You black pig, you'd stink even on ice," Diana yelled.

"If you were cut open an' me cut open you more dirty inside," Rodda retorted stoutly.

Occasionally armistice was declared and the two would chat amicably for hours on end. Then Diana would start again.

"Bombay Duck, Bombay Duck . . . " she sang out tauntingly and poor Rodda was once more on the defensive.

Isla, splitting her sides across the passage, had to admit the description was brilliant.

The association lasted two months after which the Committee took pity on the unfortunate Rodda and moved her, leaving Diana gloating victoriously with a stable to herself.

"It seems the dirtier and more unpleasant you are," Isla commented, "the better chance you have of getting a cubicle to yourself. Being decent here doesn't pay."

As for Diana, she confided to Isla: "That old woman drove me mad. I used to count ten, twenty, before I replied to her and I felt like murdering her but I respected her grey hairs like my mother's."

Diana, of course, had not the slightest respect or concern for anyone. It was quite useless to ask her to keep quiet. Even when she was alone she would talk to herself and sing at the top of her lungs "I'm an all-American girl and there are one thousand million more like me."

Another pair who were always causing trouble in Barracks 7 were Olly and her stable mate, Fatso Cohen.

Olly picked her boyfriends from the dregs of the camp. The current one at Los Baños was a violent-tempered young man who had done time in various jails. One day Isla was in the bathroom when Olly came in sobbing, covered in bruises and scratches.

"What on earth's the matter?" asked Isla as the girl stumbled towards the wash trough half blinded by a scratch that was dripping blood into her eye.

"It's Sam," she explained miserably. "I told him to go away, I wanted a siesta, but he got mad and started slapping me and pushing me about. He's jealous and says he'll kill me because of Pete but I haven't seen Pete since he stole Fatso's jewellery and . . . "

"You'd be better off in the cubicles of six in the new women's barracks," advised Isla. "Then he couldn't just come and go as he pleases. Shall I ask Mr Hodges, the Monitor, to bar him from the barracks?"

"Oh yes, *please* do," Olly begged. "I'm terrified of him."

Isla felt sorry for Olly. She was so pretty and had got herself into such a terrible mess so young. But she could not blame the boyfriend, however disagreeable, for being mad. Olly had exploited him mercilessly. Pete, who had stolen the jewellery, was one of many. Isla recalled the days in STIC when Sam would bring Olly breakfast of eggs and hot cakes. If they were the least bit cold she would fling them in the garbage can calling Sam every name under the sun.

Later, of course, Olly changed her mind about getting Sam barred.

"You see, he's apologized," she told Isla. "Anyway I'd rather he came to the stables than we had scenes outside." And she added rather pathetically: "I can't win for losing."

Fatso was an incurable giggler. Her high-pitched whinnying got on the nerves of everyone in the barracks and when she had a boyfriend it was even worse. As Monitor, Isla was always getting complaints about her giggles but there was precious little she could do about it. Fatso was on the whole of an easy-going disposition and Olly, one of the laziest girls Isla had ever known, would take advantage of her fat friend, getting her to do her garbage emptying and bathroom duties whenever she could. But as the worm turns so did Fatso and every three or four days an almighty row would break out. Invariably Diana, who hated to miss a good punch up, would rush over and join the fray. The noise, the language, the screaming were indescribable.

Once Isla heard one of them – or it could have been a new

contestant – yell out: "You're no lady." Followed by: "Nor are you." It was too much. Isla stuck her head out and yelled as loud as any of them, "We are none of us ladies, we are internees."

The few times this trio were at peace the Sniffens up the corridor would be quarrelling, either with each other or with the Ullmans from the next-door stable.

In fact Sniffen *versus* Ullman became one of the *causes célèbres* of the camp. Their quarrels always started over money or trading but before long would degenerate into slanging matches and sometimes violence, though Sniffen himself was the world's worst coward. Ullman, a mid-European Jew who had emigrated to America, brought sixteen charges against Sniffen for dishonest dealing but, due to insufficient evidence, the charges were all dismissed and Sniffen got off with a warning from the Court of Order that if any more was heard he would get six months. Sniffen then brought a charge of harassment against Ullman, who promptly levelled the same charge back at him. And the Court of Order had them both up for disturbing the peace.

Sniffen felt he had been harshly treated. As he told Isla: "Ginny and myself were having a quiet sleep one afternoon when we woke up to see a hand waving over the transom with fingers at the evil eye and heard a voice saying 'May the flesh on your bones rot'. It was that Ullman woman, I know. The thought of it keeps me awake at night and puts me off my food."

As there was no one in camp who ate better than the Sniffens, apart possibly from Shapiro, Isla thought the whole thing a great joke. She would not, in fact, have been sorry if Sniffen *had* received a touch of the evil eye. He was a nasty piece of work. It was rumoured he had started business in the Philippines by reporting back to the States that agents of various firms were not doing their jobs properly. By these sneaky methods he was said to have taken over three or four different agencies. In internment his methods were equally unscrupulous.

Like Shapiro, Sniffen built his profits on the adversity of others. He bought up supplies cheap from old men who knew no better and sold them off to the most desperate of internees – mothers with starving children, the sick, the dying – who would part with their last valuables for a few spoonfuls of sugar or klim. These ill-gotten treasures – jewels, watches, pens – were then traded with the Japs for fresh meat, milk, coffee, sugar, fruit, alcohol. There was nothing lacking in the Sniffen ménage.

One day while Isla was sitting with her new barracks friends, Roy and Copie, in their stable she heard him call out: "What'll it be, Ginny, Chase and Sanbourne or Maxwell House?"

She could not resist the temptation.

"What'll it be, Roy, Dewars or Haig and Haig?"

"Oh, I'll have the Glen Grant, thank you, Isla. How about you, cream or milk in your coffee?"

"Oh just coconut water, I'm used to it," replied Isla. It made her wild to see Sniffen and his fat wife, Genevieve – who swore she had lost a stone but could have lost half a dozen and still been fat – stuffing themselves sick while children went round covered in boils for lack of milk and meat.

How *could* the Court of Order fail to convict him? He was quite obviously trading with the enemy, undercutting his own countrymen and making profits on Red Cross goods. Guards padded in and out of his stable all night and Sniffen himself made no secret of his wealth. She supposed it must be his usefulness. Who knows? She might be forced to do a deal with him herself one day.

The wretched Fatso Cohen had just flogged him her ring for 100 pesos. He would probably re-sell at a thousand. And she knew for a fact that some earrings Gill had fancied and which he offered her for £15 had been got in exchange for a can of corned beef, a lipstick and a tin of coffee.

Since each internee's cookhouse was opposite his stable, Sniffen's was only a few doors up from Isla's and she and Gill were tortured with the delicious cooking smells that wafted over. One day Isla was horrified to see Sniffen come out with a steaming pan of hot waffles and wave it under the noses of two emaciated children who were sitting outside the Sniffen domain like animals waiting for crumbs. "Smells good, doesn't it?" he asked them. "Sorry I can't share it."

Compassion of any sort was alien to the Sniffens. They took a sadistic delight in the sufferings of others. Sniffen charged an old man, who had just been operated on and had only a quarter of his stomach left, 150 pesos (£25) for a can of klim. When the hospital made an appeal for sugar for a sick woman Sniffen offered to donate two spoonfuls for every one given by the others in the barracks, knowing full well that he was the only one with sugar to give.

"He probably thinks he's being magnanimous like the Japs," commented Isla.

It was the same with matches. Roy asked if he would sell some for the barrack light.

"I'd rather trade for food," replied Sniffen craftily.

"Come off it, Sniff," said Roy angrily, "you know we haven't any. Will you take this 40 cents? It's all I've got and the light is for the benefit of everyone here."

Hearing the argy-bargy Isla poked her head out of the stable; "Here Roy, I've only got one box but you'd better take it."

"That's right," said Sniffen. "You give a box and I'll give a box. That's fair, Roy."

"Fair!" exploded Isla. "That's my last box and you've got 2,000 stashed away in that Aladdin's cave of yours!"

"That's life," answered Sniffen, completely unperturbed. Then, just to rub salt in the wounds, he added nonchalantly: "Mind if I smoke?"

The smell of Sniffen's Virginia tobacco or his Havana cigars drove the adults to near frenzy just as the cooking smells from his shanty would wake screaming children from nightmares of hunger. For by this time anyone not on the Sniffen payroll or in league with the Japs was reduced at best to foul-tasting Filipino brands or, more often, to rolling their own using dried papaya leaves, toilet – or better still bible – paper for wrapping and laundry starch or cassava flour paste for sticking. Isla was torn between cleanliness and her craving for cigarettes, uncertain whether to sacrifice her last supply of toilet tissue. She wished she could find a Bible but such treasures in Los Baños were as rare as hen's teeth. In the event she compromised by cutting out the non-holey bits of the flimsy paper she had got for toilet purposes to use for cigarettes and proceeded to roll her own on the skilfully devised wood and linoleum cigarette maker a friend had given her.

Sniffen and Genevieve were, of course, loathed and detested by everyone in camp. There was hardly a soul not out for their blood – and their goods. One day Sniff went too far. Prowling about on his usual search for sharp deals he stuck his evil face into Bob Humphreys' stable.

"You have a nice lot of canned goods," he remarked cheerily.

"Want to part with any?"

Bob, a young man of about 30 and a friend of John Hunter, had a splitting starvation headache and was not in the sunniest of moods. "Get to hell out of here," he yelled at Sniffen. "I don't deal in canned goods."

Sniff took umbrage and that night when the usual string of clients, mostly women with young children, came round to his stable trying to trade or buy goods he told them to go and see Humphreys who would give them stuff on credit to be paid for after the war. For a week Bob put up with these callers wailing and crying for cans outside his door. Then with John Hunter and his other pal, Ned Sherrin, Bob stormed up to the Sniffen stable.

"Come out and fight, you yellow son of a bitch," he called. But Sniffen wasn't moving. He just lounged on the bed and when Bob tried to drag him up he lunged out with his foot.

Genevieve, however, was made of sterner stuff. She threw her ample form at John Hunter beating him back to the cookhouse. Meanwhile Isla, Copie and Roy and the rest of the barracks stood outside their doors shouting "Yah-boo" and "Get the Sniffs".

"If I were a man I'd hit you!" exploded the enraged Genevieve at John.

"Well, why didn't you marry one?" yelled Roy.

At last when all the uproar had died down they heard Sniffen telling his wife: "If that woman, Isla Corfield, makes any more cracks you go and hit her."

"He wants her to fight for him again," said Roy loudly.

The food situation got grimmer every day. On 20 June Isla and Gill had to go on relief for the first time. It meant a monthly handout of 70 pesos between them to supplement the canteen mush and stew. Isla's first purchase was a can of peanut butter for 7.40 pesos to mix with the tasteless, apple-like circomas – or sickomas, as Diana called them – which was about the only fruit available. Soon there would be nothing left to buy and what then, she thought dismally.

Basic canteen food was also supposed to be supplemented by vegetables grown in the camp garden – eggplant, tomatoes, pechay. Garden work was a camp detail and Isla chose this in preference to hospital, kitchen or cleaning work mainly because it was quiet and reasonably solitary. In charge of the garden was Pat Hell, a cheerful and energetic Irish-American in his late 30's, tall with close-cropped, curly, reddish hair and a wide smile. Isla liked Pat and admired his enthusiastic efforts in the unpromising garden. It was hard work battling against slugs, great nests of red ants and all manner of blights with only tobacco water in a flit-gun for pesticide. It was difficult, too, getting the seeds for they were all supplied by Filipinos outside who were attached to the Agricultural College and if the Japs were feeling in an unmagnanimous mood they would confiscate the lot.

Pat was a great optimist and always believed this month would be the last in internment. Imprisonment irked him more than most and he dreamed of rescue and escape. But these days the "pestimists", as Diana called them, were always right.

An appointment which had been rumoured for some time and which the internees dreaded was confirmed. Konichi, the STIC Supplies Officer who had made their lives there such a misery cutting down on bread, eggs, fruit and vegetables, was to move to Los Baños in the same capacity.

He even managed to dull STIC's joy at his impending departure by telling them gleefully: "I'm being replaced by my brother who is an even bigger S.O.B. than I am – he's the nastiest in the family!" When he left, STIC's reprieved tannoy played "The Drunkard's Song".

Konichi arrived at Los Baños at the end of August looking scruffier than ever. Though only a lieutenant, Konichi seemed to run the show wherever he went. A citation for fighting in China was said to be the reason he was given powers above his rank. He lost no time in getting to work. On 3 September he cut the children's rations by half. On 10 September he announced *everyone's* rations would be cut to a quarter. Coffee and mush would be served only twice a day, at 10.30 am and the balance at 4.30 pm. After that, nothing.

But the most bitter blow was that all garden produce was henceforth to be regarded as part of rations and not supplementary to them.

"A new era of starvation!" Isla wrote in her diary for 11 September. Prophetic words.

For the next two weeks "at least", the internees were told, they would have to live on a daily ration of 100 grams (about 3½ ounces) of corn or rice, 75 grams for the children. In January

400 grams a day had been promised to everyone. Now, even when starvation fortnight was up, they were told there would be no chance of this. In future 300 was to be the maximum, 150 for children.

Meat, bananas, camotes and other vegetables were to be considered "extras" supplied only in small quantities from time to time. There would be no more eggs and the allowance of one egg per day, previously granted to children of five and under, was to be discontinued.

The stunned internees took the only measure open to them: a letter of protest to Major General Ko, commanding all Philippine Island internment camps, drawn up by the new Chairman M. B. Heichert and signed by every adult member of camp. They stressed the harshness of allowing only half rations to growing children, protested strongly about the garden produce and questioned the meagre sugar ration of three table-spoonfuls a month in a sugar-producing country. Over the past four months, they said, the coffee allowance had been enough to make only one cup a week and there had been no tea at all.

Konichi gave them their answer: the authorities were having difficulty in getting supplies and any further explanation would give away military secrets. He was carrying out orders from Ko. They would just have to put up with what they got.

Inevitably the drastic reduction in rations led to a further deterioration in health. Isla broke out in hives, a maddening skin irritation, which did nothing to improve her appearance. The cause was the endless rice diet and the only cure to live on liquids. Isla decided "better to starve than scratch". Already she had two infections on her leg and one on each arm. She was just going bad.

Her stomach ached with hunger or indigestion most of the time now. She felt as though a tumour had solidified there from all the grit she had eaten in the rice. Her eyes, which had given her trouble since the start of internment, were so painful she could hardly bear to read or even write her diary. Many of her teeth were broken from champing on the bricks and stones mixed in with the abominable rice and those that remained whole felt rotten. And her teeth had been so good, so strong – once. Then her ankles started to swell. It was the first sign of beri-beri. Soon Gill showed the same symptoms. Ansie, Copie, who was so pretty, small and delicate, Margot, Don – one by one the disease got them. Only the Sniffens still looked normal in this community of distorted flesh.

Hunger drove some to madness. A case with which Isla became involved was that of a 32-year-old missionary woman called Pat. She went crazy quite suddenly one day while she was making a cake for her boyfriend, Eddie. She had put everything she had into that cake – all her cassava flour, all her eggs, all her fruit and all her love. But when she took it out of its baking tin on the charcoal stove it was heavy and flat. She screamed and she went on screaming and screaming and screaming.

As Pat could not be left in hospital with the other patients, Miss Cobb, the chief navy nurse, got her fixed up in a room in the College's former Administrative block, the only brick building with a full-flush lavatory in the place. Poor Pat had such depression it was unsafe to leave her alone and, looking for volunteers to sit with her, Miss Cobb came to Isla. She asked if Gill, who was already working in the hospital, might be allowed to do an extra shift looking after Pat.

"No, sorry, I really can't let Gill take on any more," Isla told Miss Cobb. "She's seen enough horror and sorrow. But if you can't find anyone else to help, I will."

She had just resigned her Monitor job which meant no more seat-wiping, cistern-flushing and taking the douche for sterilization, so she would have a *bit* of energy to spare. The garden kept her busy most of the day but the evenings were free. Finally it was agreed that Isla should take the 9 pm to 1 am shift with Pat.

"Well, that's settled," said Miss Cobb, obviously greatly relieved. "You can't imagine how difficult it is getting staff now. Women promise they'll come and then they simply don't turn up. We're desperate and every day the hospital gets more and more crowded. Still if the deaths go on at this rate there won't be anyone left at all!" And she swept out leaving Isla to think about her new patient.

Poor Pat was a mass of inhibitions and repressions. Like so many mishes she seemed to be obsessed with sin. On a slip of paper in her Bible she had written rather pathetically: "Let me be obscure enough to live the life I please, to dress as I please, to kiss the man I please. Save me from any reputation I may have to live up to. Give me each day some intoxication, not of food or drink but of sight or sound or some idea which will make me a little crazy."

Isla felt sorry for her – in love with a man who had a wife back in the States, desperate for his affection yet riddled by guilt. She listened with patience to her ramblings and somehow her presence had a soothing effect on the deranged woman. Gradually Pat's reason began to return. If only she could get out of this dump soon, thought Isla, she might make a full recovery.

Gill meanwhile had got herself a job at Bungalow D, the missionaries' hospital. There most of her patients were old and she soon realized she was dealing with the dying and the dead and not with those whose youth and strength could give them hope of recovery. Her first patient to die was an old Franciscan nun. She told Gill she was quite ready. Gill brought her flowers and she died holding the tiny bunch.

Her next patient was a man, Posner. He begged Gill to sit up with him and she did. He died at dawn. Hardly a day passed when some poor, emaciated ghost of an old man or woman would not give up the unequal struggle for survival and many called for Gill in their dying hours.

Isla did not like her daughter being so involved with death – after all she was still only 17 – but obviously she was able to give immense comfort and happiness to the patients in Bungalow D and, as long as Gill felt she could take it, Isla decided she would not interfere. Suffering had somehow led all the teenagers into premature adulthood. Camp rules defined a child as "10 years and under" and so it eventuated.

The missionaries, priests and nuns and defeated Italians had arrived at Los Baños in mid-July. Nearly all had been brought in from the seminaries, convents and mission houses in the Manila area and, since they had been given only a few hours to pack and in any case could only take with them as much as they could carry, they were desperately ill-equipped to face the rigours of internment.

Barracks had been prepared for them behind a sawali fence in the upper part of the camp but conditions there were even more primitive than in the main camp. There were no cement paths, no garbage cans and no water. They had to walk to a tap outside the camp gate to get both drinking and washing water. The floors of the barracks were bamboo on mud and, of course, there were no mediaguas over the windows or doors to prevent the rain, by this time in full spate, from pouring in.

Many had brought no plates or mugs with them and the other internees had to club together to send over what they could. Many, too, had no beds, just rolls of bedding, since the Japs had told them beds would be provided. The bedding got soaked lying on the rain-washed floors and soon dozens were down with colds and pneumonia.

"No human beings deserve such treatment," declared Isla, "even if they have been out of camp all this time."

Inevitably the religious area got the name "Vatican City". And one of the priests came up with "Hell's Half Acre" for the camp beyond the sawali. At first the rule was no co-mingling between "saints and sinners" but soon, for practical reasons, this was abandoned.

Mishes were Isla's pet aversion – she always thought of the incident in Nanking when the mish women were raped and the mishes refused to press charges because their business interests might suffer.

She was not remotely surprised to hear from interpreter Ernie Cummings, the only one at first allowed within the Sacred Precincts, that the nuns had quickly cleaned up their barracks, setting their few possessions neatly in order, whereas the mishes were in an awful state sitting in the midst of all their refuse reading the Bible and saying "God will help".

The other mish idiocy that drove Isla wild was that they had taken no precautions against disease, thinking they would not be interned.

"I suppose they thought God would take care of them," remarked Isla sarcastically when Miss Cobb told her they were going down like ninepins. "Well, he didn't!"

By all accounts either He or someone else had looked after them outside. The mishes were always complaining about the food saying how well they had eaten before even though prices in town were astronomical – far higher than in Los Baños. Where, Isla wondered, did all the money come from? Not, she hoped, from the Chinese missions.

Vatican City or the Holy City was aptly named. Even a cluster of Carmelite nuns had been interned there who, in order to hide themselves still from the world, the devil and the flesh, had hung sheets around their cubicles. In one barracks of sixteen stables there were sixteen altars.

One of the new arrivals to Vatican City was Father Arcaud. His knowledge of news and world affairs soon caught the attention of Isla and her friends and they invited him to join them at their evening Council of War by the hogwallow. He was an intelligent, much-travelled man and knew how to tell a good story. Vague reports of the Normandy landings in June, 1944, had reached Los Baños and the Council of War listened with rapt attention while Father Arcaud told of the dramatic eye-witness account he had heard on the radio.

Ever since the first whisper of the invasion the internees had been wild to get hold of a newspaper but, from the end of May, there had been a total ban even on the Jap-run *Tribune*. When they asked General Ko why they could no longer have papers he replied, "Because you might misconstrue the news."

The only misconstruction the caged internees did in fact put on the tiny scraps of information that mysteriously filtered through the Jap smoke-screen was that the war would be over by the end of the year.

In Europe, they thought, there could be no doubt. In August, 1944, French and American troops had landed on the Mediterranean coast and made a swift advance up the Rhône. In the same month Paris was liberated and by September France was cleared of Germans. Brussels was entered on 2 September. On the eastern front the Russians had made steady progress ever since Stalingrad and stronghold after stronghold fell before them. Soon they would be knocking on the gates of Berlin.

Nearer home, in the Pacific, MacArthur was planning the last stage in the final journey back to the Philippine Islands. Having secured the Marshalls in February, 1944, the Allies moved on to the Marianas, where on 19 and 20 June the greatest air-sea battle of the war was fought, the Battle of the Philippine Sea. The Allied victory was so great the U.S. sailors and airmen dubbed it "The Great Marianas Turkey Shoot". Little wonder General Ko was reluctant to give the internees the news, however much disguised by propaganda!

On 29 August MacArthur announced that the fight for the Philippines was on. The internees were beside themselves with excitement. Isla could not imagine freedom.

Even the Jap guards seemed prepared for the worst. One soldier told the camp blacksmith: "Last year I think Japan win but this year I think Japan lose." And St Louis, the tiny monkey-man guard with his big gun, sang merrily "Over there the Yanks are coming" – though he probably did not understand the words. He was called St Louis as he usually whistled the St Louis blues.

At the beginning of September the Japs started to build themselves air-raid shelters. The Executive Committee told Monitors to warn their barracks to expect heavy fighting any time now, big bombs and ack-ack. But, they warned, "No demonstrations". Filipinos had been shot outside for this.

On 10 September the blackouts started. From 7 pm roll call everyone was confined to barracks. There were rumours of bombings in Mindanao, the Visayas and Leyte. On 14 September the internees were told, "Stay in your cubicles. There is an air-raid over Luzon." And the Japs ran wildly about the camp their rifles at the ready. Isla packed her suitcase and urged Gill to do the same.

"Hurry, hurry, I want to go home", she told her diary.

CHAPTER SEVEN

Any Nimitz now

(21 September, 1944–6 January, 1945)

21 SEPTEMBER, 1944: "Red letter day and we've waited for nearly three years and no rumour, real bombing. First I knew was the sound of heavy guns at 8.30 then I heard the crrump of bombs and saw the doors shaking. Everyone out looking. Some say it started at 7.30. There must have been waves of bombers. One man said he saw two planes come down in flames and a lot saw a dog fight. I, of course, missed it trying to get the stable clean. The Japs went crazy, a lot rushed down to the gym for shelter . . . "

The excitement was electric. Diana burst into song with: "Hallelujah, God bless America, only the Americans will win the war, they can make or break anyone. Hallelujah, the hospitalities have started! Limitation day is near, Hallelujah!"

That night was like Thanksgiving. Everyone delved into emergency supplies and next morning the garbage cans were full of tins. Isla and Gill celebrated with a feast of curried rice with an egg on top.

The Japs were edgy and not amused. Strict blackout orders were issued and internees were warned that anyone caught "wandering aimlessly" after 7 pm or when the alert had sounded would be shot. Those who, for various reasons, had to leave their barracks must do so under armed escort.

One reason for the "aimless wandering" rule was, apparently, the fear that leaflets would be dropped and picked up and read by the hopeful internees. It was a rule particularly unpopular with the young people since internees had to stay in their own barracks – no boyfriends or girlfriends visiting other barracks and nothing on earth to do all evening.

Another rule was not to gaze and point at the sky when

Allied planes flew over, even from the barrack windows. In STIC a group of men who disobeyed were taken out to the gate and made to look up at the sky for seven hours.

The news continued to filter in, sometimes written on ducks' eggs, sometimes in Jap newspapers which had to be translated, and on 13 October even the old *Tribune* got past the guard with encouraging reports of a big battle over Formosa and devastating damage to the harbour and military installations. A great U.S. fleet was said to be in P.I. waters. Obviously a full-scale battle centring on the Philippines was in the offing.

The Japs at Los Baños were taking no chances. U.S. raiders would not wish to bomb an internee camp full of their own nationals. It was obviously the safest place and Commandant Tannaka issued orders for all internees in the men's Barracks 3 and 4 to vacate their stables and cookhouses by 15 October so the Japs could move in. Besides losing the cookhouses that had cost so much in time, money and lumber to build the unfortunate men would also lose the tiny gardens which they, like Isla, had cultivated so lovingly on the strip of land outside their stables and which were now just about to produce their first crops. The gym was to be turned into a military hospital.

Don was among the men who had to move to the new quarters in the Church and Education Barracks. It was a dump of a place and had no bathroom or toilet facilities. It was pathetic to see them struggling over with all their belongings so gaunt and tired and haggard. The years of internment had certainly told on Don. Now he looked an old, old man.

Up went the inevitable sawali fence and soon the Japs were moving in behind it with bookcases, beds, comfortable chairs and cases and cases of food. Even the sentries moved their boxes inside the camp. "Now *we're* protecting *them!*" commented Isla. It made her sick to think of it.

The internees' comfort lay in the firm belief that the boot would very soon be on the other foot. On the night of 14 October Isla dreamt she heard a British band playing at the head of troops arriving to save them. Shades of Mafeking.

But the feeling in her old bones was right. On the 15th the bombing started again. She rushed out and saw two U.S. fighters swoop over the hill. The sun shone bright on their silvery wings and the powerful roar of their engines was like a song of victory. Such a change from the oil-less and labouring phut-phuts of the enemy planes! They flew low with impunity. Not a sound of ack-ack. The Japs were all flat on their tummies, camouflage and all.

On the 18th they came again. The sky was black with planes. "Boy, what a sight," wrote Isla in her diary, "sun glinting on steel and the fighters like dolphins in and out of the bombers."

Of all the U.S. planes that flew over only one came down. In spite of the "no-looking-at-the-sky" rule the internees saw the pilot eject as his plane burst into flames. The guards rushed off to search for him and for days the internees prayed he would be safe. Then, mysteriously, the message came through – he had been picked up by guerrillas. Comfortingly the Council of War decided they must be close to a guerrilla area and that pilots in trouble had probably been advised to guide their planes in that direction.

Then – flash – the news that MacArthur had landed in Leyte. "This is the *Voice of Freedom*, General MacArthur speaking. People of the Philippines: I have returned!"

Isla was trembling so much she could scarcely hold a pen. 23 October, 1944: "We're all so excited we've most of us got goose pimples, indigestion and stomach cramp. Couldn't sleep last night for making plans. It seems it's true MacArthur landed in Leyte on the 20th with President Osmena and General Sutherland (his chief of staff). Roosevelt credited in camp with saying the eyes of America are on Manila. Why not Los Baños?"

On 25 October the Battle of Leyte Gulf, the biggest sea-fight in history, was fought and won by the Allies. It was a decisive victory for the U.S. 3rd and 7th Fleets, the former commanded by Admiral William F. Halsey and the latter by Vice-Admiral Thomas C. Kinkaid. The build up of U.S. sea power had been enormous, a veritable armada.

At Leyte some 300,000 tons of Japanese combat shipping was destroyed, a third of the surface ships of the entire navy. It was the end of the Japanese navy as an effective fighting force. Their aircraft losses were also heavy. In contrast American losses were light, less than 40,000 tons of shipping and a relatively small number of planes.

But the most horrible aspect of this whole battle had been the *Kamikaze* strikes. They were the first organized suicide attacks of the war. In a desperate effort to delay the Allied victory, hundreds of Japanese pilots deliberately crashed their explosive-laden aircraft into enemy vessels, showering their targets with bombs, sharp pieces of metal, gasoline and the flesh and bones of the dead pilots. As one American sailor wrote in his diary, the deck round him "was covered with blood, guts, brains, tongues, scalps, hearts, arms, etc, from the Jap pilots."

In spite of the obvious disaster to the Japs of the entire Leyte campaign, the Japanese papers – the only ones to get into Los Baños – continued to report success. Isla's translation read: "Tokyo, 26 October (Domei) . . . What Admiral Halsey's disaster must have meant to General MacArthur needs no explanation. Waking up on the morning of 25 October after this American débâcle in Philippine waters, General MacArthur literally found himself naked – stripped of his protective covering – and flat on his back. General MacArthur having had an unpleasant experience at Corregidor and Bataan before his ignominious flight from the Philippines at the outset of the war knows full well what fate looms for his unfortunate forces marooned amid strategic Japanese points. The world will soon be hearing of the astounding news of how the Japanese forces dealt with these would-be invaders of the Philippines."

And an editorial from the same news-sheet, claiming astronomical American losses, read: "What the Nippon Army and the Navy achieved during the two weeks between 12 and 26 October can be said to be unprecedented in world history . . . The enemy is hard pressed, so much so that he cannot even spare a few planes to raid Manila."

In fact the struggle to secure Leyte was long and hard. The American forces were hampered not only by continued *Kamikaze* attacks at sea but also by the appalling weather. Thirty-five inches of rain fell in the first forty days of the campaign, turning the island into a quagmire.

The final offensive on Leyte did not begin until 5 December. By the 25th it was all over and MacArthur was able to announce the end of organized resistance on the island. Mindoro island to the west, in MacArthur's words "the gate to Luzon", fell to the Allies on 15 December. By the New Year the whole of Leyte and Mindoro and part of Samar island were held by U.S. forces. Luzon was the next target.

In Los Baños the Music Committee struck up with "The Nearness of You" played for Admirals Halsey and Nimitz and

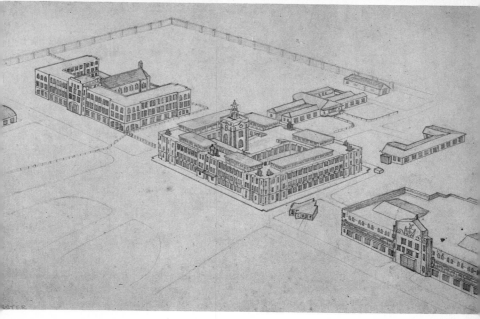

6 An aerial view of Santo Tomas drawn by internee Alan Lester, when aged eleven. Room Five was on the left wing of the centre block.

7 Isla Corfield on her bed in Room Five, which housed twenty-two women in very cramped conditions. The drawing is by Ansie Lee, William Donald's secretary.

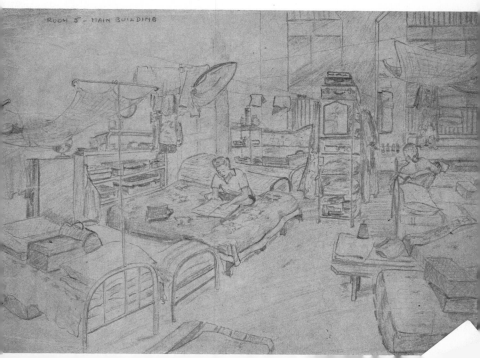

8 (*left*) A cartoon of Mrs Corfield cooking rice. This and the following three drawings are by Teedee Cowie.

9 (*above*) Gill Corfield 'milking' coconuts.

10 Bundles for Tokyo—internees were constrained to hand over all their electrical equipment to the Japanese and they naturally assumed that it was bound for the capital.

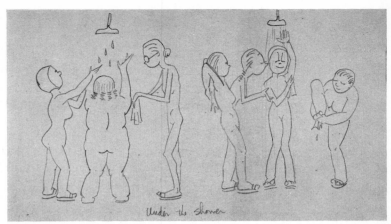

Under the shower

11 Under the shower—a humorous view of the spartan bathing conditions.

12 The patio of Isla Corfield's cabana for which she fought so desperately. The sketch was drawn by Poppy Lyman in 1943.

13 A typical advertisement from the camp magazine 'The Internitis'. Apart from suggesting the unfailing spirits of the internees, it also shows the overall design of a camp shanty.

14 Ansie Lee's representation of Mrs Corfield's cookhouse in Los Baños with her banana tree prominently in the foreground.

the current joke was "Any Nimitz now . . . "

The internees needed all the humour they could muster. With Luzon under virtual siege hardly any supply ships were getting through and it seemed anything that did went straight onto the Jap's plates. One night while Isla, Father Arcaud and the others were sitting out by the hogwallow a small boy was brought along under guard escort. It turned out that he had been caught peeping through the Commandant's window while the staff were at supper. The table was laid with big bowls of rice, camotes, squash, coconuts, beer and saki.

"After having mush I thought I felt good," the boy told Isla wistfully, "but when I saw what they were eating I didn't."

Mush. Mush with gravy. Mush with a few grains of sugar. Mush cakes that tasted like bad bread. Mush pudding. Mush and more mush to try and keep the pathetic diet up to 800 calories a day – starvation level. It was only palatable to music – and so they made a song:

> "We had mush last month and mush the month before
> We'll have it every day till the ending of the war
> And with our mush we're as happy as can be
> We add a prayer at grace for the USAFFE.
>
> Oh, it's glorious, glorious!
> One can of mush for ninety-four of us,
> Thanks be to God there are no more of us
> 'Cause one of us could drink it all alone "

It would be unfair to say there was *nothing* but mush. There was soggy rice or, worse still, lugao which was even soggier rice. It looked like runny white blancmange. The internees would take their two miserable little scoops of the stuff and lay it outside on plates to try and dry it out. Once dry it could be ground into flour to make cakes or popped and eaten as a sort of popcorn.

Gati, a form of potato, was another favourite with the canteen. That, too, was mostly water by the time it reached the internees. On good days it came served with a spoonful of gravy and even a few water-lily leaves; on bad days with sword beans, razor-edged and aptly named. All too often it was undercooked, perhaps because of the shortage of firewood, and gave the internees terrible indigestion and diarrhoea.

Isla, along with many of the others, would always try and save some lugao or mush from the morning meal so that she and Gill would have something midday. To wait from 10.30 to 4.30 with no food at all, working at the same time on a camp detail, was too exhausting. Isla was amazed how the men with their heavier work load and greater need for food managed to carry on at all.

The September protest to Ko about Konichi's starvation rations had had not the slightest effect. The Executive Committee were as helpless as the rest. All they could do was issue strict warnings not to waste anything. "If you cannot eat it, offer it to your neighbours", the notice read. "If your neighbours don't want it, see that your pig farm gets it. Don't waste it."

Food for sale at the canteen got more and more scarce. Part of the problem was that the Filipinos would no longer sell for money. They distrusted the Japanese "Mickey Mouse" peso and wanted rice or clothes, not inflated paper notes, in exchange for their eggs and vegetables. The going rate for a new pair of U.S. shorts was said to be 500 ducks' eggs, 250 for a shirt.

"I wish I could barter all my old clothes," thought Isla, "I might go nude, but oh boy, we'd eat!"

By 10 October the food had hit rock bottom. Only 600 calories. Another couple of weeks at this level and they would all be dead.

Then one day at the 4.30 meal a man did an Oliver Twist. He marched up to the Commandant with his plate.

"Look at this," he demanded indicating the tiny scoop of gati swimming in a grey liquid that passed for gravy. "One meal, starvation diet. Just look. The pigs do better in this camp!"

It was true. The pigs *were* better fed. All the yellow eggplant the internees had so recently harvested from the camp garden was taken for pig fodder. Even the potato peelings that the kitchen women scrambled for under the tables to take home for soup was confiscated for the pigs. Isla thought it high time they killed the damn things and gave the internees something to eat instead.

The "Oliver" protest had some effect. The Commandant ordered that five pigs a week should be killed starting 1 November. With seventy-five skinny porkers left in the sty that meant fifteen weeks of pig – but why wait until 1 November?

Every day people were keeling over as they waited in the chow line, faint with hunger. Don was so weak he only just managed to keep out of hospital. Headaches, palpitations, cramps, dizziness, irregular periods – Isla and Gill were spared nothing. The slightest exertion made them shake all over and though they slept heavily they always woke exhausted. As for bowels, Nance told his patients not to worry if nothing happened for ten days as the food was insufficient and he warned anyone who had laxatives not to take them as these would be weakening.

Nance, like all the other doctors, was at his wit's end. He stormed into Konichi's Supplies office and told him he could do no more for his patients. It was impossible to operate on people in such a weak condition. In the past three months, he informed Konichi, the internees had had only seven grams of meat per person a month and the calorie intake had dropped from 1,800 to 1,300 and now to 800. Over one-third of the camp had incipient beri-beri. In the hospital they were dying like flies and there was no alternative to his death certificate verdict: Starvation.

But Konichi seemed to revel in the distress of his captives. When one day the meat ration arrived late he sent it back. Another day he pulled a fast one and issued the camotes the internees had eaten the day before. He confiscated the seeds that came in for the garden.

Then he stopped the salt ration. It was the cruellest cut yet. In the tropical, almost equatorial, climate of the Philippines the body dehydrates fast, draining essential salts. The pain if these are not replaced is excruciating. Every bone in the body aches for salt and the muscles tense in unrelievable cramps. Gill would wake in the night screaming with pain.

The Executive Committee protested and, as usual, were given an excuse for an answer. Salt was apparently needed in Japan for the making of munitions – even the Japanese had to go without, they were told.

There was almost nothing the internees would not eat. Pigweed with its damnable thorns, which Isla "weeded" from the camp garden, was a delicacy compared with the strange vegetation some tucked into with seeming relish. Stewed Morning Glory leaves or stewed tomato leaves were popular though Isla thought them vile. Banana skins were one of the tastier dishes – fried they were rather like potato chips.

Dave Harvey's song "Cheer up, Everything's Gonna be

Lousy" was coming true. Soon they *would* be eating the bark off the trees.

Isla's swollen ankles had indeed been the first signs of beri-beri. Soon her finger joints, wrists and elbows were swelling painfully and then her face grew puffy giving her the evil look of a bloated mandarin. *She* was one of the lucky ones. Hers was dry beri-beri which affects only the face, legs and arms. Many poor wretches had contracted the more serious wet beri-beri which made them blow up all over as if they had dropsy. The only cure – and its success rate wasn't high – was to tap them and draw off the excess liquid. What was left of the thiamin supplies was also reserved for these acute cases.

Gill was as pale as a ghost and had started to suffer from fainting fits. She, too, was getting beri-beri in her ankles and she was as thin as a skeleton. Isla insisted she give up her job at the hospital and Gill reluctantly agreed that in her present state of weakness she had no choice.

It was essential to get more food. Isla's chance came when volunteers were called for to work on the new camp garden that had been started on some dried-up wasteland on top of the hill. Five hours' digging, weeding and planting would earn one hundred extra grams of rice. The work would be in addition to her normal garden detail but Isla felt she must try. She checked in for duty at 6.10 am on 15 November.

In her diary she wrote: "I'm so weary I don't know whether I can take it but it would be useful . . . I can't see how we can go on much longer. Really feel despondent and frightened. Have heard from so many people that the men's barracks is an appalling sight. Men lying down all day too emaciated to get up. After getting their mush they weave their way back and now if they stop and feel dizzy and faint no one helps them, they are all in the same state . . . Tonight we have got 530 kilos of gati for the whole camp – a lot of that weight is dirt – and some gravy. Konichi said in Santo Tomas he would make the Americans eat dirt and it is getting that way."

Nance warned that the garden work would not be worth the energy expended but Isla was so desperate for food for herself and Gill she had to take the risk. She was so proud when she got her first week's pay – 200 grams. It would make two good plates of rice for their supper. In addition the garden pay rice was red or unpolished rice which, unlike the polished, contains

Vitamin B, the vital ingredient in the prevention of beri-beri.

But 200 grams for hours of back-breaking work by no means solved the hunger problem. Isla decided that if the men's deputations to the Commandant had failed then it was up to the women to try. With her next-door neighbour Mrs Judge – whose real name was something unpronounceable like Winzca-linus so the camp called her Mrs Judge because her husband had been one – and two other women from the Barracks, Mrs Mora and Evelyn Clarke, Isla drew up a petition. They got an appointment to see the Commandant at 3 pm on 26 November.

Speaking through the interpreter, Mr Ito, Commandant Iwanaka, the latest Jap import, told them it was not his custom to see any of the internees except the Committee, least of all women. This interview was a great favour. The four chorused "Thank you" and Mrs Judge, the elder stateswoman of the group, read out the letter.

Mr Ito interpreted. The Commandant listened. The women pushed forward two skeletal children they had brought with them to emphasize the urgency of their requests. It was useless.

"You do not understand the situation," the Commandant told them. "The Philippine Islands are a battleground. We can get no more salt and what supplies there are must be kept for an emergency. I know your children need butter and eggs but I can do nothing for you. I take my orders from headquarters."

They filed sadly out. But they had learned something – the Japs were as worried as they were. "The admissions were worth the price of admission," remarked Mrs Judge.

By 6 December things had reached rock bottom. "God, I'm lower than a snake's belly", Isla told her diary. "Hungry, hungry all the time. No sugar to put on this vile mush. Mud everywhere, bakias get stuck, feet always muddy. Fight to keep clean and get washing done, fight against slugs eating one's poor little garden. No toilet paper so the seats are perpetually foul. No cream to help the lines on one's face and miserable char-woman hands. Nothing we've been used to. All the ordinary things of life – butter, bread, tea, sugar, salt, eggs, milk – taken from us. Fight to light these damn charcoal and wood stoves, then they smoke so they ruin the skin and one weeps all the time standing over them. Seems to me the new cemetery will soon be started. At first they decided to put it in the hospital grounds but thought it a little out of place."

She had no wish to join the dead men. She sent another yellow P.O.W postcard to the British government. "Suffering beri-beri thanks to wonderful diet. Work 5 hours for 100 grams rice. All the same hopeful. Ask Winnie to step on it."

She *must* find food. There were two other means of acquiring it – stealing and trade, both of them becoming increasingly popular. Diana resorted to the former, pinching four miserable camotes from the vegetable detail and got a sentence of twenty-five days confined to barracks from the Court of Order for her pains.

Nothing was safe, least of all the plants in the unprotected gardens and the pathetic fruit and vegetables many of the internees were trying to grow in the soil outside their stables. One man invented a brilliant burglar alarm to protect his "crop", a small and lovingly tended papaya tree. He hung the tree with tins threaded together with a piece of string and attached the other end of the string to his big toe while he slept. The trap was double-edged: the thief, he hoped, would set the tins clanking and tweak his toe at the same time. For all his scheming the papayas got stolen just the same.

Isla was sorely tempted to indulge in some duck-snatching from the poultry farm Konichi had started for the Commandant's office with 500 ducks. She felt like Brer Fox as she padded past the compound and heard their fat squawking.

Instead she decided to try trading. So far she had not parted with any of her jewellery. It was against her principles to trade on any basis with the enemy but, with starvation only weeks away, there was no choice.

"Get what you can for it," she told Ernie Cummings who was to trade her rose diamond and cabochon sapphire ring with one of the guards, "I can't eat the damn thing."

It took weeks of negotiation but at last, just before Christmas, Ernie clinched the deal: eight kilos of mungo beans and two kilos of sugar – supplies that would have cost at least £150 on the open market. The ring was no doubt worth more but Isla felt she had struck a good bargain. Later Barney, the tin sauce-pan maker, got her half a kilo of peanuts and ten little hen's eggs for her gold chain. Once again she was Mrs Rich Bitch.

Meanwhile Gill astounded her mother by pulling a remark-ably fast deal on Shapiro. With the aid of John Hunter she managed to extract 4,000 pesos from the arch-black marketeer for the white sapphire ring Doug had given her for her seven-teenth birthday in STIC. Shapiro, taking it for a diamond worth at least 6,000, thought *he* was the smart one. When he discovered it was only a white sapphire he was furious and demanded his money back. "Sorry, too late," said John giving him a dose of his own medicine. And for a time Gill, and con-sequently Isla, were the most notorious women in camp!

Christmas looked like being bleaker than ever before. The internees could talk and think of nothing but their kits. At one stage it was rumoured that the Japs had them hidden away. But the truth of the matter was there were no kits because there were no boats. Stewed cat was a more likely feast for the Christ-mas dinner table than roast turkey.

Nance had started the cat craze. He and his pharmacist, Rube Levy, quite blatantly announced their dish and recom-mended it to the other internees as delicious, just like rabbit. Isla was completely in sympathy. She believed no one had any business keeping pets now that there was so little to eat. If she had been given cat she would certainly have eaten it – but they were scarce and none came her way.

Dogs, another of Nance's recommendations, were even scarcer. Here again Isla felt he was right to have them put down and served up as stew but she considered his methods unnecessarily cruel. He snatched one unfortunate animal from the family with whom it had lived for eighteen years and killed and skinned it for the pot right outside their barracks.

It was a missionary woman who started the fashion for fried slugs. She insisted they were full of vitamins and, in hope of curing beri-beri, groups of slug hunters would roam the gardens in the early mornings in search of breakfast. Isla knew slugs were something she could never force down her throat however hungry but she kept all the ones she found for the slug brigade.

One wit suggested a Thanksgiving Day menu of: Canna Root Cocktail, followed by Roast Cat stuffed with Banana Root, garnished with Fried Banana and Calamencie Skins and served with Camote Tops and Pigweed *en branche*. Lugao with Morning Glory leaves was offered as a side salad and, to finish, the chef's *pièce de résistance*, slugs on Mush Cakes.

A week before Christmas Gill, who was feeling slightly better since her resignation from the hospital and had boosted her morale, much to her mother's disgust, with a new short, curl-less hairstyle, signed on for garden work. If she too could earn a few hundred extra grams of rice they could have a real Christmas blow-out!

Obviously the kits were a fond dream. When one internee asked a guard where their presents were, he replied pointing to the sky: "Presents? *There* are your presents."

And, indeed, as if to confirm his words a fleet of nine P38s flew low over Los Baños on Christmas Day sending the internees into transports of delight and the Japs scurrying to their trenches.

As Isla said, it was a beri-beri Christmas and a hungry New Year. The Catholic priests from Vatican City redeemed the day slightly by donating 15,000 pesos to the Executive Committee for extras and the missionaries put in another 1,500. It meant everyone got a taste of camotes, eggplant, mungo beans and even a sliver of carabao meat instead of just mush and pork gravy. Someone obviously had roast cat as a cat's head was found in the garbage bin on Boxing Day!

Strangely, though conditions could not have been worse, spirits were high for New Year 1945.

Optimism was reflected in the spate of new pregnancies and the slogan in camp was "Get to New York and beat the stork!" Jean Tullock had already had her baby, a son weighing 8 lbs, the biggest baby yet born in Los Baños.

The optimism was well-founded. By the New Year MacArthur was ready for the final stage in the battle for the Philippines. The air attacks from Admiral Halsey's powerful carrier force and General George Kenney's Far East Air Forces built up preparing the way for the landing of General Walter Krueger's Sixth Army at Lingayen, on Luzon, north-west of Manila. On 2 January the 7th Fleet, charged with putting Krueger ashore and providing initial protection and support, left Leyte for Lingayen.

The Japanese fought back in almost the only way left to them – vicious *Kamikaze* strikes. In three days suicide planes killed and wounded more than 1,000 Americans and Australians and seriously damaged a large number of ships. But the invasion pushed on. On 6 January the American force entered Lingayen Gulf.

In Los Baños the noise of bombing and straffing could be heard all day. The Japs were even more jittery than usual and the Commandant was spotted trying to camouflage his car with leaves. The rumour went that evacuee barracks had been prepared for all the internees in Leyte under Red Cross supervision.

"I can't wait", wrote Isla. "Got the mattresses out for, I hope, the last time. Tomorrow I'll have my first lie-in for over a month."

CHAPTER EIGHT

Camp freedom!

(6 January–22 February, 1945)

ISLA's lie-in ended abruptly at 3.30 am. She did not know whether she was awake or still dreaming.

"We're free, we're free!" The calls came from everywhere. "The Japs have gone. We're free. The camp is ours!"

The incredible had happened. The Commandant, Konichi, the whole pack, had cleared out in the middle of the night leaving the camp in charge of the Committee.

The first hint of the exodus came at 11.50 on the night of Saturday, 6 January. Mr Ono of the Commandant's office woke Committee Secretary George Gray, telling him to collect every shovel in camp and turn them over to the Japanese authorities by 1 am.

George was mystified but he alerted the monitors and soon forty-seven shovels were duly presented at the Commandant's office. There was obviously something more dramatic than a mammoth "dig" in the air with the Commandant's car, the Japanese international truck and the camp Oldsmobile all lined up outside the office. Gray determined to find out. No one stopped him as he marched towards the door. There was not a guard to be seen on the usual patrol round that block. The reason was that they were all inside wildly packing whatever belongings they could lay hands on.

George strode through the *mêlée* to Konichi's office. There he found the hated Supplies Officer with a towel wrapped round his head and a bottle and a great pile of Mickey Mouse notes on the table at his side. He was bundling things into a cardboard box and his gold teeth glinted in the dim, yellow light.

Had the Allies at last invaded? Were they about to be rescued?

Would the Japs leave them or shoot them? Endless possibilities raced through George's mind.

It was not until 3 am that he, together with Chairman Heichert, British Vice-Chairman Watty and senior Committee member Downs, was summoned to the Commandant's presence.

Solemnly Major Iwanaka addressed the group: "From now on internees are released from my charge. By sudden order from our superiors I release all internees from five in the morning to the Executive Committee. Your Committee is given complete charge of the entire camp. We are willing to leave all food provisions which will last for at least two months. I would suggest that your Committee keep all internees inside the camp. By our orders, within about one hour we must leave here. That is all I want to tell you."

Mr Ito, adjutant and interpreter, then handed over money and receipts which had been taken from individual internees and, rather touchingly, a personal gift for one internee, Mrs Frampton, who had taught him English in Korea.

At 4.45 they left. And at 5, under the still starlit sky, Heichert addressed his 2,224 charges and declared "Camp Freedom".

An hour and a half later at sunrise the internees assembled again for a simple ceremony outside Barracks 15. Bishop Binstead from Vatican City offered three short prayers – the Lord's Prayer, in which everyone joined, a prayer for those who had given their lives in the war and a prayer in thanksgiving for the deliverance of Los Baños. Then a boy from the Rangers sounded the reveille and the American and British flags were raised to the top of the bamboo flagstaff while the gramophone played "The Star-Spangled Banner" sung by Bing Crosby, the only version in camp, and "God Save the King".

It was a moment too deep for tears or laughter. Everyone was smiling but everyone was stunned. For a minute they stood silent in the dawn light and then the flags were lowered. To leave them flying might have invited Japanese reprisals.

They were free but, as Chairman Heichert warned: "This is potentially the most difficult and dangerous period of our internment." They were still in a war zone. Although the Commandant's crowd had left there was no indication the Japs had abandoned the surrounding area. Indeed two sentries spotted outside the gate were said to be attached to a nearby unit. No reports of Allied landings on Luzon had yet been confirmed. In the circumstances Heichert warned the internees it would be unwise to attempt to leave the camp. Roll call at 10.30 would continue though they would not be supposed to bow and blackout should be kept up. They must, he said, remain calm and maintain the organization and discipline they had practised over the past three years. Discipline was one of his greatest problems. Even before the Japs cleared out looters had broken into the chicken and pig farms and had ransacked the rice and sugar bodegas. Even the camp garden was looted and all the plants that Isla, Pat Hell and the others had worked so hard to grow were uprooted and, in many cases, eaten on the spot.

The sawali fence round Barracks 3 and 4, which the Jap garrison had so recently taken over, was torn down and the quarters stripped of all remaining property – clothes, electrical equipment, food.

In his later address to the camp on Freedom Morning Heichert appealed to the looters to give back their ill-gotten gains to the patrols. He said he realized that in the confusion some property had been acquired "inadvertently" but these supplies were now communal and were needed to feed the camp. Anyone failing to return property before noon would be prosecuted. It was a vain hope for, in the event, most loot had been eaten well before deadline.

Barracks 3 and 4 were made the administrative headquarters and all Committee members moved themselves and their belongings over.

Food was the all-important consideration. As soon as they could the kitchen staff served breakfast – double helpings of thick mush. Lunch was at 12.30 and supper at 5. It was the first time in weeks the internees had had more than two meals a day.

That afternoon the Filipino suppliers met the Committee. Apparently there was plenty of food in the area and they promised to keep the camp well stocked. The Commandant's bull was killed for beef and the carabao. Also all the pigs from the Japs' piggery. The internees watched drooling as the food came in – chickens squawking, bananas, coconuts, milk, vegetables.

On the 9th Isla wrote in her diary: "It's been worth three years of hell to go through this thrill. Full bellies since Sunday am. In fact too full, uncomfortable. Last night we had camotes, greens and rice and a big scoop of each! Curry sauce and corned beef – the curry donated by the Japs in their hurry! Amazing no either/or. Today we are going to have 700 or 800 kilos of beef instead of the 10 kilos the Japs gave the whole camp."

And later after supper: "It's fantastic, 60 hours ago we were hungry, tired and depressed. Tonight we had to take seven containers to get our chow. On the menu – boiled papaya, gravy, meat, gati, rice, tea, greens. Meat delicious, used a knife and fork for the first time in years. Only grumble came from a Communist. I've never met a Communist that didn't grouse perpetually."

The Communist apart, everyone was tremendously cheered by their full bellies, but oddly, the beri-beri did not improve; on the contrary it got worse. The doctors advised the internees to eat everything they could. The good fortune might not last for ever.

One of the first things to get started was the radio. The Commandant had left a transmitter and by the evening of the first day the broadcasting system was ready. MacArthur's station *The Voice of Freedom* came on the air. And station KGEX, San Francisco. There was news of bombing all over the Pacific. On the 8th they heard, albeit faintly, Roosevelt's speech to Congress; on the 9th Bing Crosby singing Cole Porter's latest hit, "Don't Fence Me In".

Then came the biggest news of all – the news they had been waiting for for three years – MacArthur had landed at Lingayen. He came ashore on 9 January at the head of 68,000 men of the Sixth Army. The broadcast described it as "the largest far-flung amphibious land operation". Strangely, apart from a few *Kamikaze*, there was no Japanese opposition to the landings. Resistance would come later from the chain of stubborn defences built up by the enemy inland. The collection of forty-seven shovels made sense. They would be used to help dig an intricate network of caves, tunnels and pillboxes.

There was no better medicine for the internees in Los Baños than these regular news bulletins. Most had had to make do with rumour for years. Isla was amazed when Don told her he had all along listened in to a friend's radio, a tiny gadget which he connected to his gramophone. No wonder he was always so well informed!

On the 10th as Isla was sitting in the cookhouse writing

recipes – an obsessive internee occupation – with Gill at her side peeling garlic, a tremendous burst of bombing and gunfire shook the camp. "Lumme, we *were* in the war this morning", she wrote. "Dive bombing, machine guns, bombs. Saw the planes just skimming the trees. When the cannon went off the barracks shook. Gill and I had rushed out so often we just sat in the cookhouse."

Isla and Gill may have been unconcerned but the Executive Committee decided it was no longer safe to risk public listening to the radio. News would have to be relayed to the internees in bulletins. There was no point, in Heichert's opinion, in inviting trouble.

Heichert was cautious but the heady draught of freedom was too strong for some and, in spite of warnings not to leave camp, many internees, including Gill, were going out roaming the hillside and meeting guerrillas and Filipinos to collect food.

It seemed that the guerrillas, led by an American mestizo, were highly organized. All along they had managed to maintain some sort of contact with the Americans and, according to the Captain, whom Gill met on several occasions, they had a complete plan for harassing the Japs and aiding the Allies in the last stages of the conquest of Luzon. Some of the young men in camp volunteered to join up and left. Isla could not blame them. If they had been in their own country on the outbreak of war they would have been conscripted and have had three years of action instead of a morale- and health-sapping stay in internment.

The guerrillas acted as go-betweens for the internees on the food market. By this stage no Filipino wanted money which was pretty well worthless. Clothes were their great need and they were prepared to exchange fruit, coconuts and cigarettes for the most ancient and unsightly garments.

Isla and Gill scraped together the remains of their ragged wardrobe and Gill set off up the hill to barter the wretched wares. She returned with one cigarette and two coconuts. The next day it was bananas and shrimps. On the 12th she appeared with a little black hen which was promptly named Angeline and given a nest under their bed – the safest place. With five chickens in all tethered on Isla's side of the barracks cackling and crowing it reminded her of a farm outhouse.

They settled down for the night with their future dinner

clucking contentedly on the floor beneath them, confident that any day now MacArthur's soldiers would come to take them home.

At 2.30 on the morning of Saturday, 13 January, they were woken by scuffling and shouting. It was soldiers all right, but they wore the wrong uniform.

"Important announcement, important announcement," Isla heard a man's voice saying. "Konichi, the Commandant and his staff are back and soldiers are all round the camp."

Well, they had had a good six days and it *was* the 13th. But freedom had seemed so near.

It had been a nasty shock for them all but poor Watty's experience was the worst. In the move back to Barracks 3 and 4 he had taken over Konichi's old quarters and he woke in the night to see that fiend among warders leering down at him. He thought it was a nightmare and turned over but the dreaming had to stop when he felt Konichi's grubby hand on his shoulder and smelt his fetid breath, heavy with stale booze.

The internees were told to be ready for roll call at 6.30 am. They waited till 7. When the Japs finally crawled out to inspect them Isla had never seen such a bunch of ragamuffins in her life. Their uniforms were torn and filthy, their bakias broken and trailing, their faces grey with exhaustion. She wondered where on earth they had been and why they had come back.

Konichi gave the Committee *his* answer. He told them the Japs had been away on a mission and had now returned to protect them. He proposed to start his special care of his charges by giving them their orders. First Barracks 3 and 4 were to be cleared for Jap use and new barriers erected. All mattresses, bedding and electrical equipment taken from these barracks was to be returned, together with the radio and amplifying equipment. All the rice that had been shared out among the internees on the Japs' departure to use as they thought fit was to be given back.

"These instructions are to be obeyed without delay," he snapped. "Otherwise dire punishments will follow. Understood?" And he returned to picking his mud-engrained toenails.

"One more thing for your protection," Konichi's eyes glinted bloodshot and cruel. "You are forbidden to trade with the Filipinos. Anyone seen leaving this camp will be shot. Out."

It didn't seem possible that only a week ago the camp had

resounded to the strains of "The Star-Spangled Banner" and "God Save the King". The Los Baños Japs were obviously going to take their resentment at Allied successes out on their captives.

That same afternoon at two o'clock a second roll call on the hospital road was announced. No one was excused. Soldiers surrounded the internees with machine guns making the most horrible animal noises and for nearly two hours they were kept lined up on the road under the hot sun while the Japs searched their poor stables. Luckily Isla and Gill's cubicle was left untouched. The diary was still safe in its hiding place at the bottom of a suitcase. Even the three hens – in spite of the Japs' return they had been able to acquire another two – were still tied to the bed. But other stables looked as though a tornado had hit them. Even the floorboards had been pulled up.

The excuse was that a second radio was missing from the Jap quarters. Konichi stressed that this was military equipment and therefore in the same category as rifles or pistols. Retention of the radio would be treated as a hostile act and could result in the gravest consequences. In vain the Committee protested that only one radio had been taken and that had been returned. The "hostile act" phrase could so easily be twisted into an excuse for shooting the entire camp population before the Americans could save them.

Other important missing items were Commandant Iwanaka's chow bowls painted with the Imperial flag. He disliked eating from anything else and kept interrupting meetings to ask whether they had been found.

The taste of freedom – and good food – had been too much for some of the internees. Pat Hell was determined that no one was going to stop him collecting his chicken and vegetables from the friendly Filipinos outside. He had a secret hole through the fence and told Gill that she was welcome to come with him on his forage.

On Sunday the 14th while most of the Japs, exhausted from their mysterious six-day trek, were still asleep Pat and Gill crept out. Dodging from rock to bush they soon reached the rough, wooded path which led up the mountain to their appointed rendezvous. Within 40 minutes they were back in camp, Gill with two fat chickens, Higgledy and Piggledy.

Gill told her mother she had got the chickens from Pat and

Isla was delighted to add them to her "stores". A couple of days later Gill turned up with another chicken, Gertrude, and eight coconuts.

The prospective feasts were more than welcome but Isla worried that Pat was still risking foraging expeditions after Konichi's warning that anyone leaving camp would be shot. She would have been even more worried had she known that Gill was going with him.

On the morning of the 17th Isla was outside her stable when Pat came along bringing her a little withered pepper from his stable garden. She decided to try and reason with him.

"For God's sake, Pat, don't take any more risks. It can't be long now and you have a wife and family at home."

"I've had chicken for a week and I am going to go on having it," he replied and there was an odd gleam in his eyes. "Sorry, Isla, I know you only meant to help but I must go on."

That afternoon there was a terrific raid, more straffing and bombing than they had heard since the beginning of the war. Silence followed. Then, in the unnatural stillness that hung heavy in the battered air, four rifle shots rang out.

Pat Hell was dead. Three of the four bullets had got him in the chest. He was on his way back in, just 200 metres from the fence, when the guard shot. Gill could so easily have been with him. It was one of the few expeditions he made alone. Isla was aghast when she heard how close her daughter had been to death. To come this far through internment and be killed for a chicken – it was horrible.

Pat's death hurt Gill and Isla more than they could say – or, indeed, feel in their stunned condition. The funeral was the following morning and Isla and Mrs Mora, who had been one of her companions in the food deputation to the Commandant, sat up all night making a wreath. He was buried in the new cemetery – Jan Howard Hell, age 38, 17 January, 1945.

"It's a damn shame", Isla wrote in her diary. "He's done so much for the camp in the garden and there are many individuals who can thank him for much."

Roll call revealed that four young men had left camp – obviously to join the guerrillas. At least they missed the misery inside.

"Never have we gone through such hell", wrote Isla on 24 January. "It's all so terribly slow. Food is a worse problem than ever. This rice we're getting is just blobs of gum. Hard to digest and difficult to re-cook. Our last two coconuts were bad which is an awful blow. If only we could get some sugar this rice would go down easier. Everyone has colds. I'm aching everywhere."

Angeline and Higgledy and Piggledy had long since exchanged bedpost for pot, with their skin and bones for stew and of their offal pâté made. Delicious, but now just a memory.

They were back to two meals a day – wallpaper paste lugao and mush if they were lucky. Blackout lasted from 7 pm to 7 am. Wood was in such short supply the beautiful acacia tree by the gate had to be chopped down. Once again the Committee emphasized the importance of garden work. It was to continue even when the alert was on and only to be stopped if the Japanese guard gave the order.

Even Masaki, one of the friendly guards, admitted to Copie that he was worried about the camp. In his opinion the Commandant was a coward and Konichi a crazy drunkard. They had left, he told her, not on orders but because the Commandant was frightened and when they got to Manila they were told by the military to go straight back and clear up the mess.

The internees just wished they would take fright again. This time they were all ready to leave, suitcases packed and desks pushed back, but every morning it was a case of "Still 'oping, but 'ere they still are".

On 28 January Isla woke to the crack of a rifle shot. Automatically she thought "Another of our internees" and sure enough it was. George Lewis, a friend of George Gray, had been out on an early morning food hunt. He was shot in the shoulder as he climbed back over the fence which marked the camp boundary.

Within minutes Gray and Dr Nance were on the scene. Nance insisted on seeing him and treating him but every time he and Gray made a move towards the poor man, who was bleeding profusely and was obviously in great pain, the guards threatened to shoot.

For one and a half hours he lay wounded on the ground. Then at 8.25 the guards said they had orders to shoot him. In vain the Committee pleaded for his life on the grounds that, under the terms of the Geneva Convention, the Commandant had no powers to impose the death penalty on any internee for any offence whatever. But the Commandant refused to see them and the guards insisted they must obey orders. They carried George Lewis, alive but semi-conscious, down to the bamboo grove and put a revolver to his head. Even the Catholic priest was refused permission to go with him and give him the last rites.

"It is plain murder by the Bushido Japs", wrote Isla. "A man isn't shot *coming into* camp by a decent, civilized nation. He may be jailed, solitary confinement etc. But if he's wounded they don't just murder him."

The odd thing was that George's friends had seen the guard with his rifle at the ready and had tried to warn him shouting: "Don't come over, George. There's someone watching. Don't come over." But, light-headed with hunger and sickened by beri-beri, George had not heard their cries. He came blindly, deafly on – on to join Pat Hell in the camp cemetery.

It might be against the Geneva Code to sentence a civilian internee to death but there was no doubt they had been warned. Again and again the Committee had stressed the danger of violating the camp boundaries and attempting to trade or communicate with anyone outside. The Commandant had made his orders clear: the garrison troops were to shoot on sight anyone attempting to escape and this meant anyone who, for whatever purpose, was found outside the camp boundaries.

In a fresh appeal to the internees to recognize the seriousness of the situation the Committee posted yet another notice urging them to obey the rules "in order to avoid the severe penalties which undoubtedly will be visited upon them as individuals and the possibilities of repercussions upon the camp as a whole".

At the same time they sent a strong letter of protest to Major Iwanaka at the manner of George Lewis's death.

"You, as Commandant of this camp," they wrote, "have no power to order the imposition of the death penalty upon any internee here for any offence whatever. We call your attention to Articles 60 to 67 of the Geneva Convention of 1929 which soon after the outbreak of the present war your government agreed with the government of the United States to follow in its treatment of civilian internees. Under those articles only a court may order the death penalty. The procedure is prescribed. In such cases notification must be given to the protecting power of the institution of the case, the right of the prisoner to defend himself is safeguarded as well as his right to have counsel and to appeal and these articles expressly provide that no death penalty may be executed until three months after the protecting power is notified of the imposition thereof. You have disregarded all these provisions in ordering the execution of Mr George Lewis this morning."

It continued: "From no point of view was Mr Lewis guilty of any offence involving the death penalty. At the worst he could only be considered as in the act of escaping when first shot. The facts are to the contrary. He was actually returning to the camp and hence was not an escaping prisoner. In any case, under Articles 47, 50, 51, 52 of the Geneva Convention of 1929 an attempted escape is only an offence against discipline and the punishment thereof may not exceed 30 days' arrest . . . There can be no doubt that the refusal to permit medical attention to be given Mr Lewis after he was first shot, the order for his execution within an hour and a half thereafter without any court action whatever constitute a record unlawful, inhumane and shocking."

In Isla's opinion, not only Iwanaka deserved to be shot but also the head of his bureau for sending a Commandant who did not know, or would not obey, international law.

Up till now Isla and Gill had managed to steer clear of any trouble with the Japs. They had traded indirectly through John Hunter, Ernie Cummings, Shapiro and even Sniffen. In fact at that very moment Isla had a "dove" out with John Hunter in the shape of a ring to try and get some sugar. But neither had ever tried to operate without a middleman.

Then one night towards the end of January a Jap knocked on the stable door.

"Meestere Sneefin?" he queried as Isla popped her head out.

She indicated the Sniffen abode. But the Jap seemed in no hurry to go.

"You gottee watchee, you gottee Parker pen, you gottee gold?" he asked, his wide grin betraying the cavernous teeth he would no doubt like to fill with precious metal.

Isla was tempted. Obviously her dove was not bringing home the bacon. Surely a small, quick deal could do no harm? She arranged for him to call back later that evening and, after a bit of haggling, exchanged her fountain pen for sixty precious grams of sugar which he brought in his filthy cap.

Having found a good source of trade the Jap naturally was reluctant to abandon it. He came to the stable again and again pestering Isla for gold lighters or watches. He particularly wanted her gold propelling pencil. With his toothy grin and nervous twitch the man terrified her. She began to wish she had never had anything to do with him. Then she had a crazy impulse. Mr Barnes, Pat Hell's successor in the garden, had given her a map showing where Pat had made a cache of coconuts. He had buried them during Camp Freedom week in the ground near Barracks 3 and 4, now reclaimed by the Japs. If she could get her toothy little guard to uncover the cache and bring it to her it would be worth the gold pencil.

Isla put her proposition when he called on the night of 29 January. Gill handed him the map and he promised to return the following day with the coconuts.

Isla's emotions were on a seesaw. Having done the deed she was seized with panic. She got out her diary and wrote: "I suppose internment lowers resistance, hunger makes one cuckoo; anyway, I have done the stupidest, most dangerous thing of my life. Have no excuses to make except that I didn't think and if it turns out all right I'll change and if it doesn't I won't have a chance of changing."

Next morning a sergeant from the Commandant's office arrived at the stable with an interpreter. Isla was in the middle of her cleaning. Gill was out at the hospital.

"We want to see your sister. You go get," the interpreter translated. He meant Gill.

Isla had no choice. She hurried off to find her daughter. As they made their way back to the stable she told her: "It's that damned map. For God's sake tell them everything. You know they never question without knowing it all. Tell the truth, admit we gave the guard the map and tried to trade. It's our only hope. At the same time we must protect Barnes. I'll say Pat Hell gave us the map."

Gill preceded her mother into the stable.

"I *would* be found out the first time I try trading with the Japs," she said plonking herself down on the bed next to the two officials.

The sergeant looked unimpressed. He turned to Isla just coming through the door. "Out, out," he rapped.

"Oh no, I'm her mother," retorted Isla. "I'm not leaving."

The sergeant gave a curt nod for a reply and Isla squatted down on the floor in the corner. There was no more room on the bed. The questioning began.

"Name? Where do you come from? How many times have you met this man? What have you traded? How did you get this map?"

"That map was given to me by the man you shot last week," Isla replied. "It is mine. Yes, I gave it to the guard because we are hungry, we don't get enough food."

"We know everything so don't lie," the sergeant, now speaking without the interpreter, told them. "We shall punish you if you lie."

"It's the truth," protested Gill. "It's our map."

"If either of you do anything wrong again, never mind, man or woman, we will shoot you," warned the sergeant.

Gill was indignant. "What *did* we do wrong? It is on the board we can trade with the Japanese. We didn't trade with anyone else. Can't we speak or trade with a Jap?"

"If you ask him if he has my permission," the sergeant replied coldly. He turned to Isla: "How many coconuts?"

"I don't know."

"Well, you can have them if you want." Isla was bewildered. This man was known as a stinker and now he was offering them coconuts. He must have believed their story. He went on: "We throw them away. We have them at the office but we not want them."

After all the terror it would have been foolish not to collect the spoils. So, accompanied by the two officials, Gill marched off returning with a bag of eleven rattling coconuts.

As she walked back across the camp with her obvious load she heard women hissing: "Trading with the enemy! Traitor!" "She'd sell her soul for a bag of coconuts!" "Playing footsie with the Japs!"

But Isla and Gill were unabashed. They knew very well that there was hardly a man or woman in camp, Vatican City not excluded, who had not tried to strike a bargain with the enemy. Conscience may make cowards of us all but not hunger. Five of the coconuts were bad. The remaining six they shared with Barnes who had given them the map.

But were two miserable coconuts each worth their peace of mind? Now their names would be on the list of suspects. Any day they might hear the knocking on the door which could mean Fort Santiago or the death sentence.

"Now I really know what people under the Nazis went through", wrote Isla. "They say the matter is closed but they break their word too often. It's part of my nightmares, I think, the beginning part."

And she took her diary, now thirty-five large exercise books, and hid it under the floorboards of a friend's stable. It would be safer there until the fuss died down.

How she wished she had not been such a damned fool! To show a map of all things to a Jap with their phobia over maps and the written word. And just towards the end too!

The next day, 31 January, was Gill's eighteenth birthday and her fourth in internment. In celebration they killed Gertrude, the last of the chickens Gill had brought in from outside. She was delicious in spite of the fact she was fried in rancid fat. Poor Gertrude! Her demise was such a relief. It had been so messy with her living in the stable and all the time Isla was worried she would be looted and grace someone else's pot. They boiled her bones four times for soup.

By the beginning of February Camp Freedom seemed more like a lost mirage than a real happening. Had the twin flags of Britain and the United States really fluttered proud in the dawn breeze? Was it MacArthur's voice they had heard on the radio telling them to keep up their courage, he was coming to set them free? Had they really dined off beef, carabao, chicken and fruit?

To make matters worse Isla seemed to have landed yet another complaint to add to the already impressive list – a sort of mange or fungus on her head. It itched and ached like a boil. The only thing the hospital could offer was gentian violet. They had no other antiseptic left and half the camp seemed to be walking round with deep blotches of gentian staining legs, arms and faces. Isla was terrified she would have to shave off all her hair. She looked freak enough already and baldness would be the final indignity. Once again she was saved by a friend's generosity. Helen, one of the hospital nurses, gave her a tiny piece of Lifebuoy no bigger than a thumbnail. It must have been the last bit of soap left in Los Baños but, using it every day, the leprous infection cleared.

The same could not be said for beri-beri. Every day the hateful disease grew more disfiguring, more painful. Isla and Gill woke in the morning with faces like suet puddings and by evening the water had descended to their ankles. One young man told Isla that when he got up he weighed 128 lbs, by mid-morning he was 160 lbs, and by evening 190 lbs – all water.

Strangely, the gruesome spectacle of the beri-beri victims did not deter the Japs from taking their propaganda photographs. Isla could only suppose that in black and white the pathetic wet beri-beri victims, with their bloated faces, stomachs and limbs, would look fat and prosperous. The camera's eye was blind to the deathly yellow-grey pallor that characterized the skin of the dying.

MacArthur was as impatient as the internees to recapture his beloved Philippine Islands but the Japanese resistance, which had at first appeared to be light, showed its teeth as the invading armies marched inland towards Manila.

In charge of the defending Fourteenth Area Army was General Tomoyuki Yamashita, the victor of Singapore and Malaya. His force of 275,000 men was far larger than the 25th Army which had taken Malaya and almost twice the strength estimated by MacArthur's Chief of Intelligence, General Willoughby. With this army divided into three strategically placed groups, Yamashita believed he could hold off the Americans for months or even years.

Placing himself at the head of the *Shobu* group – with 152,000 men the largest of the three – Yamashita had set up his headquarters in the mountains at Baguio to defend the northern part of Luzon from Lingayen Gulf to Aparri. The *Kembu* group of 30,000 troops under Major General Rikichi Tsukada was concentrated on the central area north and west of Manila and was responsible for Bataan and Clark Field. The third group of 80,000 troops, the *Shimbu*, under Lieutenant-General Shizuo Yokoyama, was set to defend the area south from Manila to the Bicol peninsula – an area which included Los Baños.

Krueger's Sixth Army, consisting of the U.S. I Corps, 6th and 43rd Divisions, under Major-General Innis P. Swift, and the U.S. XIV Corps, 37th and 40th Divisions, under Lieutenant-General Oscar W. Griswold, pushing inland from Lingayen after the 9 January landings, encountered the *Shobu* to the north and the *Kembu* to the south.

It took Griswold's troops almost a week to penetrate the

defensive network of caves and tunnels protecting the Clark Field complex and the airfield was not in Allied hands until 31 January.

Manila was the next target. "Go to Manila," MacArthur urged the gallant XIVth. "Go around the Nips, bounce off the Nips, but go to Manila." The battle for the capital started on 1 February. By 3 February the Americans were in the city but a month's hard fighting lay ahead before the U.S. could claim to have wiped out enemy resistance.

Meanwhile what had become of STIC and its 3,500 internees? Isla had been right in thinking Santo Tomas was better placed for a rescue operation than Los Baños. The internees of Santo Tomas were freed on 3 February by the 1st Cavalry division. Later that same day the P.O.W.'s in Bilibid were rescued. Cabanatuan to the north was captured in a daring night operation on 30 January and its 500 or so emaciated prisoners of war set free. In Los Baños they heard the news with elation. Surely their turn would come soon? And as Manila fell the Japs retreated south. South towards Los Baños.

The battle now was all about them. At the Council of War tempers grew short as one councillor estimated, from the time-lag between gun flashes and bangs, that troops were fifteen miles away, while another said thirty and another more like fifty. On other occasions the experts nearly came to blows over whether the noise was bombing, naval guns or artillery.

Isla was just thankful relief was near. "If we don't have trouble with the retreating Japs we'll pull through", she wrote on 4 February. They knew only too well that desperation might lead their captors to massacre them where they were. It had happened before. Even now gangs of rioting sailors in flight from Manila were raping and bayoneting women and children in a last drunken fury of defeat and setting fire to their homes. All about Los Baños the native barrios were going up in flames in an effort to "smoke out" the guerrillas.

The important thing, the only thing, was to keep alive until MacArthur came.

The Executive Committee were at their wits' end on how to cope with the food situation. Unofficial trading between Japs and individual internees indicated that supplies must be available but somehow they were not getting through to camp rations. After a week of fruitless requests to see the Commandant,

Chairman Heichert, Vice-Chairman Watty, Mr Downs and Harris, the Food Administrator, got an interview with Mr Ito of the Commandant's staff on 9 February. It was depressing in the extreme.

"I recognize that your present diet is inadequate," Mr Ito told the assembled four. "It is barely sufficient to sustain life. But in the last few days this has become an area of actual conflict. There appears to be little hope of improvement. No one can say who will win and, until a decision is reached, there is little hope of any increase in the supplementary food arriving in camp."

The Committee pointed out that even the inadequate grain supplies would run out by 19 February. What would happen then?

From Mr Ito's reply it was obvious that their guess was as good as his. "The Japanese Army recognizes its responsibilities and will do its utmost, but, of course, cannot at the moment make specific promises."

Isla decided to trade anything and everything she could. Gill was desperately hungry and she would prefer to part with all her jewellery than see her suffer. The sickening thing was the Japs preferred the cheap and flashy stuff and all Isla's things were good quality.

Gill was the expert in bargaining. "You gottee mungo beans? You gottee sugar? You gottee lice?" she asked the little Jap guards as they hurried on their way to and from Sniffen's where business was brisker than ever.

In exchange Isla offered her beautiful eternity ring studded with tiny diamonds. But, with the whole camp on the trading racket, the Japs were spoiled for choice. There might be a lot of diamonds on the ring but they were unimpressively small.

Yaki, Gill's contact, looked disdainfully at the £80 ring (1939 value): "No biggee stones," he told her. "No lice, no mungo bean. Bottle whisky – Golden Rose."

"I want to eat not drink," Isla told him. And the deal was abandoned.

Finally, after days of hard bargaining, Gill pulled off a triumph. The ring was exchanged for four kilos of rice and one of sugar.

"I feel like a dog with two tails", wrote Isla in her diary for 12 February. "Couldn't sleep all night was so elated. It'll take us to the 19th anyway . . . What a difference sugar can make besides giving one a little energy to carry on."

She still had two nice rings – one diamond and one platinum and pearl – and a pair of beautiful diamond and sapphire earrings her father had given her. She also had the gold propelling pencil that had been offered for the coconuts. But as the days went by and the war situation became more imminent she realized that trading them for any reasonable quantity of food would be next to impossible. With the battle almost on top of them the Filipino suppliers had simply fled into the mountains. Now even the Japs were unable to get extra food and to exchange what little sugar, rice and coconuts they had in store for uneatable jewels became impracticable.

On 19 February the grain supplies ran out. As a substitute the internees were issued with unhusked rice or palai rice. Gill and Isla were given 500 grams between them. The problem was unhusking the stuff. It took Isla and Gill two hours' hard work with a makeshift pestle and mortar and after all that they had only 50 grams left – about two ounces.

It was amazing to see the different ways people went about de-husking. Some did it with bottles and a stick, some with two boards, some pounded it in a jar, others soaked it first. The clatter all over the camp was worse than an army of crickets. George Harris, the Food Administrator, organized a husking shift system and, with nine men working in three continuous shifts all day, fifteen kilos was produced.

In vain the Committee protested. It was too bad, they were told, there was nothing else. They asked if the palai could be sent out for grinding in a local mill but this too was refused on the grounds that all the mills were in operation – no doubt for the benefit of the Japs. There was nothing to do but make the best of it. Eat palai or die.

Many, thought Isla, would eat palai *and* die. The de-husking was so tiring and such a strain on the eyes that the old and the chronically sick would probably abandon the unequal struggle and eat the stuff husks and all . . . and the husks were like powdered glass. The only practical thing that could be done with them was to boil them up and drink the "soup" or tiki-tiki as it was known, in the forlorn hope that a trace of Vitamin B1 might lurk among the brittle.

On the 19th, too, the last pig was killed and put in the pot.

Isla and Gill were lucky – they got a bit of hide! One pig between 2,100 people.

It was their last feast. After that there was nothing except palai and sour mush mixed with the deceased pig's copra meal.

All Isla and Gill's stores had gone. The garden was cleaned out. The salt was finished. The water was off again and, because of the war situation, the internees were told, the pipeline could not be mended. The electricity was cut and even the hospital had no power.

To make matters worse it was raining again. The dry season seemed a fiction in this godforsaken country.

In the hospital the death toll mounted. One beri-beri victim was said to have eaten his pants in a frenzy of starvation. And the man who had talked so much about slug protein and had boasted of having eaten over 3,000 slugs was now on the danger list.

Hampered by lack of water and no electricity the doctors and nurses were unable to continue the tapping of wet beri-beri victims. Other operations were also impossible. Nance predicted: "If they don't come now we won't be able to dig graves fast enough." Already they had run out of coffins. So many people were going crazy one of the bathrooms had to be converted to a psychotic ward.

As for Isla, the beri-beri had affected her face so badly she could neither see looking down for the mountains of flesh nor lift her eyes up owing to the heaviness of the swelling above. To keep sane she wrote her diary and – perhaps, she thought, this *was* some form of madness – copied out endless recipes. All the women were doing it and the more exotic the dish the better. Needless to say, none of them contained rice and the most popular recipes were the really sweet and creamy ones – strawberry and walnut cream cake, cassata ice-cream, pears in red wine. By the time Isla finished with the recipes she was cross-eyed and drooling at the mouth and her very bones ached with hunger. Perhaps it would have been better to ignore them but somehow even the faintest connection with food was obsessive.

By the 21st the gnawing pains were unbearable. Isla reckoned she had lost nearly a stone in weight in a week. It was agony even to lie down on her thin, scrawny body.

Sniffen offered her two tablespoonfuls of rice for her £100 gold cigarette case. She gave it to him. Even by Sniffen standards it was daylight robbery. The going rate outside for a 110 lb bag was now 20,000 pesos compared to the eight paid before the war. On this basis Isla should have got about three pounds of rice for her gold case – but Sniffen had to make his profit, hadn't he?

Copie, now in hospital, sold her solitaire diamond ring for a few grains. Mrs Judge traded her diamond ring, all the jewellery she had, for a pittance of mungo beans. They were stolen.

Every day the bombing and gunfire grew nearer. Bud Ewing swore it came from just across the Laguna. Then George Gray appeared with a shiny one-cent American coin. It was dated 1944! The guerrillas must have made contact with the troops!

At first Isla was too bemused with pain and hunger to make the connection – that their salvation was just the handing of a coin away. The problem was how could the Americans ever get through to them, surrounded as they were by retreating Jap troops, not to speak of the area army and the Los Baños garrison itself?

On 21 February Commandant Iwanaka made an anouncement that could only mean, one way or another, the end was in sight. If the Japs should leave again, he told Chairman Heichert, and the internees contacted the Filipinos or the guerrillas, for whatever purpose, the whole camp would lose its non-combatant status individually and collectively. So it had come. The excuse to shoot them all.

"What they are asking for is a demonstration and people to go over the side, then they can shoot – they are itching to do it", wrote Isla.

Already several of the young men had escaped to join the guerrillas, dyeing their skin with permanganate of potash to give them an "Asiatic" appearance. Would another escape condemn the whole camp to death? Obviously the surviving 2,146 sick and hungry internees were a dreadful encumbrance to their captors.

"Oh God, let the troops come soon . . . "

That night they heard a tremendous explosion in the direction of Manila as if the whole city was crumbling under the force of a gigantic earthquake. It was the Japs blowing their vast ammunition stores in the tunnels of Malinta Hill on Corregidor.

On the 22nd Isla took to her bed. Gill ran down to fetch Nance but he was too busy to leave the hospital. Isla knew now for sure they were dying of starvation.

"Dear God, this terrible hunger pain . . . ", she wrote, her swollen beri-beri fingers could hardly hold the pen, " . . . they have informed us they will not give us grain tomorrow . . . "

CHAPTER NINE

Glad to see you

(*23 February–15 April, 1945*)

IT was still dark when Isla woke on the morning of 23 February. She could hear Mr Mora, the Monitor, calling "6.30 roll call, 6.30." She felt worse than ever with a headache that seemed to stretch as far as her toes. Her body was a lead weight, disconnected from her mind, an instrument refined by an expert in pain which for some diabolical reason she had to carry with her, a wheel of torture. Perhaps it was the effect of the beri-beri: for wherever the eye's orbit ranged the view was obscured by mounds of puffy flesh. Every movement was an effort of will as if she was in a drugged coma or gripped by a paralysing nightmare. If lying down had not been so painful she would have stayed in bed. Robot-like she programmed herself to crawl up to the cookhouse to start warming the breakfast lugao.

It was 7 am, daybreak, and something was happening. She heard screams and looking up saw planes in the sky. Tiny figures stepped into the air and, as the first parachute opened, a volley of shots rang out. The hillside ran rivulets of troops moving purposefully towards the garden.

Over the camp a plane flew low with the word "RESCUE" on it.

"Oh well," she told herself philosophically, "there'll be no roll call this morning. Better get the stove going."

Hunger had so numbed her senses Isla could scarcely feel excitement. It was simpler to concentrate on the business of existence. Anyway, she reasoned, they were bound to be stuck in Los Baños for at least a month while things were sorted out. They couldn't move them all in a day. If the Allied invasion had got this far it would simply be a change of status, as in STIC, from "internment" to "rehabilitation" camp. No point in abandoning breakfast.

Bullets whistled past the open cookhouse as Isla crouched over the stove struggling to coax a flame from the impoverished charcoal. The shots came from the direction of the garden close to the spot where the Japs did their morning exercises.

"Take cover! Get inside!"

She took no notice. The Committee had warned them to hide under their bunks at the first sound of shots but since she had never "stopped one" yet she was not going to bother now.

"*Why* won't this damn fire light?"

The noise roused Gill from her customary morning dormouse act. Pulling on her slacks and shirt she belted over to the cookhouse.

"Mummy, something's happening. Why didn't you wake me?" She was furious at having missed out on the excitement. Isla started to explain how everything had happened at once but the next thing they knew Snooks was calling from her stable: "Isla, Gill, come on, we're all leaving!"

Isla handed the fire arrangements over to Gill – she was much better at it anyway – and ran back to the stable. She flung aside the passage door and found herself looking into the face of a young man. What a good complexion he had! How white his teeth were! He looked healthy. He was smiling. It was 7.20 – the moment they had dreamed of for over three years: RESCUE.

"Bless you," said Isla. "Bless you. We *are* glad to see you."

"Not half so glad as *we* are to see *you*," replied the young man. He was a parachuter from the famous 11th Airborne. "Come on, you've got five minutes to pàck and get out. We're taking you across the lake to safety. Like a cigarette?"

Isla and Gill, who had followed her mother down to the stable, both took one. How strange, it was a Philip Morris!

Life was odd. Nearly thirty-eight months of waiting and now only five minutes to get out. They were both packed. Isla had made sure of *that* when the bombing first started in September. It was crazy but she had decided then that whatever else she left behind she would take her diary – now thirty-six bulky notebooks – with her. It had been her comfort, her friend, the thing that had kept her sane. It was part of her, like an unborn child, and wherever she went it must go too.

Her one regret was the banana tree which Owen had planted

for her outside the cookhouse almost a year ago. She cast one last reproachful look at its green fingers, now nearly ripe to eat, and wished it had been a papaya – so much quicker to mature!

She staggered out with her two heavy suitcases. The place looked like Victoria Station on Bonfire Night. From every direction people were rushing towards the main gate dragging or carrying curiously shaped packages and bundles. Still Isla could hear the occasional crack of a rifle shot like a Guy Fawkes rocket. Then Barracks 3 and 4, the Jap quarters, and the guard houses went up in flames. Was Konichi the Guy? Already several internees had claimed to have killed him.

The fire spread. It was American policy to leave nothing behind for the Japs. Soon Barracks 8 was burning. The nipa and sawali quickly shrivelled in the roaring flames like paper in a grate. Huge sparks flew off and landed before Isla's feet. The heat was intense.

Suddenly she remembered she had forgotten Gill's little red suitcase and their barracks was the next for the bonfire. She rushed in to fetch it. Seconds later Barracks 7 was in flames. Stable 40, with its superior wooden partitions, would be more resistant than the others, she thought abstractedly. She was conscious now of fire all about her. She was being hurried through a street of flames, the old road to the canteen, towards an amphibian truck which stood revving its engine at the gate. It was the last in a convoy of about twenty and already its companions had left and were chugging down the rough track towards the Laguna. Isla and Gill hurried to scramble aboard but there was no room – no room in the last truck. They stood bewildered as more than 2,000 of their fellow prisoners were driven off to the Laguna.

After what seemed hours, but was in fact ten minutes, a soldier came over and addressed the little group of fifty or so men and women still clustered pathetically at the gate, the last of the Los Baños internees.

"Sorry, you'll have to walk. We can't risk staying here any longer. Any minute we're expecting a bunch of 20,000 Nips over the hill. It's not far."

Not far. The walk was to the shores of Laguna de Bay and it was six kilometres. From there they were to be ferried by the amphibians north across the lake to Mamatid, beyond Calamba, in American-held territory. After that trucks would drive them a further eighteen miles up the coast to Muntinlupa, where quarters had been prepared for them in New Bilibid women's prison.

Isla found herself carrying the heavy suitcase with the diaries and another big box. Gill had her red case and a few oddments tied up in a bundle. Then, to Isla's intense relief, the nurses offered her a bit of luggage space on the rubbish cart they had managed to commandeer.

With parachuters in front and guerrillas on either side Isla helped to push the rubbish cart through the gate – to freedom. She didn't look back. She had no feeling about it at all. Gill walked ahead with John Hunter.

From all about them came the crack of rifles, the thud of explosions, the noises of war. Obviously they were still way behind enemy lines. The Allies had not, as Isla had first thought, taken this territory. No wonder they were being hustled out so quickly! It began to dawn on her that she was part of some very special rescue operation.

The rubbish cart rattled and bounced along the rough road, helped not at all by its groggy wheel. Soon it became obvious it would have to be abandoned. Isla, summoning every last ounce of strength, heaved her two cases off the cart and, bakias flapping on unsteady feet, began to lug them along the road. But it was no good. They were too heavy. She would have to ditch the diary. She stopped at the side of the road, opened the case and braced herself to throw away three years of her life. "Oh God," she sighed aloud. "Poor old diary!"

A hand touched her arm. "Hi, Missy, can we help?"

Two little guerrillas, no taller than their rifles, were standing there smiling. The diary was saved! Later, as she plodded along, Isla saw a bamboo pole by the side of the road which she presented to her tiny friends so they could carry the cases Chinese fashion.

It was gone 10.00 by the time they reached the Laguna. Isla had never felt such unutterable weariness. Her ankles were more swollen than ever. Her feet were raw and blistered from the long walk, and one of her toes was badly bruised. The nail would not last long. She sat down wearily on the scrubby shore. It would be an hour or so before the amphibians, which had already taken the majority of internees across the Laguna to safety, would return for their second load.

As she gazed out across the water, a huge inland lake, she heard a forgotten but familiar voice. "Isla, thank God I've found you!"

She looked up and Clark Lee, her old friend from Associated Press, was standing there, rather more weather-beaten than when last seen at the Manila Club three years ago, but otherwise the same, cheerful Clark.

"It's been a long time but I've come back to get you," he said, obviously moved by her changed appearance. "I looked for you at the camp and called your name again and again but I couldn't find you. But I knew you'd be somewhere. You wouldn't let those Nip bastards break you. Where's Gill?"

Isla called her daughter over. She had been scarcely more than a child when Clark last saw her. Now she was eighteen.

Soon Isla was catching up on news. Clark had covered all the war fronts since Pearl Harbor and Isla told him how she had often seen his name in the Jap papers. It was so good to see an old friend!

There seemed to be a lot of military activity just off the beach and Isla could hear guns and explosions coming from the direction of the track they had so recently taken. There was no time to lose. As the first returning amphibian appeared on the horizon the internees were lined up and given their instructions. It was 11.45.

"There are Japs either side of us," a soldier addressed them. "We've got to get everyone, you and the troops, into the amphibians so we can only allow one small piece of hand baggage each. You must leave the rest and we'll try and bring it on to you."

Isla dug in her cases to see what was most precious. It was her three years' diary. It had been her burden all this time and she thought "I'll stick to it". She wrapped it up in a towel and clambered into the waiting amtrack.

"I suppose this is what it was like at Dunkirk," she thought as the strange, scaly, alligator-like tank pointed its nose north. "Thank God, Los Baños is near a lake. It's made our rescue possible!" She could not know then just how right she was.

It took about two hours to get across the lake to Mamatid, a distance of just over seven miles. By three that afternoon all the internees, as well as the attacking force, were safe at Mamatid beach.

"Thus ended the rescue of the Los Baños internees," read a XIV Corps report, "an operation brilliantly conceived and meticulously executed, in which 2,146 American citizens and Allied subjects were liberated from the Japanese and brought to safety."

It *was* brilliant. As Isla later wrote in her diary, "We were literally snatched from the jaws of death in the most spectacular way. For efficiency, organization and timing it was outstanding and if I had seen it in a movie I would have said it was too fantastic!"

On Palawan island, another of the Philippine group, 150 American prisoners of war had been brutally massacred in December, 1944, when the Japanese garrison believed invasion imminent. Only five escaped to tell the story of how they were herded into underground shelters, soaked with gasoline and then set fire to by their frenzied captors. When they tried to get out they were mowed down with machine guns. It was a fate the U.S. Army feared might be in store for the Los Baños internees. A surprise attack was therefore vital and it was this necessity that led to the spectacular and daring air, land and water operation which had so astounded Isla Corfield and her fellow prisoners.

From the start a parachute/amphibious tank manoeuvre seemed the only possible way of saving the internees, trapped as they were behind enemy lines. They would have to be plucked out. To attempt a rescue by land would, as the XIV Corps report put it, "have resulted in evacuation of the internees by the enemy, if not more extreme measures".

As early as 4 February the mission had been assigned to the 11th Airborne Division. They had landed at Nasugbu, south of Manila and west of Los Baños, on the last day of January and were heavily engaged with the enemy in the South Manila area. Although unable to release sufficient troops for an immediate attack on Los Baños – at that stage still fifty miles behind enemy lines – a detailed plan of action was prepared.

On 10 February the 11th Airborne was placed under the control of Griswold's XIV Corps. By the 12th the rescue plan had been completed and a date set. A special force, the Los Baños force, was formed and placed under the command of Colonel Robert H. Soule, commanding officer of the 188th Glider Infantry Regiment.

On 21 February, 1945, Field Order No. 18 was issued: "The LOS BAÑOS Force will move to LOS BAÑOS by airborne, motor, amphibious, and foot, and will relieve the LOS BAÑOS internees and return them to MUNTINLUPA Hospital."

The ground work had been well done. As soon as the mission was assigned Major Vanderpool, GHQ representative with the guerrillas in Batangas Province, was contacted and, with the help of guerrilla patrols, escaped internees and Filipino civilians living in the area, a detailed plan of Los Baños internment camp was drawn up. The exact location of every sentry, the Commandant's headquarters, the guards' barracks and the building containing weapons and ammunition, were all specially marked. Covered approach routes were also detailed so that small groups of troops could creep up unseen to surprise and kill the sentinels. A parachute dropping ground was chosen only 800 yards from the camp boundary and, on the shores of the Laguna, a group from the 127th Airborne Engineer Battalion reconnoitred a landing site suitable for the amphibious craft.

Secrecy was of paramount importance. It was known from intelligence reports that the enemy had some 6,000 troops in the Province of Laguna with the heaviest concentration in the hills south of Alaminos, about ten miles from Los Baños. The camp itself was guarded by some 250 soldiers – guards and garrison troops – and 3,000 yards to the west, in a gravel quarry, was at least one enemy company with two 105 mm howitzers and four machine guns. To the north along Highway 1 and just south of the San Juan River at Calamba – by 23 February American troops had got as far as the north bank – another enemy force blocked the way. If the slightest hint of a rescue plan leaked out the internees' chances of survival would be minimal.

Complete surprise meant split-second timing. The attack on Los Baños was planned for 0700 exactly. This hour was chosen because it was known the enemy would be in the middle of their morning callisthenics and a minimum number armed. The plan – and it worked flawlessly – was for a simultaneous landing of troops by parachute and from amphibious craft, co-ordinated with an assault across the San Juan River by land troops.

To ensure everything worked smoothly a Division Reconnaissance Platoon, accompanied by two escaped internees and a guerrilla group, went ahead to prepare the way. They landed at San Antonio, near Los Baños, in native bancas thirty-six hours before H-hour (7 am) and split into three groups. The first, after wading through the thick mud of the paddy fields, secured the parachute drop zone; the second secured the beach-head for landings; the third moved up to within fifteen yards of the camp guards at the main gate, concealing themselves in a deep ravine which ran just outside the camp boundary on the hospital side.

The planes – nine C47s – took off at 0630 from Nichols Field – secured by the Allies just four days before – with the parachute infantry aboard. At 0658 the reconnaissance group at the drop zone sent up two columns of white phosphorous smoke indicating all was well. The men jumped. Seventeen minutes later they were at the camp.

Meanwhile the group hiding in the ravine had been busy. As the first parachute opened they started to fire on the Japs. By the time the parachute infantry arrived to help out there was scarcely a soldier left in camp. Minutes later the entire garrison of 243 Japanese soldiers had been annihilated.

It fell to the second group of the Reconnaissance Platoon to signal the all-clear to the fifty-four amphibian tractors which had set off from Mamatid at 0515 that morning. The smoke signals went up at 0658. One minute later – and a minute before H-hour – all the troops had landed. The journey across totally unfamiliar water had been made in pitch darkness, with adverse wind conditions and with only a compass for guidance.

If all the tanks could have gone full speed ahead to Los Baños camp the rescue would have been a comparatively easy matter. But the area was thick with Japanese troops – the *Fuji* branch of the *Shimbu* group – and they had to be dealt with if the internees were to stand any chance of getting through to the Laguna alive. The task of securing the rescue route fell to the first waves of amphibians to land. One group moved straightaway to Mayondon Point to rout an enemy force before proceeding to Los Baños town to establish a defensive block, while another took the road to Bay and occupied the high ground dominating the approaches from the east. Meanwhile on the beachhead, field artillery fired on enemy machine guns operating from Mayondon Point. (See map.)

The remaining amphibians drove straight to the camp,

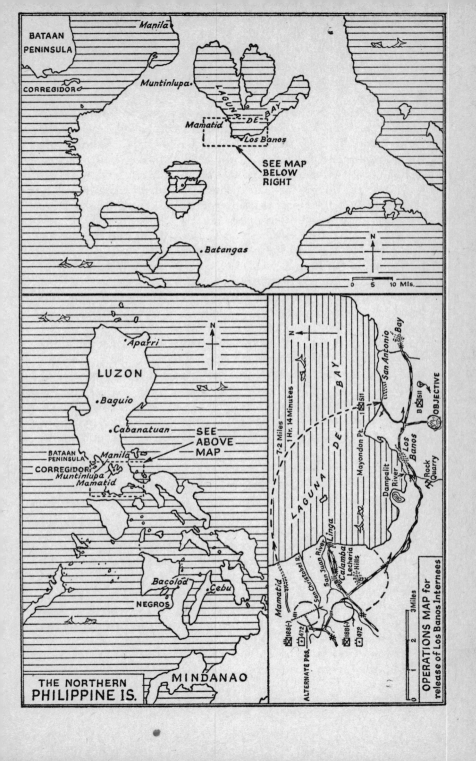

BATAAN
PENINSULA

Manila

CORREGIDOR

Muntinlupa

LAGUNA DE BAY

Mamatid

Los Banos

SEE MAP
BELOW
RIGHT

Batangas

N

0   5   10 Mls.

LUZON

Aparri

Baguio

Cabanatuan

SEE
ABOVE
MAP

N

BATAAN
PENINSULA

CORREGIDOR

Muntinlupa

Manila

Mamatid

Bacolod

Cebu

NEGROS

MINDANAO

THE NORTHERN
PHILIPPINE IS.

San Antonio Bay

N

511

B 511 OBJECTIVE

Los Banos

Rock Quarry

LAGUNA DE BAY

Mayondon Pt.

7.2 Miles

1 Hr. 14 Minutes

Dampalit River

Mamatid

San Juan River

Linga

Calamba

Lecheria

Hills

188(-)

472

472

188(-)

ALTERNATE POS.

San Christobel R.

0   1   2   3 Miles

OPERATIONS MAP for
release of Los Banos Internees

wisely preceded by mine-detecting engineers, to meet up with the parachute infantry and guerrillas and rush as many internees as possible – with priority for those unable to walk – back to the lake.

Meanwhile, to the north, at 0700 exactly, infantry forces crossed the San Juan River and seized the bridgehead on the south bank. By 0745 they had taken Lecheria Hill dominating the road to Los Baños. By noon Allied troops had reached the Dampalit River, only a couple of miles from the camp, had overcome the enemy force in the nearby quarry and were ready to help with the evacuation of internees should any disaster have overtaken the amphibious operation.

In the event their services were not required and they withdrew behind the San Juan bridgehead. But their reassuring and enemy-distracting and destroying presence was a vital ingredient in the rescue plan.

The 15th Air Force also backed the rescue, bombing and straffing the quarry west of Los Baños at H-hour and providing fighter cover for the whole of the operation.

The army reports all agreed that whirlwind speed and split-second timing, hitting from all angles at once, had made the success of the mission and saved the prisoners from torture and death.

In the entire operation two of the Los Baños force were killed and three wounded and out of the 2,146 rescued internees only three were slightly wounded. The Los Baños force had made history.

As Isla climbed out of her amtrack onto Mamatid beach she could scarcely believe her good fortune. Less than twenty-four hours ago she had gone to bed almost despairing of ever rising again.

But the journey was not over. They were still within enemy artillery range and a counter-attack might be mounted any moment. In all eighteen ambulances and twenty-five two-and-a-half-ton trucks had lined up on Mamatid beach to drive the internees, under guard escort, the eighteen miles to Muntinlupa. Thankfully Isla and Gill clambered into one of the trucks, Isla still clutching the towel with her diaries. All the way Filipinos lined the route shouting "Victory" — "Mabuhay".

It was evening by the time they arrived at New Bilibid Prison, their rescue quarters. They registered, were given a packet of cigarettes and two packs of chocolate each and were assigned to Prison 4. It was an open cell with fifty-three other women occupants. There they were issued with a stretcher and two blankets and told the way to the showers and the canteen. Later, to their amazement and extreme gratitude, the luggage they had had to leave behind on Los Baños beach was delivered. They had thought they would never see it again.

That night, in spite of the desperately uncomfortable and narrow stretchers which slotted into double-decker iron bunks, and the scratchy army blankets, Isla and Gill slept like two drugged logs. They were free again.

There was no doubt that the prison was uncomfortable, horribly so. It was much hotter than at Los Baños and terribly dusty in spite of the water truck that went round spraying. Also there were no chairs and one of the worst things, in Isla's opinion, was having to sit on the hard ground when "our tail bones aren't well covered yet and I have a boil on mine!" Every night in the cinema there were grunts and groans as the floor-seated audience shifted painfully from cheek to cheek.

But at least there was water, even though the pressure was not as good as it might be. And food. It was incredible to see it again. Bread and butter and sugar and coffee and meat. Chocolate and chewing gum. Candies and cookies and tea. In Los Baños Fred Satterfield had kept the same bit of chewing gum for five months. Now there were fresh packets every day.

Sensibly, the Red Cross, who were in charge of the ex-internees, had not given them too much at first. Even ordinary helpings could have proved fatal with their shrunken stomachs and systems so unused to animal fats and any form of richness. Indeed in STIC three people were said to have died from over-eating.

For the first week or so in Muntinlupa the food was dropped in packages by parachute. Sometimes a parcel would burst open and the former internees, still conditioned to acute scarcity, would rush to scoop it off the ground. It was a reflex action to food that many would keep in some degree all their lives. It took at least a week, too, before the Los Baños crowd stopped grubbing round the garbage cans. It was not that they were hungry: simply a case of old habits dying hard.

Every day there was an issue of something – towels, tooth-brushes, soap, magazines. Unfortunately for Isla all the magazines were American and she was longing for some news of home, but she devoured what articles there were and began to feel a little less cut-off. The daily news-sheet and radio bulletins also helped to keep them in touch with the world outside.

At last it was Cosmetics Day. The queue was immense. Even the nuns were waiting for their handout of Helena Rubinstein face-powder, lipstick, nail polish and a hair brush.

Money was, as ever, a great problem but here, once again, Isla's friends came to the rescue. Fred Satterfield had managed to get some cash released from his Manila bank and he was able to lend her a few pesos to carry on. She shuddered to think what her war debt would be – at least £2,000 she reckoned.

Poor Fred. The first news he heard on release was that his wife, Lewis, whom he adored, had died in the States. He was shattered by the tragedy and, trying to comfort him in his grief, Isla dreaded to think what her news might be.

She still kept her diary though now it was reduced to bits of Red Cross paper. With all the supplies, no one had thought to send any note books.

"It all seems so far away and yet I still can't take it in", she wrote a fortnight after the rescue. "It seems so strange not to feel the Japs around, to see the flash and then count till you hear the guns and say 'That comes from Calamba'. To hear the news and it's no rumour, not to worry over food and not to feel hungry, and to get toilet paper and soap given you . . . All I want now is a hot bath, shampoo and a permanent. Comfortable chair and bed, whisky-soda and my family around me – no more, no less. It isn't much to ask after three years."

There was still no indication of how long their stay in Muntinlupa might be. Isla could only suppose it was a vast military secret. They were still very much in the front line and not many days went by without the sound of machine-gun fire and bombing. It was going to be a long job smoking the Japs out of their foxholes.

Fred was by no means the only one whose release was marred with stories of tragedy and disaster. Sully, Isla's first friend in the Philippines, met a terrible end. While he was in church one day the Japs broke in and dragged him and two priests outside, bayoneted them, cruciform, to the church door and shot them. Whether they had been operating a radio or had been in contact with the guerrillas no one ever learned.

Santo Tomas had its share of horror. Only hours before the rescue Chairman Carroll Grinnell and two others were taken out and shot. Again no one seemed to know the reason. Father Kelly received the same brutal treatment as poor Sully.

Others, including kind Dr Foley, the only mish Isla had liked, were killed in a terrible shelling raid four days after STIC's liberation. The Jap shell hit the corner room of the Main Building in camp. Foley was killed outright and Mrs Foley lost an arm.

Santo Tomas was liberated by the 1st Cavalry Division on the evening of 3 February. Isla heard the full story when she got a jeep lift over to see her friends on 17 March.

All day the STIC internees had heard the noise of battle growing nearer. By afternoon the Japs were really edgy and had herded them all into the Main Building and Education Building, warning that anyone going outside would be shot.

They heard the tanks roar round the stockade. Were they about to be rescued or massacred? Then from outside came the unmistakable sound of an American voice shouting: "Where the hell's the front gate?" It was blocked and barred but they found it and the tanks came crashing through one after another.

Then an internee voice yelled: "If you're Americans turn a flash light on your face." One man did so.

"My God, it's Carl Mydans!" gasped the voice.

Sure enough, it was Mydans, the *Life* photographer, who had himself been a Santo Tomas internee with his wife, Shelley, in the early days. For some months after his dramatic "revelation" Mydans could not go anywhere without someone clapping him on the back and saying: "My God, it's Carl Mydans!"

Soon the internees in the Main Building were free. But across the way in the Education Building Jap soldiers were holding nearly three hundred men and boys hostage, among them Wyndham Stopford and his eldest son Neville, now 12. The Japanese Commandant demanded safe conduct for himself and his men to their own lines – or else.

Negotiations seemed endless. May Stopford, who was waiting outside with Craig and Anne, told Isla she aged twenty years in those few hours. In the end the Japs got their safe conduct and were allowed to leave the camp unmolested though rumour had it the Filipinos got them later. The hostages were led to freedom – by Stanley, the man everyone had suspected of being in league with the enemy. Isla's feeling about him had been well-founded. He was a British Intelligence Officer and all along had been feeding out information to the Allies. It was thanks to Stanley that many of the messages to and from the P.O.W. camps had got through.

Over 3,500 internees were rescued from Santo Tomas. Among those quickly reunited with their families was Virginia Hewlett, U.P. correspondent Frank Hewlett's wife, whom Isla had helped to look after before her move to Los Baños. In the middle of his long dispatch to the office Hewlett reported simply: "I found my wife today, recovering from a nervous breakdown . . . Her weight has dropped to eighty pounds. But I found her in excellent spirits. It was a reunion after years about which I do not want to think."

MacArthur lost no time in getting to the camp where he was greeted with cheers and cries of "He's back!" Broken men hobbled towards him to touch his uniform. Women embraced him; one kissed him on the cheek. His aide, Colonel Sid Huff, later described the scene at Santo Tomas in a book.* "We stopped in horrified silence when we saw, coming toward us, emaciated men and women dressed in torn, limp clothes. Hoarse cries came from their mouths. Tears flowed down their cheeks. I thought I had never seen such an unhappy sight, until I realized that this was not a demonstration of sorrow; it was an outburst of pure, unalloyed joy!

"Men I had never seen before threw their arms around me. Or had I seen them before? Yes, there was Sam Howard, the British engineer who had worked on our torpedo boats and whom I had known like a brother. I had to look again to be sure that this living skeleton of about one hundred pounds was the same man who, when last I saw him, weighed one hundred and ninety pounds. His thin arms cut into my flesh as we embraced."

Rescue stories were the talk of the day. Isla heard how at Cabanatuan the 486 survivors of the notorious Bataan Death March had been half carried from the liberated camp by the U.S. Rangers. There were 121 Rangers to some 150 Japanese and when the news of the attack got out 2,000 more Japanese were rushed up from a nearby village – for Cabanatuan was then still deep behind enemy lines. "But", as Carl Mydans reported, "out from the trees came Filipino guerrillas. This was

* *My Fifteen Years with General MacArthur.*

their job . . . Their orders were to stop the Japs and they did. No Ranger will accept congratulations on a job well done without saying, 'Thanks, but don't forget those Filipinos. We broke into the camp but the Filipinos got us through.' "

Another amazing rescue was that of the nuns at the convent by Santo Tomas. The Japs had them all lined up against the wall to be shot and were just lifting their guns when the Americans appeared over the top of the wall. The nuns all went flat on their faces and the Japs were shot instead. Only one nun was killed in the affray.

In her turn, Isla told the story of the Los Baños rescue. Her STIC friends were amazed at the fantastic escape. No one had ever expected to see them alive again. Even the army, she was told, had reckoned on fifty killed and two hundred wounded. Just three slightly wounded was a stupendous achievement.

Isla stayed the night of 17 March at Santo Tomas sleeping on a spring mattress that May Stopford had found for her. It was the first time in three years she had bedded down on anything more exalted than thin horse hair and, for all its bliss, she found it too comfortable for sleep!

The jeep ride through Manila had shattered her. There was hardly a landmark left. The Japs' policy of turning every major building into a minor fort had resulted not only in their own destruction but that of the city. It was devastation on a scale Isla could never have believed possible.

The fortification and subsequent demolition of Manila had not been Yamashita's idea. Blockaded in his northern stronghold at Baguio, Yamashita had no wish to involve his troops in a bloody and unprofitable attempt to hold the city and he recommended evacuation. The Japanese naval commander, Rear-Admiral Sanji Iwabuchi, however, was determined to fight to the death for the capital. It was he who organized the massive demolition of the city when the 37th Division first entered Manila at the beginning of February.

The struggle for Manila lasted one month, till 3 March, and cost the Americans 1,000 killed and 5,500 wounded. Almost none of the 17,000 Japanese in Manila survived. No toll could be made for the Filipino civilians but it was thought as many as 100,000 had died either in the fierce battle or the victims of Jap atrocities.

As they talked about all the terrible things that had happened since Isla had left for Los Baños nearly a year ago once again she had the sensation that she was discussing someone else, somebody else's friends. She was brought back to reality by the mention of Don. He, with Ansie, was one of the first to be rescued from Los Baños and on his arrival at Mamatid beach he had been taken direct to Santo Tomas. Isla badly wanted to see him and say goodbye before they left the Philippines. At last she tracked him down in Santa Catalina, the hospital block, looking almost the old, tough Don again in spite of his frail and wasted form. He told her he had heard from the Gissimo and Madame Chiang Kai-shek and would be getting priority to leave with Ansie for the States. Ansie, he understood, was planning to marry Henry Sperry just as soon as he could get a divorce from Olly's sister, Chris.

Soon it was time to catch the bus back to Muntinlupa. That night there was a tremendous party, the 5th Cavalry Dance. "What a party!" wrote Isla. "Shut my eyes and it was Gone with the Wind. Never saw so many 'live' bottles of all kinds – G.I. gin, Cointreau, whisky. I stuck to Cavalry Punch! Danced very badly, head and feet not co-ordinating yet. As I was the only Limey there they sang 'Bless 'em All' unexpurgated for my benefit! I'd never heard of it before – pretty raw! Next morning didn't feel so good but after all these years a party to remember!"

Two days later Isla and Gill were told they would be leaving the next day by air for Leyte where a ship would take them to Australia. From there they would probably be able to get transport to India or the United Kingdom. Once again there was a luggage restriction, only fifty pounds were allowed. Isla's diaries, her magazines and illustrations, and her score or so newspapers together weighed nearly twenty pounds. Taking them would leave little room for anything else. Once again the diaries won the day. She would simply have to jettison other things and, the decision made, two boxes of shoes and all her washing promptly joined the rubbish pile.

Isla and Gill flew from Nichols Field to Leyte where they were taken immediately to a transit camp right on the beach. It was strict segregation and the men were all hustled off to another camp sixteen miles away.

Strangely, at this last camp there were more rules than ever before. No men were allowed in the compound – consequently named the harem – and lights had to be put out at 10 pm. The Red Cross did their best to make the evacuees comfortable but the tents on the sand were desperately primitive and the lavatories just horrible pits crawling with maggots. Isla was informed the latter had their uses but they just made her feel sick. At night the smell was appalling. During the day, in spite of the pouring rain, most people spent the time on the beach swimming. But, like a fool, Isla had thrown away the two bathing costumes she had hung on to for three years, along with the shoes and washing, the day they left Muntinlupa.

The saving grace, or graces, of Leyte camp were the Three Musketeers, an incredible trio of Damon Runyon characters all from the Bronx, who were convalescing at the rest home nearby. During the four days Isla was at the camp they became firm friends. She hardly understood a word they said but what she could make out was incredibly entertaining. They also taught her to play pinochle which, as she was a good bridge player, was not difficult and whenever they wanted a fourth for their game they would call her over the tannoy: "Mrs Corfield, please come down to the beach!"

While she was on Leyte, too, she received her first telephone call in three years. Willie Clifton, a man they had known in Shanghai and who was now RAF liaison – his wife had taught Gill the piano – had spotted their name on the list of those rescued. He came forty miles just to see Isla and Gill for a few minutes and give them news of old friends and a few tips and addresses for Australia.

26 March, 1945: "We're off – left the P.I., that's the astounding thing. I'm in a daze and this 'ere *David C. Shanks* is a dream ship. I'm pretty sure I'm on board – she's rolling and pitching . . .

"*David C. Shanks* whoever he was or may be must rate high because this ship is wonderful. I'm in a cabin for eight, beauty rest mattress etc., two bathrooms – a *real* bath, eight lockers, bedside lights and reading lights. Can't get over it – s'wonderful!"

The food was wonderful too – lamb chops, peach pie, apple pie, cheese and as much coffee as they could drink for their first dinner on board. The women and children ate in the officers' saloon and were waited on by ship's stewards. There were cloths on the table, napkins, glasses, spoons, forks and knives – it was another world. That first night was like a toddlers' tea party with everyone stretching out both hands right and left, reaching, picking, stuffing food. Gill grabbed and guzzled with the best of them but Isla, though hungry, found she couldn't eat. But a roll wouldn't hurt. She stretched a long arm about three feet down the table narrowly missing her neighbour's flailing knife and fork. Suddenly she realized what she was doing. She would have to go back and teach herself – and Gill who was far, far worse – good table manners before they got to Australia!

The second day on board Isla spent one and a half hours under the hot showers trying to scrub off three years of camp dirt. She reckoned four soapings a day in water as hot as she could stand would get her clean before landing day. Improving her appearance was going to be a far more difficult operation. How she longed for a beauty parlour! When she read in a Sydney paper that Helena Rubinstein had a salon in town she was elated hoping some drastic beauty aids could be applied before meeting up with T.D. again.

They sailed in a convoy of about fifty ships, four hundred releasees and about the same number of troops going on leave. Their destination was Townsville, Eastern Australia, from where a train was to take them on a four-day journey to Sydney. The war was still on – indeed the Japs were still in Philippine waters – so they had to wear great, unwieldy life-jackets, a sort of bra-cum-corsets, wherever they went. Every day there was boat drill.

Every day, too, there were pills to try and pump back life into the still sickly ex-internees. Beri-beri had left its mark on Isla as on others. Suddenly she lost the use of her left hand. A cigarette was about as much as she could hold. Her eyes were still bad and her hair, where the septic patch had been, was coming out in handfuls. She was terrified of going bald. She had boils, and her legs, arms and face still ached from the beri-beri. She was painfully thin. But thiamin shots, vitamin and iron pills, good food and rest, gradually restored her.

Gill was looking much better, quite pretty again, and her healthy appetite was bringing out all the curves. Almost every night she had a date with one of the soldiers. Isla often worried how the whole experience of internment would affect her. She had lost so many years of education, so many carefree years. She had leapt from childhood to adulthood with nothing in between.

She wondered, too, where and when they would be able to meet up with T.D. and Richard, what had happened to their home in Shanghai, how they would get back to England.

Still it was not real. "I can't believe I'm at sea and feel I may wake up and find myself wondering what Konichi is going to do next . . . I can't believe we're on our way leaving the P.I. never to return – I hope."

29 March: "Time is so funny these days. It's only five weeks to the day tomorrow that we were rescued, five weeks ago we didn't know when or what would happen. A week ago today was our first day in Leyte. It all seems another world away and yet the days pass quickly. Such distances have been covered and we've done so little. I feel more rested now. In Muntinlupa I was hideously impatient and jittery. On board I know, or rather feel, I can get no news and can do nothing towards getting it so have given in."

Luckily there was a big library on the *David C. Shanks* and Isla was able to catch up a bit on her reading although her eyes were still giving her hell. She was struck one day by a little poem in the *New Yorker* by Lewis Mumford:

> "Happy the dead!
> If we do ill
> They will not know we lied.
> Happy the dead!
> If we do well
> Their death is justified."

On Easter Sunday, 2 April, they docked at Hollandia, New Guinea, and, with tongues hanging out, watched crate after crate of beer coming aboard. They were told they would be in Australia by the end of the week.

Isla's excitement at the prospect of being a free agent again was tinged with fear and apprehension for the big world outside, now so unfamiliar.

"I realize it won't be all beer and skittles", she wrote. "In fact it rather terrifies me. Crossing roads, clearing up debts, finding news good and bad, buying clothes, having to make decisions, carrying money and paying cash – all the things that in prison didn't come into the picture. In other words a terrific readjustment . . .

"There'll be rationing of this and that and all the things we've been looking forward to will be difficult to get. But it's good news I want and I'll take the rest . . . "

On 5 April they sighted Australia.

"I wonder what is in store for us? But, anyway, it's civilization and freedom from the Japs . . . I still can't take it in."

CHAPTER TEN

Thirty years on

IT was five months before Isla got her wish to be home with "a comfortable chair and bed, whisky-soda and my family round me".

The war both in Europe and in the Far East was still on when she and Gill docked at Townsville, North Queensland, in April, 1945. They had no idea what to expect but their exuberant reception surpassed their wildest dreams.

The people of Townsville fêted them like conquering heroes. Isla had never seen anything so lavish, so magnanimous, as the banquet at the town hall. Rationing was still in force yet the tables were groaning with rich butter, cream, meats, cakes – families from all over the state had sacrificed their rations and clubbed together to make this home-coming a feast of feasts.

The kindness was overwhelming. Families gladly took in the evacuees offering to give them a home for as long as they liked. But Isla was anxious to get to Sydney where both ships and news might be more accessible. It took four days to travel the eight hundred miles from Townsville to Sydney. At the stations en route people crowded onto the platforms to try and get a first-hand account of the camp, the rescue, the tortures. Isla was angry when officials tried to bar their way. She felt they had a right to know and ask questions. After all, it was *they* who had footed the bill for the banquet!

They came to help as well as hear stories. At every stop women ran forward to take off the babies and small children and clean them up before the next stage of the journey. The men brought offerings of food and drink.

At last the evacuees reached Sydney and, dressed in the new jumpers and skirts given them by the Red Cross at Brisbane, they were taken to Federation House for the grand reunion.

Reunion for some but not for Gill and Isla. They had no relatives in Sydney and there was still no news from T.D. or Richard.

Reporters and photographers crowded round. "What happened at the rescue?" "How did you feel?" "Were you ill treated by the Japs?" "What was the worst moment of internment?" In spite of feeling like death with a terrible cold Isla could not avoid the cameras. Gill spoke of the coconut cache incident when the guards had threatened to shoot them and of the tragic death of Pat Hell whom she could so easily have been with on that fateful morning.

She described the food and the way they used to steal banana skins from the Japanese garbage cans, they were so hungry. Had she put on weight since release? "Yes, 15 lbs!"

The Duke of Gloucester, then Governor-General of Australia, and the Duchess sent a message of welcome and the Corfields found themselves guests at another Freedom party.

Luckily they had friends from Shanghai in Sydney with whom they could stay and soon life settled into the familiar pattern of waiting for a ship. It was a time for catching up on news and debts and health.

The *Anhui*, on which they had sailed from Shanghai three and a half years ago, *had* safe conduct as Isla thought all along. If only Captain Evans' orders had got through they could have gone with her and been spared the nightmare of internment. As for all their luggage, including a load of valuable table silver, that had departed in the *Anhui*'s hold, it had been looted and, in spite of the theft being admitted, Isla was never able to get it back.

The war had cost her a fortune. She had £2,000 of debts to settle with the friends who had lent her money – the Stopfords, the Lennoxes, Fred Satterfield, Frank Hanson and the executors of Carroll Grinnell. Her hundred dollars bridge winnings from Fred – the product of three years' hard playing – were a welcome drop in the financial ocean.

Later she learned their beautiful Shanghai flat had been turned into an oil dump by the Japanese. They got £50 for it.

Isla had always wondered why none of the British had been repatriated from the Philippines. Now she learned it was because the Australian government had refused to release fifteen Japanese pearl divers.

The war in Europe ended in May, 1945. The surrender was signed on 7 May at 2.41 am at a long wooden table in a bare school room in Rheims. Hitler was dead, Berlin was in ruins.

Japan remained. It was a bitter struggle. As the "island-hopping" Americans got nearer to the Japanese homeland resistance built up. In the month-long assault on Iwo Jima in February–March 1945, the Americans suffered thirty-five per cent casualties. The capture of Okinawa, only 320 miles from South Japan, produced a similar casualty percentage with 40,000 Americans dead or injured.

By the end of July it was obvious that hundreds of thousands of American lives would be lost in attempting to subdue Japan by conventional warfare methods. Deep in the Arizona desert scientists prepared a new secret weapon.

Impatiently Isla and Gill Corfield waited for their ship home. At the beginning of August they were told they could take the *Stirling Castle* sailing to Liverpool. As they neared Madras they heard the news that the most powerful weapon of destruction the world had ever known, the atomic bomb, had been dropped on Hiroshima. Two days later a second atomic bomb fell on Nagasaki. On 14 August, 1945, Japan surrendered. The war was over.

Strangely, in the Philippines, Yamashita still held out in the rugged mountains of northern Luzon. He heard the news of Roosevelt's death, he heard of his country's capitulation after Hiroshima and Nagasaki. But the Tiger of Malaya would not give in until he had formal notification from Tokyo. He finally agreed to surrender on 2 September, the same day as the official surrender ceremony on board the battleship *Missouri* in Tokyo Bay. Ten months later, on 4 July, 1946, the Philippines received their independence from the United States.

It was a grey and drizzling September afternoon when the *Stirling Castle* docked alongside the Prince's landing-stage in Liverpool. T.D. and Richard were waiting. It was a reunion that all four had separately feared might never happen. It was too deep for words and Isla wrote none.

She never returned to the Philippines and has no desire to do so. Indeed, she has no wish ever to live anywhere remotely rural. London has been her home from that day. Now T.D. is dead, Richard and Gill are both married and Isla herself is a great-grandmother.

What happened to the people she knew so well?

Konichi escaped to Manila where he was found, tried and hanged.

Isla's greatest friend, Don, lived only fourteen months after his release. He never finished the memoirs he started with Ansie on the yacht before the outbreak of war. If his notes are ever found and published they will make fascinating reading. He wrote his last letter to Isla on 23 April, 1946, from the Country Hospital, Great Western Avenue, Shanghai – the hospital where nineteen years earlier Gill was born.

"Now I am laid by the heels. Without knowing it my right lung collapsed and the tissue began disintegrating. This must have happened in camp. I found it out by accident in Tahiti where shortness of breath caused me to go for an X-ray . . .

"The doctors chased me out of Tahiti . . . They told me I had about run my race and what was left of my future must be spent in bed . . . Chiang and Madame demanded I come home and so here I am . . ."

In fact the Gissimo and Madame had cabled him "Come home" as he lay sick in Honolulu whence the Tahiti doctors had banished him. Back in Shanghai Madame flew to his bedside from Nanking. When he died a few days later, aged 71, the Chinese nation mourned him and honoured him with the Grand Blue Cordon of the Order of the Brilliant Jade.

Ansie married Henry Sperry of the National City Bank in Manila after taking courses at first Berkeley and then Columbia Universities in the States.

Isla never heard again from the Stopfords or the Ewings or the Selphs, repatriated from STIC, or from her Los Baños friends Roy and Copie. Clark Lee, the journalist, is dead. Her only contacts with those far-off days, beside her diary, are Ida Lennox and Fred Satterfield, both living in America.

Gill, herself a grandmother, lives in Sydney, Australia. "Fortunately," she says, "one mostly remembers the happy and amusing incidents – Mary the Holy Roller and Diana, the old prostitute whom she hoped to convert."

Internment at the age of fourteen with full adult responsibility at sixteen, she feels, deprived her of adolescence and made her behave like a belated teenager in her early twenties. Lack of education she sees as another consequence of internment. The memory of acute hunger has never left her.

"I still have a slight sense of urgency if I get too hungry," she admits. "For years after it was a real problem of panic."

But Gill does not hate the Japanese. "I can't understand hate. The Japs were doing a job, on many occasions I was most kindly treated by guards . . . No, I feel no animosity and I admire them for the way they have rebuilt their country."

Isla feels very much the same way. She likes the Japanese and thinks that, apart from Konichi and his kind, they all too often got more consideration from the Japs than from fellow internees.

She still can't bear the thought of waste or to see a grain of rice left in the pan. She remembers the three and a half years vividly, perhaps because of the diary which, through all her moves, she has kept safe by her. Most of all she remembers the day of the rescue and the face of the young parachuter with his white teeth and healthy complexion. "We *are* glad to see you."

Bibliography

The Philippines by Raymond Nelson
The Battle for the Pacific by Donald Macintyre
MacArthur, 1941–1951, Victory in the Pacific by C. A. Willoughby
and J. Chamberlain
The Untold Story of Douglas MacArthur by Frazier Hunt
Total War, Causes and Courses of the Second World War by Peter
Calvocoressi and Guy Wint
Triumph in the Philippines by Robert Ross Smith. U.S. Army
History
Inside Asia by John Gunther
The Four Samurai by Arthur Swinson
My Fifteen Years with General MacArthur by Sid Huff with Joe
Alex Morris
Illustrated World History edited by Esmond Wright and Kenneth
M. Stampp
Purnell's History of the Second World War:
  Fall of the Philippines by John Vader
  Fall of Corregidor by Fred Stolley
  Midway, the Turning Point by A. J. Barker
  The Liberation of the Philippines by Stanley Falk

Extracts from the reports of the following units on the Los Baños
rescue operation by courtesy of the United States of America
General Services Administration, National Archives and Records
Service, Washington National Records Center, Washington,
D.C.: 6th U.S. Army, Luzon Campaign; 6th U.S. Army, 6–3
Journal; 11th Airborne Division; XIV Corps; 511th Parachute
Infantry Regiment; 188th Glider Infantry Regiment.